Malta

WORLD BIBLIOGRAPHICAL SERIES

General Editors:
Robert G. Neville (Executive Editor)
John J. Horton

Robert A. Myers   Hans H. Wellisch
Ian Wallace   Ralph Lee Woodward, Jr.

John J. Horton is Deputy Librarian of the University of Bradford and was formerly Chairman of its Academic Board of Studies in Social Sciences. He has maintained a longstanding interest in the discipline of area studies and its associated bibliographical problems, with special reference to European Studies. In particular he has published in the field of Icelandic and of Yugoslav studies, including the two relevant volumes in the World Bibliographical Series.

Robert A. Myers is Associate Professor of Anthropology in the Division of Social Sciences and Director of Study Abroad Programs at Alfred University, Alfred, New York. He has studied post-colonial island nations of the Caribbean and has spent two years in Nigeria on a Fulbright Lectureship. His interests include international public health, historical anthropology and developing societies. In addition to *Amerindians of the Lesser Antilles: a bibliography* (1981), *A Resource Guide to Dominica, 1493-1986* (1987) and numerous articles, he has compiled the World Bibliographical Series volumes on *Dominica* (1987), *Nigeria* (1989) and *Ghana* (1991).

Ian Wallace is Professor of German at the University of Bath. A graduate of Oxford in French and German, he also studied in Tübingen, Heidelberg and Lausanne before taking teaching posts at universities in the USA, Scotland and England. He specializes in contemporary German affairs, especially literature and culture, on which he has published numerous articles and books. In 1979 he founded the journal *GDR Monitor*, which he continues to edit under its new title *German Monitor*.

Hans H. Wellisch is Professor emeritus at the College of Library and Information Services, University of Maryland. He was President of the American Society of Indexers and was a member of the International Federation for Documentation. He is the author of numerous articles and several books on indexing and abstracting, and has published *The Conversion of Scripts and Indexing and Abstracting: an International Bibliography*, and *Indexing from A to Z*. He also contributes frequently to *Journal of the American Society for Information Science*, *The Indexer* and other professional journals.

Ralph Lee Woodward, Jr. is Professor of History at Tulane University, New Orleans. He is the author of *Central America, a Nation Divided*, 2nd ed. (1985), as well as several monographs and more than seventy scholarly articles on modern Latin America. He has also compiled volumes in the World Bibliographical Series on *Belize* (1980), *El Salvador* (1988), *Guatemala* (Rev. Ed.) (1992) and *Nicaragua* (Rev. Ed.) (1994). Dr. Woodward edited the Central American section of the *Research Guide to Central America and the Caribbean* (1985) and is currently associate editor of Scribner's *Encyclopedia of Latin American History*.

PLYMBRIDGE

VOLUME 64

Malta

Revised Edition

David M. Boswell
and
Brian W. Beeley

Compilers

CLIO PRESS
OXFORD, ENGLAND · SANTA BARBARA, CALIFORNIA
DENVER, COLORADO

British Library Cataloguing in Publication Data

Boswell, David Mark, 1937-
Malta. – Rev. ed. (World bibliographical series; v. 64)
1. Malta – Bibliography
I. Title   II. Beeley, Brian W. (Brian William), 1935-
016.9′4585

ISBN 1–85109–269–2

ABC-CLIO Ltd.,
Old Clarendon Ironworks,
35A Great Clarendon Street,
Oxford OX2 6AT, England.

ABC-CLIO Inc.,
130 Cremona Drive,
Santa Barbara,
CA 93117, USA.

Designed by Bernard Crossland.
Typeset by Columns Design Ltd., Reading, England.
Printed and bound in Great Britain by Bookcraft (Bath) Ltd., Midsomer Norton.

THE WORLD BIBLIOGRAPHICAL SERIES

This series, which is principally designed for the English speaker, will eventually cover every country (and some of the world's principal regions and cities), each in a separate volume comprising annotated entries on works dealing with its history, geography, economy and politics; and with its people, their culture, customs, religion and social organization. Attention will also be paid to current living conditions – housing, education, newspapers, clothing, etc. – that are all too often ignored in standard bibliographies; and to those particular aspects relevant to individual countries. Each volume seeks to achieve, by use of careful selectivity and critical assessment of the literature, an expression of the country and an appreciation of its nature and national aspirations, to guide the reader towards an understanding of its importance. The keynote of the series is to provide, in a uniform format, an interpretation of each country that will express its culture, its place in the world, and the qualities and background that make it unique. The views expressed in individual volumes, however, are not necessarily those of the publisher.

VOLUMES IN THE SERIES

Dedicated to
PAUL XUEREB

- University of Malta, Librarian 1965-97
- Malta Library Association, sometime Chairman
- Commonwealth Library Association, President 1979-84
- Malta Book Fair Committee, Chairman 1988-96
- Action Committee on the National Library and
  National Archives (Malta), Chairman 1997-
- *The Sunday Times* (Malta), Drama Critic 1964-
- Manoel Theatre, Valletta,
  Management Committee Member 1992-

Contents

Contents

Contents

Introduction

The Maltese archipelago, comprising the islands of Malta, Gozo and Comino and the tiny uninhabited islets of Cominotto, Filfla and St. Paul's Island, is situated in the Mediterranean Sea, about 60 miles (96 kilometres) south of Sicily and 180 miles (288 kilometres) north of the African coast. Malta is the largest island in the group, accounting for 77 per cent of the islands' 313 square kilometres, and its highest point is only slightly over 800 feet (247 metres) above sea level. The island has no lakes or rivers and few trees. Moreover, no mineral resources have been discovered apart from salt. Its strata of coralline and globigerina limestone provide the local building material. Fresh water is scarce, extracted from the aquifer below its layers of limestone or created from the sea by reverse osmosis.

Notwithstanding this, historically Malta has played a significant part in international affairs, because of its strategic importance and its fine natural harbours. Over the centuries many nations have taken control of the islands in order to secure these advantages. Not surprisingly perhaps, the country's avowed aim today is to pursue a neutral foreign policy, and to create a viable economy, based not on the island's military value, but especially on tourism, electronics, and 'offshore' finance. The 1995 population of the islands was 376,000, representing an increase of 9 per cent over the previous decade. The conurbation, centred on the two great harbours (Grand and Marsamxett), accounts for most of the population, though the inner harbour area – notably the capital, Valletta, and nearby districts – is losing residents.

Despite its remarkable prehistoric structures, little is known about the country until it was taken over by the Phoenicians in about 800 BC. It was then colonized successively by the Carthaginians, Romans and Arabs. Around 1090, Malta was occupied by the Normans of Sicily and this was the beginning of a period of great hardship for the islands. In the 15th century Malta suffered piratical raids and pestilence as well as a disastrous famine. In addition, in 1488, it endured the first concerted attack by the Turks.

In 1530, the year in which Emperor Charles V offered Malta to the Knights of the Order of St. John of Jerusalem (now known as the Sovereign Military Order of Malta, with its headquarters in Rome), the country was impoverished and desolate. However, since being expelled from Rhodes in 1522, the Knights had been searching unsuccessfully for a base in the Mediterranean and were in no position to turn down the Emperor's offer. When the Knights arrived few Maltese would have dared to hope for the protection and prosperity their rule would ultimately bring. The Order's early years were spent in fortifying the island, as they feared another assault by the Turks, the first, in 1551, having almost depopulated Gozo. Their apprehension was justified when, in 1565, the Turks launched an attack which became known as the Great Siege of Malta. Vastly outnumbered, the Knights nevertheless hung on to their positions and the Turks became increasingly demoralized as a result of heavy casualties, sickness and food shortages. Eventually they were forced to leave the island and after the Battle of Lepanto (1571), which checked the Turks in the Mediterranean, a period of relative tranquility ensued.

The Knights made Malta into a naval bastion and a thriving trade and communications centre. After the Siege the Knights built a new town, with what it was hoped would be invulnerable fortifications. The town, which replaced Mdina and Birgu as the capital of Malta, was called Valletta, after Jean de la Valette, the Grand Master who had led the victory against the Turks in 1565. Successive grand masters continued the process of improving the island's defences and building new settlements, particularly around the Grand Harbour. Annual predatory naval *corsos* were undertaken against Turkish warships and trading routes. The Knights' wealth brought prosperity to the island and their rule was, by the standards of the day, fair and enlightened. Maltese settlements expanded and it was an era of great artistic and architectural development, despite a severe earthquake in 1693.

However, in the 18th century, the Knights became less monastic and more worldly. With this came financial weakness, when in 1792 their extensive possessions in France were confiscated. In 1798, Napoleon invaded Malta and, without much resistance, the Knights departed. French rule was harsh and, in 1800, the Maltese rebelled and appealed to the British for help. This was duly given with the help of Sicilian troops, and two years later, the Maltese asked to be placed under British sovereignty. Under the Treaty of Paris (1814), Britain formally annexed

Malta, having previously refused to hand the islands back to the Order under its new but short-lived Grand Master, the Russian Czar Paul.

Malta was extremely valuable to Britain because of its strategic importance and the Maltese economy flourished intermittently throughout the 19th century, with the installation of military bases, the expansion of the shipbuilding industry and the improvement of harbour facilities. During this period, a succession of constitutions brought varying degrees of local representation to the governing council as the islanders agitated for greater political freedom. In 1921 Malta was granted a constitution which gave the country considerable self-government, although Britain retained responsibility for the islands' foreign affairs. This constitution was suspended in 1930 and again in 1936, after further political crises, and in 1939 Crown Colony rule was re-established. The predominant position of the Roman Catholic Church in Malta was acknowledged by the British authorities, but was also a major source of tension in local politics as well as constitutional negotiation.

During the Second World War, Malta played a crucial role in the Allies' Mediterranean strategy. The island was subjected to very heavy bombing and a naval blockade by Italy and Germany. Thousands of people were killed or wounded by air raids and starvation became imminent. As a recognition of the great courage which the Maltese had shown in withstanding the bombardment, King George VI awarded the George Cross to the whole island. Leading nationalists, including the Chief Justice, had been deported to Uganda for the duration.

After the war, the desire for independence grew and throughout the 1950s there were various proposals regarding the future status of Malta. In 1955, the integration of Malta with Britain was proposed at the Round Table Conference in London, but there was no consensus within Malta over the form that the future government of the island should take and negotiations with Britain proceeded slowly. Finally, in 1964, a constitution was approved in a referendum. The British Government agreed that Malta should become independent under this constitution and, on 21 September 1964, Malta became an independent state and a member of the Commonwealth.

After independence, Malta was still used as a military and naval base by the United Kingdom and NATO and, when the Labour Party came to power in Malta in 1971, Prime Minister Dom Mintoff threatened to break ties with the West if Britain did not increase rental payments. After discussions, an agreement was reached whereby Britain and NATO would supply economic aid to Malta in return for the use of its naval base. This agreement was operative until 1979, when the last British service personnel left the island.

Introduction

Since independence, Malta has officially been pursuing a policy of non-alignment, though Mintoff argued that if his country was to survive the closing of the naval base, he would have to seek new allies and assistance. The Nationalists stressed a role for Malta within a Western European union but Mintoff proposed that Malta form part of the non-aligned block in the United Nations. In 1972 Malta signed a cultural agreement with Libya and received oil at concessionary rates, of which any surplus could be sold to Malta's advantage. Malta's own oil prospecting was, however, curtailed and the dispute with Libya about the delimitation of maritime boundaries taken to the International Court at The Hague. Work for the Drydocks and manufacturing enterprises including shipbuilding were obtained but throughout the decade these tended to fade out in common with much new private manufacturing which could only compete with northern Europe and the United States.

In 1987 Labour rule was replaced by that of the Nationalist Party, with Eddie Fenech Adami as Prime Minister. Settlements were reached with the medical profession and the position of the University of Malta re-established after a decade of direct confrontation with the previous government. The Church had already handed over landed property in return for the maintenance of grant aid to its schools. This government opened the free-port that its predecessor had constructed, but in foreign policy made a major switch from non-alignment to European integration. After its defeat in 1992 the Labour Party elected Alfred Sant as its leader and he became Prime Minister when the Labour Party was re-elected to power in 1996. One immediate result was the reversal of Malta's policy regarding the European Union. Where the Nationalists had favoured membership, the Labour administration advocated maintenance of Malta's associated but separate status. The issue of the islands' ultimate place in Europe therefore remains undecided.

Economically, Malta has had considerable success in developing tourism. British visitors relax in the bars once frequented by the UK service people or they enjoy the facilities in the hotels and other holiday – and long-stay – accommodation which have become prominent features of the landscape. Half of the million or more annual visitors to the islands are from Britain. The emphasis has been on mass tourism, with some 43,000 beds available. In an attempt to diversify the source of tourists, Malta has been able to attract a considerable number of German tourists in recent years. It is now hoped to reduce numbers of arrivals, while maintaining income, by stressing higher quality accommodation and the provision of specialized holidays. This follows the realization that Malta's landscape has indeed suffered from the demands of tourism for space and buildings. Certainly a major part of the islands' economic success has been due to tourism though the Maltese do not lose sight of the fact that this continues the dependence on outsiders which prevailed in pre-Independence times.

A noticeable feature of the islands is the rapid and extensive expansion of its built-up area, mainly for residential purposes but including large churches in Malta and more recently in Gozo. Already well developed before the Second World War around the harbours, since Independence the process has been ubiquitous. Coastal resorts have been built for tourist hotels and self-catering apartments, and local use as second homes and residences. Considerable internal migration has populated the more prestigious villages with a fringe of villas, following a pattern first established in the 1960s by expatriates in retirement. And since the 1970s many villagers have themselves removed to larger properties built on the outskirts of their original settlements in common with Maltese emigrants returning from Australia, Canada, etc. with the pensions they have earned abroad. To date most of this building has taken the form of low-rise terraced housing and apartments with external cladding in one of Malta's few natural resources, the easily quarried and honey-coloured limestone. No assessment of the local economy can overlook the scale of this investment in real estate. It remains to be seen what impact the implementation of recent planning legislation will have had on this pattern of urban development.

Among other areas which it is hoped to develop is Malta's potential as an international conference and communications centre, given its central Mediterranean location, its separate national identity between Europe and the Middle East, and its small area. Certainly the islands seem set to continue to demonstrate a cultural energy and creativeness – including the production of writing in English – out of all proportion to their small size.

The bibliography

This bibliography has been annotated from works written in the English language and published, in most cases, from about 1983 to 1996. The vast majority are by Maltese scholars and have been printed in Malta. They are most easily found in the National Library of Malta and/or the Melitensia collection of the University of Malta. The volume is therefore concerned primarily with recent publications and differs from J. R. Thackrah's *Malta* volume in the World Bibliographical Series (1985), which was potentially devoted to all the publications on Malta in previous years and was drawn especially from the extensive historic holdings in the Royal Commonwealth Society, the Scicluna Collection of Melitensia at Rhodes House, Oxford and other libraries in the United Kingdom. Where new editions or reprints of classic works have been published, we have included them and we have listed again some of the previous entries that remain as major standard works. Essentially, however, this is a review of more recent publications and therefore complements Thackrah's bibliography.

The most significant collections of earlier books on Malta in Britain may be found in the one-time library of the Royal Commonwealth Society, which has been transferred to the Cambridge University Library (as a collection with its own catalogue), and official publications at the Institute of Commonwealth Studies and the British Library of Political and Economic Sciences. Especially important is the substantial collection of publications donated by Sir Hannibal Scicluna to the University of Oxford and held at Rhodes House with its own catalogue which also includes the relatively small number of books on Malta donated subsequently. Sir Hannibal, a notable Maltese centenarian and previous Librarian of the then Royal Library in Valletta, was himself the author of an encyclopaedic volume on the conventual church of the Order of St. John in Valletta, now the co-cathedral, and editions of documents on Napoleon's acquisition of Malta and the subsequent British-supported Maltese rising against the occupying French troops.

The library of the Venerable Order of St. John of the British Realm, housed at the Museum of St. John's Gate in Clerkenwell, London, is also a significant source of reference to works on Malta as is this Order's own museum, where much has been exhibited and catalogued in the last decade. However, we have only been concerned with the Sovereign Order of St. John as it relates to Malta, notably between 1530 and c.1800, and not to its general history, etc. That excepted, a brief note on archival sources in Malta is worth making for those whose study of publications on the islands is the prelude to more intensive research. The most important may be found in the following depositories. The archives of the Sovereign Military Order, from its foundation in Palestine until its expulsion from Malta in 1798, may be referred to at the National Library of Malta in Valletta. The volumes themselves are in a catalogue list but the contents of only some of them have so far been published by the University of Malta. During the 1990s the hitherto 'current files' of Maltese government departments during the period of British rule, 1800-1964, began to be transferred to the good conditions of the ex-Santo Spirito Hospital in Rabat, where they can for the first time be referred to in an archival search room. Catalogues are being compiled. Until very recently even Maltese researchers had to use the Public Record Office in London.

There are two primary archival collections of the Roman Catholic Church in Malta. The diocesan archives are at the Curia in the ex-Jesuit retreat house in Floriana, and include the *Status Animarum* parochial censuses. But much material concerned with church court cases as well as the Cathedral Archives and copies of several parochial registers may be found by reference to the Cathedral Museum in the ex-seminary in Mdina. The Notarial Archives in Valletta are a primary source of much data on both property and disputes. The primary sources of demographic data and much architectural as well as local history are the registers of baptisms, marriages and funerals and other records of the churches of the parishes and religious orders of Malta. With the single exception of the Bonavita papers that may be referred to at the University of Malta library, the private papers of no Maltese families are in the public domain. Where guides to, or catalogues of, archives have been published they are included by subject.

However, it is important to issue one caveat to English-speaking readers. The archives of the Order use ecclesiastical Latin, French, Sicilian/Italian and relevant vernacular languages. Church records are in Latin and Sicilian/Italian as are the Notarial Archives which also use many conventional abbreviations. And although many of the archives from the British period are in English, the language of the law courts and the Maltese *professionisti* was usually Italian until the 1920s/30s, when Maltese and English were made the two official languages. Since Independence in 1964 these two languages have kept this status so that government publications are usually printed in English, or in bilingual publications. But the language used in Parliament, in court cases, and in most communications, has increasingly been Maltese with the result that verbatim reports in English-language newspapers printed in Malta are often translations by the journalists from Maltese. English is widely spoken and printed in Malta. But researchers will not find that English is always sufficient for studying the country's history or its more recent politics, religion and expression of ideas and literature, although the librarians generally offer to help translate particular passages.

Two libraries have legal depository status for publications in Malta. These are the National Library in Valletta and the Public Library in St. Francis Square, Vajringa Street, Victoria, Gozo. Two copies of publications in Malta are obtained for each library. The National Library also buys two copies of each foreign title on Malta or the Knights. Malta does not have a parliamentary library – but there is talk of one. The Islands' Library Association (Għaqda Bibljotekarji) is affiliated to the Commonwealth Library Association.

The National Library's compelling appearance has probably changed little since it was completed in the early years of British rule – though its founding collection goes back to 1763. It operates a closed-stack system for all readers (who are not normally asked for references, etc.). There is a book-style listing of earlier titles and a card index for more recent items. In 1991, the 20th edition of the Dewey Decimal Classification replaced the 19th which had been in use since 1984. A substantial *Melitensia* collection is being developed and reorganized. From 1983 the National Library has published a (usually) annual update of items of eight or more pages, along with a review of periodical articles.

The *Melitensia* collection at the University of Malta (Ta'Qroqq, Msida) is also a closed stack. It is expanding rapidly and, since 1992, acquisitions have been electronically listed, while material back to 1981 has been added to the new system. The committed staff in this library endeavour to obtain locally published works on Malta and Gozo, despite the lack of depository status. Relevant titles appearing abroad are also acquired as far as possible but there are inevitably gaps in the coverage.

The University's *Melitensia* rooms contain a fast-growing array of local theses and dissertations on Maltese topics. Some areas are much more complete than others, depending on the diligence of academic departments and individuals in presenting copies and information. Most theses written in Malta nowadays are in English. Some are in Maltese, for example, studies of the language itself, and a few are written in French, Italian, etc. Some theses on Maltese topics written abroad are available, depending on initiatives from authors or from *Melitensia* staff. A card index of available theses and dissertations is maintained and attempts are made to note relevant titles missing from the library. The coverage is being extended as much as possible for both contemporary and older titles and it is hoped that the whole area of thesis material will have begun to be computer-listed as soon as possible. Meanwhile, copies of foreign theses 'published' to order by a facsimile agency are in the general catalogue as are several original copies of such theses presented by the authors. Several faculties require undergraduates to submit a final year dissertation and also have similar submissions for their masters' programmes. Some are lodged in the *Melitensia* collection of the University Library. Others may be found in the relevant departmental offices while some can be found in the supervising professors' offices. Only the dissertations submitted to the Faculty of Law have their own published catalogue. These researches often provide the only information on their subject but of course vary in quality, sometimes cover the same ground as earlier dissertations and do not necessarily focus on Malta. In this bibliography we have included some representative thesis titles by topic. Where a thesis has subsequently appeared in published book form we have aimed to list the latter.

A small number of bookshops and dealers in the islands trade in *Melitensia*. The best-established of these is Sapienza's bookshop (Republic Street, Valletta) which has a growing business of titles in print devoted to matters of local interest (mostly in English). The shop produces useful lists of current and recent titles.

In the United States there is a major collection of *Melitensia* in the Malta Study Center of the Hill Monastic Manuscript Library at St. John's University, Collegeville, Minnesota 56321. The Center maintains a microfilm collection of some 13,000 documents covering the period since the 12th century. The coverage includes the Archives of the Inquisition and of the Knights, materials in the Mdina Co-Cathedral Museum and in the National Library in Valletta, together with those held by the dioceses of Malta and Gozo, plus musical compositions. The Center continues to acquire a range of antiquarian and modern publications dealing with Malta's history, literature and culture, along with materials pertaining to the Order.

Elsewhere in the United States there is an accessible, representative collection of titles on Malta at the Library of Congress, Washington, DC. Also in that city is the Catholic University of America with *Melitensia* material in its Mullen Library (Room 2006, Washington, DC 20064). Another accumulation on Malta is to be found at the New York Public Library (Oriental Division, 5th Avenue and 42nd Street, New York 10018).

In Australia mention can be made of the State Library of New South Wales (Macquarie Street, Sydney, New South Wales 2000).

Although there has been a thriving publication of newspapers and periodicals in Malta since the British removed censorship in the early 19th century, the production of books and academic journals has followed the developments and vicissitudes of the University of Malta and of education in the islands in general. Since about 1980 there has been a remarkable increase in the number and standard of well-illustrated and scholarly books published in Malta, mostly in English, in addition to the parochial histories and biographies which have usually been published in Maltese. In addition to beautiful picture- and guidebooks for the tourist market, Malta's primary industry since the closing of the British base in 1979, the emphasis has been on art, architecture and Maltese local history. Some have been published at reasonable cost but others at prices apparently unwarranted by the format and in small print-runs. Hence the importance of an annotated bibliography because few editions can remain in print for many years. Midsea Books have reprinted standard-sized facsimiles of many of the classic works of reference on Malta in Italian and English and some histories and archaeological guidebooks have been reprinted in Malta on the same lines as their original publication in England.

For a 'city-state' the size of Sheffield or Newcastle-upon-Tyne, the production of work published in English is impressive enough. When one adds the larger quantity of publications in Maltese, this productivity is astounding. Even the city of Leeds, which effectively covers much of the West Riding conurbation, has only one local history journal and a few locally relevant publications over several years. In just over a decade Malta has produced more than ten-times that quantity in the field of history – much of it of high quality. This says much for the education, self-consciousness and resolve of Maltese writers and the enterprise of local publishers and printers.

It also indicates several characteristics of this small-scale society. Malta is a place in which anything political is also of personal import and vice versa. This is nothing new. The pre- and post-war Nationalist Party favoured *Italianità* and Malta's Roman past. The Church had St. Paul's shipwreck. And Lord Strickland's party and newspaper backed the British connection and postulated an image of Malta's ancient Punic past. The Malta Labour Party had its own history and introduced compulsory Arabic in schools and research into Malta's Islamic experience. History and politics are therefore entwined as they are in local studies, and in the relations between Church and State which have repeatedly been problematic in Malta. However, it would be quite mistaken to assume that Malta's publications are therefore only of local interest. It seems highly likely that the finest of Malta's neolithic temples are some of the earliest stone buildings to be found in the world. And the legacy of the Order of St. John to Malta has included a wide range of Mannerist and baroque churches, palaces and other buildings as extensive as any great Italian city or a state capital of a far larger country, in addition to the spectacular series of fortifications extant from the Middle Ages until the end of British rule. No wonder these are the topics covered in many recent publications!

Maps and other cartographic material constitute another special category. We have listed some as appropriate to their topic but can add here a general comment on the wealth of material available. Under the Knights (1530-1798) plans were drawn for estates, built-up areas and – especially – for sites with particular naval or military importance for the Order. Under British rule the defensive imperative remained clear but, between 1858 and 1863, the United Kingdom Ordnance Survey produced a full map (1:2,500, for Malta only, surveyed by the Royal Engineers) entitled 'Fortress of Malta'. At the end of the 19th century another directly surveyed and beautifully hand-drawn coverage was completed by the UK General Staff. These '25-inch' surveys have been the standard basis for land-use registration, transfer, and – more recently – for planning and zoning. These sheets were subsequently revised while, from about 1911, a '6-inch' (1:10,000) version of the basic survey also became available.

For many decades the map mostly in general use has been the popular '2.5-inch' (1:25,000) covering the islands on three sheets and resembling the OS maps for Britain itself. The 1957 edition of this issue was, belatedly, updated in 1984 to reflect the rapid expansion of the built-up area and road network. Air-photographic coverage of Malta and Gozo in 1988 (at 1:15,000) formed the basis for a new map at 1:25,000. It is being computer-drawn by the Mapping Unit located within the Planning Authority in Floriana. Contours will be in metres and these maps will be progressively updated: they will be generally available from 1998. The Mapping Unit includes sections for Mapping, Geodetic Surveying, and Geographical Information Systems and is now established as the national cartographic centre undertaking work for the state and for a variety of other clients.

Notable among modern special maps are those showing surface geology, soils, planning zones, housing developments, local council boundaries, bus routes, etc. There is also a growing range of 'popular' maps aimed at the visitor to Malta, together with street guides to the islands' burgeoning built-up areas. Some of these are listed in the sections of this bibliography to which they relate.

As with maps, we have attempted to indicate major statistical documentation in appropriate sections of the bibliography. Once again Malta is extremely rich, with a range of available data extending over a considerable period. The coverage is, however, not without gaps. Successive Maltese governments have produced an array of statistical reports and publications. The provision has become progressively more systematic and complete since the 1940s. In that decade (1946) appeared the first *Statistical abstract of the Maltese Islands* to be published by the Central Office of Statistics in Valletta – which continues to issue the full range of 'official' material (available through a public sales outlet in Castille Square, Valletta). From 1961 the *Statistical abstract* became the *Annual Abstract of Statistics* (since 1960 there has also been a *Quarterly Digest of Statistics*). Other series have undergone similar name changes but these present no difficulty to the inquirer seeking continuity of data. The sections of the *Abstract* are each drawn from a major branch of activity for which special data and reports are available. Reports on several of these, for example, education, national accounts, production, shipping and aviation, and the statistics office itself, first appeared in the earlier 1950s. A few are much older: *Trade of the Maltese Islands* (1875 to 1966), for example, became *Trade statistics* from 1967. Some series have been less durable. The *Census of agriculture,* which was first produced in its modern form in 1955, has not been published since 1983, though estimates of major farming trends continue to be available. Statistical series have been included in this bibliography according to topic.

The best-documented area of all is population and demography. There has been a series of censuses since 1842 – at intervals of ten years from 1851, with an interruption at the time of the Second World War followed by censuses in 1948, 1957, 1967, 1985, and 1995. Coverage of the Census has been detailed and varied and a range of associated reports, on housing, social welfare, etc., have sometimes been made available. Representative recent titles are included where appropriate in this volume.

The traditional openness of access to information in Malta means that unpublished data are often available on special request to official and other agencies – subject to the limitations arising from rules governing personal or commercial anonymity. Equally, statistical data have been collected for centuries by agencies of the Church, the Order of St. John, and the British colonial administration.

Reference has already been made to the general principle we have followed in entering items related to maps, statistics, research, theses and directories under the subject heading to which their contents refer rather than to separate sections. General dictionaries and bibliographies are entered in their own sections. Most books and articles published in, and on, Malta have included either footnotes, terminal notes and references, and/or bibliographies. For the sake of convenience we have always used the term 'bibliog.', at the end of an entry's publishing particulars preceding the annotation, to cover all these ways of listing sources.

Acknowledgements

During the many years that both the compilers have been researching and visiting Malta, we have built up debts of gratitude to colleagues, authors and other friends. Several members of staff at the University of Malta and other researchers kindly provided us with their bibliographies and others have answered specific requests. In particular we should like to thank Paul Xuereb and Eric German of the University of Malta, Donald Sultana and Joseph Bonnici of the National Library of Malta, Pamela Willis of the Venerable Order of St. John's Museum and Library in Clerkenwell, London and the Sapienza family whose bookshop services in Valletta have helped to keep us abreast of new publications.

At the Open University we have been well served by the secretarial support of Pauline Turner, Beth Bissett and Philippa Hopkins and we thank John Hunt for preparing the map. We are pleased to acknowledge the support we have both received in small grants from the University's Faculty of Social Sciences' Research Fund to assist this bibliographical and other research in Malta. And we benefited from the advice of our publishing editors, Dr. Robert Neville, Julia Goddard and Anna Fabrizio, with whose guidance we have adopted the World Biblio-graphical Series' standard system of classifying entries, and from the first edition of this bibliography by J. R. Thackrah whose introduction we have amended and updated for this one. But the selection of titles, and therefore the omission of items, has been our own and we hope that it both represents the bulk of publications on Malta in the English language since about 1983 as well as a range sufficient to provide the basis for any contemporary student of Malta.

The Country and Its People

1   **A nation's praise: Malta: people, places and events: historical
     sketches.**
     A. E. Abela.   Valletta: Progress Press, 1994. 232p. bibliog.
The title well expresses the nature of this book – a large number of unrelated pieces of
information gathered from public records with well-reproduced illustrations of the
people, buildings and events in these accounts. Appendices list the men of Malta who
lost their lives in the First World War, as are recorded on the memorial in Floriana,
and Maltese recipients of the Royal Victorian Medal as well as members of the Royal
Victorian Order 1903-54. There is an extensive bibliography (p. 214-26) of the many
and various sources.

2   **Della descrittione de Malta isola nel mare Siciliano con le sue
     antichità ed altre notitie: libri quattro.** (An account of Malta island in
     the Sicilian sea with its antiquities, and other things of note: four books.)
     Fra. Gio. Francesco Abela.   Malta: Paolo Bonacota, 1647. 573p.
     Facsimile reproduction, Valletta: Midsea Books (Melitensia Book Club),
     1984.
This remarkable book was published in excellently clear Italian by a Maltese member
of the Order of St. John a century after its establishment in Malta. It is the classic of
Maltese studies. The four books comprising this single volume are devoted to the following topics: a description of the topography of the archipelago and antique sites; an
account of the succession of settlements and conquerors in Malta from its origins until
the arrival of the Order of St. John; an historical description of the diocese, parishes
and religious foundations in Malta; and notes on office holders from 1350-1530, the
old families of Malta and other famous men. It is a significant study of Malta and the
Maltese rather than an account of the Order's activities and is illustrated from copper-
plates of maps, buildings and antiquities to be found in the islands. It was published
with a substantial index.

3 **Annual abstract of statistics, 1993.**
Valletta: Central Office of Statistics, 1995. 258p.

This is no. 47 in a series which has appeared since 1947. It is subtitled 'an annual review of main statistical data on demography, labour, industry and other economic, financial and social subjects'. Text is limited to brief explanations of the major sections of tables on area and climate, population, justice and crime, education and culture, elections and referenda, labour and prices, foreign trade, agriculture and fisheries, transport and communications, industry, national accounts and balance of payments, banking, insurance and public finance.

4 **The story of Malta.**
B. W. Blouet. Valletta: Progress Press, 1993. 7th ed. 253p. bibliog.

This is an updated edition of a general historical and geographical survey, which first appeared in 1967. It continues to be an accessible introduction to the Maltese Islands. There are maps and figures and a bibliography (p. 229-44).

5 **Gozo and its culture: proceedings of the 1995 Löwenbrau Seminar.**
Edited by Lino Briguglio, Joseph Bezzina. Blata l-Bajda, Malta:
Formatek Ltd. for the University of Malta Gozo Centre and the
Foundation for International Studies, June 1995. 162p. bibliog.

The nine main papers include four devoted to aspects of local culture in prehistoric times (recently excavated findings), Gozo in classical literature, the social milieu of the island before the arrival of the Order of St. John, and the development of village settlements since then. The next four comprise papers on local folklore, the role of the church in education and cultural expression, village dialects, and patterns of artistic patronage in Gozo. The editor concludes with the cultural impact of economic conditions in Gozo. Many relevant tables and photographic illustrations accompany the texts and there are useful lists of references with each paper.

6 **Gozo. The roots of an island.**
Edited by Charles Cini, with photography by Maurizio Urso. Valletta:
Said International Ltd., 1990. 211p. maps. bibliog.

This magnificently illustrated, large-page volume has five main chapters. Anthony Bonanno deals with the archaeology and history of Gozo to the early Middle Ages, while Godfrey Wettinger brings the story up to modern times. Mario Buhagiar deals with painting, Denis de Lucca with the built environment and Marlene Mifsud-Chircop with Gozitan folklore. A substantial index makes this well-referenced work accessible. It is perhaps the most important recent publication on Gozo.

7 **A focus on Gozo.**
Edited by Joseph Farrugia, Lino Briguglio. Blata l-Bajda, Malta:
Formatek Ltd. for the University of Malta Gozo Centre with the Ministry
for Gozo and the Foundation for International Studies, 1996. 217p.
bibliog.

The fourteen papers on various aspects of Gozo are based on a series of lectures delivered in a course of 1994-95. They covered topics including: the geology and flora; archaeological research and religion; the 1551 Siege of Gozo and repopulation of the island and the experiences of a parish priest; the institutions of the Order in Gozo; problems in locating the site of the island's ancient town; windmills and flour production; local music; a 19th-century account of British rule in Gozo; and a review of development options for the island. Many relevant illustrations are included in the text.

8   **Towns and villages in Malta and Gozo (part one): the twin harbour area.**
     Charles Fiott.   Rabat, Malta: Religjon u Hajja (Conventual Franciscans), 1994. 161p. bibliog.

First of a planned four-part work (see also item no. 9) – three on Malta and one on Gozo – this deals with the localities bordering the two main harbours, Marsamxett Harbour and Grand Harbour. The book aims to give a very brief account of major historical sites, supported with maps, photographs, coats of arms, a bibliography (p. 133-34), and reference lists of terms, events, people, sites, etc.

9   **Towns and villages in Malta and Gozo (part two): the south.**
     Charles Fiott.   Rabat, Malta: Religjon u Hajja (Conventual Franciscans), 1996. 212p.

The second of a planned four-part work (see also item no. 8), this deals with twenty-one villages south of the main harbours. The text on each village is supported by a sketch-map and photographs. This is a readable yet information-filled account which captures much of the essence of the communities. The work is illustrated and has a useful glossary (p. 187-92) and indexes of events, personalities, sites, etc. (p. 193-212).

10   **Malta: culture and identity.**
     Edited by Henry Frendo, Oliver Friggieri.   Malta: Ministry of Youth and Arts, 1994. 272p. bibliog.

This volume of thirteen essays by members of the University of Malta staff and some other experts provides the best introduction to the history of the Maltese nation, its language and institutions of law and medicine, many facets of its past and present cultural history and achievements, its economy since Independence and past patterns of emigration. Useful selected bibliographies are provided by each author. However, specific attention is given to neither the significant place of religion and the Roman Catholic Church in Malta nor to the social characteristics of the population and their internal demographic dynamics.

11   **Maria Calleja's Gozo: a life history.**
     Edited by Micheline Galley.   Logan, Utah; Paris: Utah University Press and UNESCO Publishing, 1993. 245p. bibliog.

An oral history recorded after 1987, this forms one of the UNESCO collection of representative works. The twelve chapters cover Calleja's memories, events and impressions since her birth in 1915, with an introduction and explanatory notes by the editor. The text is illustrated with relevant photographs. Two appendices include a long letter from a Maltese who knew Miss Calleja in Australia, and the text of a folk poem in Maltese and English.

12 **Malta.**
Adrianus (Adriannes) Koster.   In: *Southern European studies guide.*
Edited by John Loughlin.   London: Bowker-Saur, 1993, p. 118-31.
bibliog. (Area Studies Guide Series).

This chapter is the best available brief English-language introduction to recent and
contemporary study of life in Malta. There is a – mostly annotated – list of sixty-five
representative titles (p. 125-31), in support of a valuable text review (p. 118-24).

13 **Malta and Gibraltar illustrated: historical and descriptive,
commercial and industrial, facts, figures and resources.**
Alistair Macmillan.   London: W. H. and L. Collingridge, 1915.
Facsimile edition, Valletta: Midsea Books (Melitensia Book Club),
1985. 516p.

This is a comprehensive survey of Malta (up to p. 397) in the second decade of the
20th century. It is evocatively illustrated with black-and-white photographs, including
now long-gone images of the Grand Harbour full of warships. More than fifty per cent
of the text relating to Malta deals with history. Nearly twenty-two per cent is devoted
to commerce, agriculture and fisheries. The commercial coverage is especially interesting since it gives details on individual enterprises. Fifteen per cent of the text
covers aspects of society, administration and government, education and medicine.
Remaining pages provide information on geology, climate and flora, and include a
short section on Gozo as well as some biographical notes.

14 **Malta.**
In: *The World Book Encyclopedia.*   London: World Book International,
1996, p. 121-23.

A succinct factual coverage of the Maltese Islands, and their people, society and history. Related short articles in *The World Book Encyclopedia* include those by G. Borġ
Olivier, C. Camilleri, F. Ebejer, E. Fenech Adami, D. Mintoff and A. Sciortino; there
is also an entry about the city of Valletta.

15 **Malta.**
In: *The New Encyclopaedia Britannica.*   Chicago: Encyclopaedia
Britannica Inc., 1997, 15th ed., vol. 7, p. 744-45.

Provides a brief factual description of Malta's land, people, economy, government,
culture and history. See also the entry under 'Knights of Malta'.

16 **Quarterly digest of statistics, April-June, 1994.**
Valletta: Central Office of Statistics, 1995. 44p.

This quarterly issue is no. 138 of a series which first appeared in 1960. Apart from an
explanatory 'Commentary' of a few pages, it is made up of summary tables on the economic, social and demographic topics covered in the *Annual Abstract of Statistics* (q.v.).

Geography and Geology

Geography

17   Malta: at the crossroads of the Mediterranean.
E. W. Anderson (Guest Editor). *Geojournal* (Amsterdam), vol. 41, no. 2 (1997), p. 99-191. bibliog.

The ten articles in this themed issue cover selected aspects of both the physical and human geography of the Maltese Islands. In the first contribution, C. O. Hunt gives examples of typical Mediterranean Quaternary lithofacies, including tufa and slope, fluvial, coastal, aeolian and cave deposits. E. W. Anderson writes about the *wied* valley landform as a predominant feature in Maltese geomorphology, while P. J. Schembri provides a valuable account of climate, vegetation and landscape. P. J. Atkins offers a paper on the Maltese food system, looking at nutrition and health implications within the wider socio-economic context. Louis F. Cassar takes a historical view of settlement patterns, concluding with the proposition that sensitive spatial planning is now a moral obligation. Douglas Lockhart writes on tourism in the islands since the 1960s – see also his 'Tourism in Malta and Cyprus' article (q.v.) – here stressing recent efforts towards achieving quality improvements. Malta's external security is Dominic Fenech's topic; he notes that the contextual focus since the 1980s has been on relations with the European Union. Ian R. Baggett develops this concern with an article on 'Malta: macropolitical threats' and Gerald H. Blake follows on with a discussion of the islands' maritime boundaries and sea areas of special influence. N. Birdi concludes this collection with a paper on water scarcity *within* Malta; the island has no rivers or lakes. He considers responses – such as reverse osmosis – to the over-exploitation of groundwater. Together these ten articles – each indicating useful references – provide important coverage of much of the islands' geography; individually they are valuable contributions to their respective fields.

18   **A new geography of the Maltese Islands.**
Anton Azzopardi.   Birkirkara, Malta: St. Aloysius College, printed at
Progress Press, 1995. 341p.

This is an attractive secondary-school text, covering both physical and human components of the subject. It is well written and illustrated and presents a general account of
each topic followed immediately by a detailed presentation regarding Malta and Gozo.

19   **Comino, Filfla and St. Paul's Island.**
Stanley Farrugia Randon, Robert Farrugia Randon.   Malta: The
Authors, 1995. 40p.

A compact descriptive history of Comino is followed by a brief survey of flora and
fauna. St. Paul's Island is best known for the tradition of the AD 60 shipwreck, when
St. Paul landed there, introducing Christianity to the islands. Filfla, once used for
target practice, has been a Natural Reserve since 1988. Both of these uninhabited
islets are described in some detail.

20   **Malta: a book and a map in one!**
Geo Data (cartography), Paul Otto Schultz (text), L. D. Legg
(translation), Vaclav Cerny (photographs) et al.   Munich: RV Reise
und Verkehrsverlag, 1995. map.

This is the second edition of this two-map sheet which folds to 25 × 13cm. The main
coverage is at 1:50,000 and there are urban plans of Floriana, Sliema, Valletta,
Cospicua, Senglea, and Vittoriosa at 1:10,000.

21   **Malta and Gozo: including plans of Valletta, Sliema, Victoria,
Mdina and Rabat, Buġibba: also including coastal and country
walks.**
Edinburgh: Bartholemew Clyde, 1993.

This useful map, in the 'Bartholemew Clyde Leisure Maps' series, folds to 22 × 13cm.
It is in colour and has a text in English, Italian and German.

22   **A geography of the Maltese Islands.**
N. Ransley, A. Azzopardi.   Birkirkara, Malta: St. Aloysius College,
1988. 4th ed. 150p.

This is a comprehensive school text which was first published in 1973. It covers the
physical environment, agriculture, fishing, quarrying and building, manufacturing,
trade, tourism, communications, settlement, water and energy.

Geology

23 **A review of the physical geography of Malta and its significance for tectonic geomorphology.**
David Alexander. *Quaternary Science Reviews*, vol. 7, no. 1 (1988), p. 41-53. bibliog.
The Maltese Islands constitute an example of the Quaternary evolution of limestone scenery of uncomplicated lithology and heavy dependence on vertical tectonic movements. In addition to discussion of these phenomena, this article includes a very useful review of relevant literature and a bibliography (p. 52-53).

24 **Accretion sets in the lower coralline limestone of the Maltese Islands.**
Christopher M. Davies. *Journal of Sedimentary Petrology*, vol. 46, no. 2 (1976), p. 414-17.
Discusses accretion sets generally 1-3 metres thick occurring in western exposures of the Lower Coralline Limestone which elsewhere in the islands is masked beneath karstic terrain. This brief account is illustrated.

25 **Oligo-Miocene stratigraphy of Malta and Gozo.**
Robert Felix. Utrecht, the Netherlands: Rijksuniversiteit te Utrecht, 1973. 115p.
The marine Tertiary sediments of the Maltese Islands and their foraminiferal faunas form the topic of this doctoral thesis (typescript available at the University of Malta Library). After an introduction to the geological structure there are substantial sections on lithostratigraphy and biostratigraphic zonation.

26 **Geological map of the Maltese Islands.**
Valletta: Department of Information, 1992.
This map in two sheets and at a scale of 1:25,000 has an improved informational coverage compared with the earlier 1:31,680 *Geological survey of the Maltese Islands* produced by the War Office in London (1953. 3rd edition).

27 **Graben formation – the Maltese Islands – a case history.**
J. Henning Illies. *Tectonophysics*, 73 (1981), p. 151-68.
Describes how the structural setting of the islands is governed by two rift systems of different ages and trends and the interference of both. Accompanying faults, exposed along cliffs, are among the world's most spectacular examples of rift faulting. The superimposition of the two rift structures is explained by rotation of the controlling stress regime about ten million years ago.

28 **The preservation of the shells of *Sepia* in the middle Miocene of Malta.**
R. A. Hewitt, H. M. Pedley. *Proceedings of the Geologists' Association*, vol. 89, part 3 (1978), p. 227-37.
Hewitt and Pedley explain that the general scarcity of fossil cuttlebones (*Sepia*) results from the limited range of marine environments in which they may be fossilized and

the destruction of post-mortem drifted shells on shore-lines. *Sepia* are found in the Maltese Islands at the top of the Blue Clay formation.

29　**The Maltese Islands: a tectonic-topographic study.**
William Herbert Hobbs. *The Scottish Geographical Magazine*, vol. 30 (1914), p. 1-13.

A brief, illustrated study of relief elements and the system of fractures within the rock basement, based on fieldwork in February 1913.

30　**The geology of the Maltese Islands, with special reference to water supply and the possibilities of oil.**
Herbert P. T. Hyde.　Valletta: Lux Press, 1955. 135p. bibliog.

This accessible and concise survey includes a bibliography (p. 114-24) and an index (p. 125-35). It is illustrated with figures and plates and remains a valuable review despite its age.

31　**Phosphorites, hardgrounds and syndepositional solution subsidence: a paleoenvironmental model from the Miocene of the Maltese Islands.**
H. M. Pedley, S. M. Bennett.　*Sedimentary Geology*, vol. 45 (1985), p. 1-34.

An illustrated account of the two major phosphorite horizons which occur throughout the islands within the Lower-Middle Miocene *Globigerina* limestone formation. The lower conglomerate lies directly upon a hardground and both conglomerates include lithoclasts of hardground material.

32　**Mineralogy and origin of the carbonate beach sediments of Malta and Gozo, Maltese Islands.**
Allessandro Turi, Marcello Picollo, Gigliola Valleri.　*Bollettino Società Geologica Italiana*, 109 (1990), p. 367-74. map.

Reports on how the contents of aragonite, calcite and high-Mg calcite, as well as the content of $MgCO$ within the calcites, were determined by x-ray diffraction analyses in samples of Recent sandy sediments collected on beaches. This paper includes tables.

33　**Pioneers of Maltese geology.**
George Żammit Maempel.　Birkirkara, Malta: Mid-Med Bank, 1989. 302p.

This provides accounts of the careers, scholarly works, geological and palaeontological research of the following British residents of Malta: T.A.B. Spratt (1811-88), a Royal Navy hydrographer; Sir William Reid (1791-1858), a Governor of Malta; Andrew Leith Adams (1827-82), a military surgeon; and John Henry Cooke (1862-1933), an educationist and pioneer aviator. The author had already published an account of Spratt's production of accurate charts and maps and the earliest correct account of Malta's geological structure in 1843 and excavated Quaternary deposits in 1867, with a list of his publications and charts in 'T.A.B. Spratt and his contribution to Maltese geology', in *Melita Historica*, vol. 9, no. 3 (1986), p. 271-308.

Travel Guides

Guidebooks

34 Malta.
Edited by Geoffrey Aquilina Ross, Lyle Lawson (photography), Brian
Bell (editorial director). Singapore: APA Productions, 1991. 355p.
bibliog. (Insight Guides Series).

This is a colourfully illustrated comprehensive introduction to the Maltese Islands. See
also the *Insight Pocket Guide* by Lyle Lawson which gives the 'essentials' in 93
smaller-format pages.

35 The maze. A handy guide to the streets of Malta and Gozo.
Frans A. Attard. Birkirkara, Malta: Uptrend Publishing, 1994. 400p.

This is a revised version of Attard's *The maze: guide to streets of Malta and Gozo,
complete with a quick guide to Maltese towns and villages* (Birkirkara, Malta: Uptrend
Publishing, 1992). It is the best street plan currently available though it suffers from
lack of full clarity in some areas and, inevitably, cannot hope to keep up with the construction of new roads and buildings. There is an index of streets starting on p. 20.

36 Berlitz Malta.
Martin Gostelow (text), Martin Gostelow and Richard Boyle
(photography). Princeton, New Jersey: Berlitz Publishing Co. Inc.,
1996. 2nd ed. 124p. (Berlitz Pocket Guides).

The best 'pocket-guide' to Malta and Gozo, with information and advice for the visitor together with background description of the islands' past and present, illustrated
with photographs and maps. Several editions have appeared since 1980 in English and
other European languages. The next best after Berlitz in the pocket-guide category is
probably *Malta* by Hilary Hughes (see item no. 43).

37 **Malta and Gozo.**
Susie Boulton (original photography by Philip Enticknap).
Basingstoke, England: Automobile Association Publishing, 1994. 192p.
(Thomas Cook Travellers' Guides).

This title is an accessible illustrated introduction to where to go and what to see. It bills itself as 'up to date, easy to use, and packed with hints and tips'.

38 **Visitors' guide, Malta and Gozo.**
Geoffrey Brown, Alistair Morrison (cartography). Ashbourne,
England: Moorland Publishing, 1993. 192p. (Holiday islands).

This is an attractive guide to travelling in and around Malta and Gozo, with colour illustrations. It was published in the United States by Hunter Publishing Inc., Edison, New Jersey.

39 **Essential Malta and Gozo.**
Carole Chester. Basingstoke, England: Automobile Association
Publishing (Valletta: Miller Distributors), 1994. 128p.

An effective pocket-guide on what to see and how to get around in Malta and Gozo.

40 **Malta, Gozo and Comino.**
Brian Dicks. Moreton-in-Marsh, England: The Windrush Press, 1991.
175p. (Windrush Island Guides).

An informative handbook on visiting the islands.

41 **Malta, Gozo and Comino.**
Simon Gaul, Anna Grima (illustrations). London: Cadogan Books,
1993. 372p. bibliog. (Cadogan Island Guides).

This is a straightforward aid to getting about in the islands, with plans of places of interest. References are listed on p. 362-64.

42 **Illustrated guide to Malta and Gozo with a short history of the Maltese Islands.**
Joseph Gott Rutter. Malta: The Colonial Library, c.1934. 154p.

A comprehensive, standard form of guidebook with sharp, half-tone illustrations, many references to the modification of buildings and public spaces during the British period, and eighteen pages of local advertisements, which are themselves of historical interest.

43 **Malta.**
Hilary Hughes, photographs by Phil Springthorpe, cartography by Susan
Harvey Design. Glasgow: Harper Collins, 1991. 126p.

This is another convenient pocket-guide, similar to *Berlitz Malta* (q.v.).

44   **Malta and Gozo: travellers' guide.**
Christopher Kininmonth, revised edition by Robin Gordon-Walker.
London: Jonathan Cape, 1987. 4th ed. 224p. (Travellers' Guides).
An informative, popular, pocket-sized aid to seeing the sights of the islands.

45   **Landscapes of Malta, Gozo and Comino: a countryside guide.**
Douglas Lockhart, Sue Ashton, photographs by the author, maps by
John Theasby, drawings by Sharon Rochford, John Theasby.   London:
Sunflower Books, 1989. 120p.
There is a step-by-step account of fifty-seven long and short walks together with general information about preparation and access. There are outlines for three tours by car and over thirty picnic suggestions. This is the most effective pocket-guide of its type: it is well illustrated and includes some effective locality maps.

46   **Blue Guide. Malta and Gozo.**
Peter McGregor Eadie (text), John Flower (maps and plans).   London:
A & C Black; New York: W. W. Norton, 1995. 4th ed. 148p.
This compact and illustrated guide and introduction packs in a lot of information in typical 'Blue Guide' style.

47   **Mdina: the old city in Malta. A supplement of *Heritage*.**
Edited by John Manduca.   Valletta: Midsea Publications Ltd., 1991.
29p. bibliog.
A useful outline of the history of this little walled city and its buildings, with a substantial article on the Middle Ages by Stanley Fiorini and shorter items on an altarpiece at Sta. Scolastica, and the cathedral. Coloured illustrations are used as well as reproductions of prints, plans and architectural drawings. The publication makes a convenient and inexpensive guide but lacks a contemporary map of the buildings mentioned in the text.

Photo-books

48   **Malta. Mediterranean crossroads.**
Valentina Amico, English translation by Merven J. Grealey, photographs
by Bruna Polimeni.   Rome: MP Graphic Formula, 1995. 96p.
A collection of excellent photographs with introductory text on p. 2-5.

49   **Images of Malta.**
Geoffrey Aquilina Ross, photographs by Eddie Aquilina, Daniel Cilia.
Sliema, Malta: Miranda Publications, 1990. 124p.
Text, up to p. 34, is followed by an array of evocative colour photographs of a variety of Maltese scenes.

50 **Malta and its islands.**

Aldo E. Azzopardi, photographs by Bruna Polimeni. Terni, Italy: Plurigraf, 1989 and 1995 (distributed by Miller Distribution Ltd., Valletta). 128p.

This is a beautifully illustrated 'glossy' guide with some text (p. 2-15 in the 1995 edition). A shorter version also appeared as *Malta: a new colour guide.*

51 **Malta. Gem of the Mediterranean.**

Aldo E. Azzopardi. Terni, Italy: Plurigraf, 1995. 95p.

Excellent colour photographs with accompanying text.

52 **The Maltese Islands from the air.**

Jonathan Beacom (photographs), Geoffrey Aquilina Ross (text). Balzan, Malta: Proud Publishing Limited, 1994. 159p.

Fine colour photographs, with explanatory text, make this a visual feast of the landscape, towns, villages and farms of Malta and Gozo. Some of the pictures are printed across a page and a half: this enhances their size but impairs their quality as images.

53 **Gozo and Comino 360 degrees.**

Attilio Boccazzi-Varotto, Daniel Cilia (photography), Joseph Bezzina (text), Nicola Paris (sketches). Ivrea, Italy: Priuli & Verlucca, 1992. 160p.

This contains a varied selection of large, magnificent colour photographs with supporting text.

54 **Legacy in stone: the architecture of the Knights of St. John in Malta.**

Daniel Cilia, Michael Ellul. Sliema, Malta: Miranda Publications, 1991. 50p. + 48 full-page plates.

The extravagant format of this large book belies the simplicity of its actual layout. Notes by Ellul on the architecture are interposed between the richly coloured and glossy plates by Cilia, many of which are remarkable wide-angled shots of the fortifications and interiors as well as exteriors of some churches and palaces.

55 **Gozo: a journey in the past.**

Edited by Charles Cini, with Giuseppe Castelli (presentation), Francis Cremona, Joseph Cremona, Joseph Vella (photography), Paul Curmi (captions). Victoria, Gozo, Malta: Ars Nova Publications, 1992. 129p.

An album of excellent historic photographs with special reference to local work and customs, religious celebrations and the British royal visits of 1954 and 1967. Unfortunately few of these images are dated, though there are descriptive captions.

56 **Malta.**
    Claude Gaffiero (text and captions), Kevin Casha (photographs), Alison
    Jewell (maps).   Valletta: Miller Distribution Ltd., 1992. 116p. maps.
This is a collection of superb colour photographs of contemporary scenes (p. 25-116)
preceded by an introductory descriptive text (p. 9-24).

57 **Malta, Gozo and Comino.**
    Nicosia, Cyprus: Ghinis Publishing Limited (distributed in Malta by
    Haster International Ltd., St. Julian's, Malta), 1994. 144p.
This is a collection of beautiful colour photographs with some text (p. 2-17). There is
no specific author credit.

Travellers' Accounts

58   A visit to Germany, Italy and Malta 1840-1841 (A Poet's Bazaar I-II).
Hans Christian Andersen, translated by Grace Thornton.   London: Peter Owen, 1985. 182p. bibliog.

Andersen's journey from 31 October 1840 to 22 July 1841 included a short stop in Malta which is described on p. 167-74. There have been more perceptive visitors to the islands.

59   A tour through Sicily and Malta.
Patrick Brydone.   Edinburgh: William and Robert Chambers, 1840. 88p.

Brydone (born 1743) visited Malta in 1770. His account, including some description of the island and of the Knights, was published in 1773, 1790, and 1840. He noted *inter alia* that 'the industry of the Maltese in cultivating their little island is inconceivable'. Another version of this account appeared in two volumes in Paris in 1780 as a series of letters.

60   Life and letters of Robert Clement Sconce.
Compiled for his grandchildren by his daughter Sarah Susanna Bunbury.   London: Cox & Wyman, 1861. 2 vols.

As secretary to Admiral Sir J. Duckworth, Sconce (1787-1846) spent a significant part of his career in Malta. Dealing with the second quarter of the 19th century, his account covers a period often ignored by those focusing on the earlier years of British rule.

61   Some 19th century hotels in Malta.
J. Cassar Pullicino.   *Melita Historica*, vol. 8, no. 2, 1981, p. 110-24.

A review of the information contained in British travellers' accounts of hotels in Malta, mostly Valletta, the first flutter of the now dominant tourist industry.

14

62 A Poet's bazaar: Hans Christian Andersen and his visit to Malta in 1841.
Erik Dal.   Valletta: Malta International Book Fair, 1991. xiiip. bibliog.
This essay is the introduction to a 40-page catalogue of 161 books etc. exhibited at the 1991 Malta International Book Fair, mostly related to Andersen, Denmark and Malta at the time of his visit in 1841.

63 Voyages and travels in the years 1809, 1810, 1811.
John Galt.   London: T. Cadell & W. Davies, 1812-13. 435p.
This book, 'containing statistical, commercial and miscellaneous observations' (from the subtitle) has twenty pages (p. 116-37) on Malta. Galt notes that 'the produce of [Malta] is inadequate to support its population above a few months though the land is cultivated to the utmost . . .' and there are perceptive comments on Malta's prospects in imperial and world trade.

64 Daddy, we hardly knew you.
Germaine Greer.   London: Penguin Books, 1989. 311p.
The author's quest for evidence of her father's actuality, which turned out to be very different from the accounts told, or left untold, by her parents, includes three chapters (p. 153-94) devoted to his time as an RAF Secret and Confidential Publications Officer working on the Ultra programme under the Lascaris bastion in Valletta in 1942. He was invalided out with a psychological disorder and shipped home to Australia.

65 A voyage in vain: Coleridge's journey to Malta in 1804.
Alethea Hayter.   London: Robin Clark Ltd., 1993. 188p. bibliog.
When Coleridge set out for Malta he had great hopes of recapturing an ideal self but was sick with dejection by the time he arrived. This account is based on the poet's diary and the letters of his friends and interweaves his and their thoughts and activities with those of Nelson and his warships in one of which Coleridge was voyaging. There is a section of eight illustrations.

66 The General: the travel memoirs of General Sir George Whitmore.
Edited by Joan Johnson.   Gloucester, England: Alan Sutton, 1987. 244p.
This is the only substantial available source on the life, works and opinions of the senior Royal Engineer to whom can be attributed most of the 'baseless Doric' neo-classical buildings of significance erected in Malta and Corfu between 1812 and the early 1830s. It is well illustrated from Whitmore's sketches and caricatures of the buildings, landscape and characters witnessed on his travels and postings, but fails to indicate sections of his memoirs which have been omitted, some of which are of great interest to Maltese historians.

67 The moon's a balloon: reminiscences.
David Niven.   London: Hamish Hamilton, 1971. 312p.
This, the first of the actor's two-volume autobiography, includes reflections of his posting to Malta with the Highland Light Infantry between the world wars (chapters 5-7). Both the incidents and the young officer's attitudes provide an instructive as well as amusing picture of army life in the stone frigate.

68   **Viaggio del sud/Journey to the south 1664-1665.**
      William Schellinks, edited by Bernard Aikema.   Rome: Edizioni
      Elefante, 1983.141p. map. bibliog.

Although several drawings of Malta by this artist have been dispersed, the majority
remain within the fifty volumes known as 'Prince Eugen's Atlas' in the Austrian
National Library at Vienna. Sixty-one of these have been reproduced here on a splendidly large scale with an introduction in French by Yves Bonnefoy. The account of the
project and Schellinks's role, as well as the intensive notes on each drawing, are in
Italian and English. Figures 45-60 reproduce the first extensive series of landscapes,
buildings, shipping and activities in the Grand Harbour, Rabat and other parts of Malta.
The appendix provides a calendar of the catalogued drawings from 4 May 1664-6
February 1665.

69   **Malta 1796-1797: Thorvaldsen's visit; based on the unpublished
      diary of Peder Pavels.**
      Edited by Sven Sorensen, Joseph Schiro.   San Ġwann, Malta: Beck
      Graphics, 1996. 120p. bibliog.

Pavels accompanied the renowned neo-classical sculptor on a Danish frigate bound for
Italy and his account is one of the last during the era of the Order of St. John. The
December feasts are described as well as features no longer extant in Mdina and
Rabat. The text has thirty illustrations and six essays from Danish and Maltese schol-
ars and includes a discussion of British monuments in Malta in which Thorvaldsen
may have been involved.

70   **The journey of Sir Walter Scott to Malta.**
      Donald Sultana.   Gloucester, England: Alan Sutton, 1986. 190p.
      bibliog.

An account of Sir Walter's journey to London, passage to Malta, quarantine and stay
in Valletta in 1831, a year before his death. The appendices include the full text of
Mrs John Davy's diary of Scott's visit, and poems and prose arising from Scott's
Mediterranean journey. The plates illustrate places and people associated with Scott or
Malta.

71   **The journey of William Frere to Malta in 1832, preceded by a
      sketch of his life and of the Frere family, with particular reference
      to John Hookham Frere.**
      Donald Sultana.   Malta: Progress Press, c.1988. 178p.

An important source of information on the Anglo-Maltese intellectual circle around
J. H. Frere as well as on his brother in England and the form of such latter-day 'grand
tours'. It includes a description of the consecration of St. Paul's collegiate church in
1844 as well as the score of Mrs William (Mary) Frere's *Te Deum*, which was composed for the occasion and sung again at the cathedral's 150th anniversary service in
1994. J. H. Frere had retired to Malta for the sake of his wife's health. He built a large
villa on the sea front at Piétà with an extensive garden and was much involved in the
redevelopment of the university and its medical school as well as the establishment of
what is now the National Library, which was under construction when the Order of St.
John was expelled by Napoleon.

72 **Byron's visits to Malta.**
Peter Vassallo. In: *Byron and the Mediterranean: papers selected from the tenth International Byron Seminar.* Edited by Peter Vassallo. Msida, Malta: University of Malta Press, 1986, p. 20-30. bibliog.
This article provides information on aspects of Byron's visits and some of the people he encountered. Malta was an important staging post for voyagers to the eastern Mediterranean including Lady Hester Stanhope and the Greek marbles *en route* to various destinations.

73 **Malta in the 19th century: a selection of visitors' accounts.**
Compiled by Paul Xuereb. In: *VI Malta International Book Fair (22-25 October).* Valletta: Ministry of Education, 1987, p. 35-59. bibliog.
A useful selection of quotations by seventeen, mainly British, visitors, preceded by a brief note on each author.

74 **'The Arabian voyage 1761-67' and Malta: Forsskål and his contribution to the study of local natural history.**
George Żammit Maempel. In: *Proceedings of History Week 1992.* Edited by Stanley Fiorini. Malta: The Malta Historical Society, 1994, p. 35-76.
Petrus Forsskål (1732-63), the renowned Swedish naturalist, visited Malta in 1761 on a specimen-collecting expedition to the Levant. He provided the first list of fish found in Maltese waters as well as a short list of local wild plants and a list of fossils. He died of plague in the Yemen but his collections were taken back to Denmark although they do not seem to include any of the Maltese material.

Flora and Fauna

75   **Discovering nature in the Maltese Islands.**
Alfred E. Baldacchino, Edwin Lanfranco, Patrick J. Schembri.   Blata
l-Bajda, Malta: Merlin Library, 1990. 104p.
An easy-to-read introduction, which is informative and well illustrated, to the flora
and fauna of the islands.

76   **Birds of the Maltese archipelago.**
David A. Bannerman, Joseph A. Vella-Gaffiero.   Valletta: Museums
Department, 1976. 550p. bibliog.
This remains the definitive volume on its subject and is the first comprehensive
description of species seen in the islands. It is profusely illustrated and gives species
names in the scientific form and in English, Maltese and Italian. The work documents
the role of Malta and Gozo in bird migration between Europe and North Africa.

77   **Descriptive flora of the Maltese Islands, including the ferns and
flowering plants.**
John Borg.   Valletta: Government Printing Office, 1927. 846p.
In addition to the Classification (p. 69ff.) there is a comprehensive introduction (p. 1-68)
which traces the development of the study of Maltese flora and provides an overview
of geology, soils, water and climate as they relate to plants.

78   **The marine shelled mollusca of the Maltese Islands (Part One:
Archaeogastropoda).**
Charles Cachia, Constantine Mifsud, Paul M. Sammut, with illustrations
by Alfred Caruana Ruggier.   Marsa, Malta: Grima Printing and
Publishing Industries, 1991. 113p. bibliog.
Most of this well-illustrated volume consists of a systematic account of the species (p. 29-
102) and a substantial bibliography (p. 103-08). The authors promise further volumes.

79 **A study of the Maltese *Kelb Tal-Fenek*.**
Cecil S. Camilleri.   Valletta: Progress Press, 1995. 180p. bibliog.

An extensive review and analysis, in two sections, of the evolution and history, and the anatomy and physiology, of the Maltese domestic hound, with a third section of coloured plates of various places in Malta. The text is illustrated with many line-drawings and photographs.

80 **The millipedes of the Maltese Islands (central Mediterranean): Diplodopa.**
Henrick Enghoff, Patrick J. Schembri.   *Bolletino Società Entimologica Italiana*, vol. 120, no. 3 (February 1989), p. 164-73.

This study is based on a collection of some 600 millipedes, amassed between 1975 and 1987, by systematic collecting of all Maltese habitat types. It summarizes present knowledge of the Diplodopa of the islands.

81 **The non-marine molluscs of the Maltese Islands.**
Folco Gusti, Giuseppe Manganelli, Patrick J. Schembri.   Turin, Italy: Museo Regionale di Scienze Naturali (Monografie xv), 1995. 607p. bibliog.

This elegant, illustrated and comprehensive coverage of its subject starts with valuable introductory sections on the physical geography of the islands (p. 15-25), on vegetation (by Edwin Lanfranco, p. 27-29), on non-marine fauna (p. 31-44) and on Malta's biogeography (p. 45-49). Then follows an account of the general organization and morphology of the gastropods and bivalves. The main part of the book consists of a catalogue of over 78 species (p. 100-512). Following this is a concluding section and appendices. There is an extensive bibliography (p. 544-87) which can be used in conjunction with the 'Brief history of malacological research in the Maltese Islands' (p. 87-90).

82 **Malta's plant life.**
S. M. Haslam.   Valletta: Progress Press, 1969. 120p.

A survey of the physical and climatic setting of the islands' flora and consideration of the impact of man in general terms, accompanied by illustrations. For a full account of species see *A flora of the Maltese Islands* (q.v.).

83 **A flora of the Maltese Islands.**
S. M. Haslam, P. D. Sell, P. A. Wolseley, with contributions by J. Borġ, H. Micallef, M. Rix.   Msida, Malta: Malta University Press, 1977. 560p. bibliog.

After a succinct review/overview of the physical and climatic setting of plants (p. vii-lvii), this comprehensive description of plant species in the islands is followed by forty-six pages of line-drawings (between p. 490 and p. 491), an excellent glossary (p. 494-518), bibliography (p. 519-20) and an index. This remains the major source on flora.

84   **The fish around Malta (central Mediterranean).**
      Guido G. Lanfranco.   Valletta: Progress Press, 1993. 132p. bibliog.
An excellent handbook on 288 different fish with their specific families and names as
well as their Maltese names, sizes and distinct characteristics. The colour plates illustrate all the entries but without a scale. The book updates several earlier versions by
the author.

85   **Red data book for the Maltese Islands.**
      Edited by Patrick J. Schembri, Joe Sultana.   Valletta: Department of
      Information, 1989. 142p.
This important reference work offers nothing less than an inventory of the flora and
fauna of the islands, with a very useful introductory text (p. 1-4). The work, which is
illustrated – partly in colour – draws attention to questions of the conservation of bio-
logical resources and of concern for rare and endangered species.

86   **The fauna of the Maltese Islands. A review and analysis.**
      Patrick J. Schembri.   In: *Collected papers, contributed by members of
      the academic staff of the University of Malta.*   Edited by Roger
      Ellul-Micallef, Stanley Fiorini.   Msida, Malta: University of Malta,
      1992, p. 541-73. bibliog.
Reviews the study of terrestrial and freshwater fauna carried out since the 1914
account by Giovanni Gulia ('Uno sguardo alla zoologia delle Isole Maltese': IXe
Congrès Internat. de Zoologie, Monaco, 1913, 1914 – A glance at the zoology of the
Maltese Islands: 9th International Congress of Zoology, Monaco, 1913, 1914). The
stress is on endemic species and those with restricted or disjunct distributions in the
Mediterranean but the information available is not consistent so that only a preliminary analysis of Maltese faunistics and biogeography is possible at present. There is
an extensive bibliography (p. 562-73).

87   **Diversity and conservation of the non-marine molluscs of the
      Maltese Islands.**
      Patrick J. Schembri.   In: *Biodiversity and conservation of the
      Mollusca: proceedings of the Alan Solem Memorial Symposium, Siena,
      Italy, 1992.*   Edited by A. C. van Bruggen, S. M. Wells, Th. C. M.
      Kemperman.   Oegstgeest-Leiden, the Netherlands: Backhuys, 1995,
      p. 217-22. bibliog.
Nearly 100 species and subspecies of non-marine molluscs – about a third of them
thought to be endemic – have been recorded for the Maltese Islands, though precise
details are still obscure in some cases.

88   **A new guide to the birds of Malta.**
      Joe Sultana, Charles Gauci.   Valletta: Ornithological Society, 1982.
      207p.
This provides information on birds which breed in Malta and on migrant species in the
context of habitat restrictions and continuing trapping and shooting. The volume is not
intended as a guide to identification.

89   **The biogeography of the Maltese Islands, illustrated by the Clausiliidae.**
M. A. Thake.   *Journal of Biogeography*, vol. 12, no. 12 (1985), p. 269-87. bibliog.
Published data on the geology and biogeography of the islands are reviewed. The Maltese biota closely resemble the biota of Sicily, though there are several endemics. A few species occur in Malta and North Africa but are not found in Sicily. This paper interprets Maltese biogeography in terms of sea level changes and tectonic events which established or severed land connections with Sicily.

90   **The moths of the Maltese Islands.**
Anthony Valletta.   Faringdon, England: E. W. Classey, 1974. 118p.
This essential reference work provides a comprehensive record for the period 1858 to 1972, incorporating the work of Valletta and others.

91   **Additions to the known Lepidoptera (Heterocera) of the Maltese Islands.**
Anthony Valletta.   *Entomologist's Record*, 96 (1984), p. 45-48.
This is an unannotated bibliography, listing mostly English-language, but some Italian, German, etc., works. See also Valletta's 'Bibliography of the Lepidoptera-Heterocera of the Maltese Islands', *Melita Historica*, vol. 2, no. 1 (1956), p. 41ff.

92   **Hazardous Mediterranean fish.**
Louis Żammit.   Malta: The Author, n.d. 29p. map. bibliog.
This short book comprises notes on each of thirteen fish which are illustrated by pen drawings and a note on eight kinds of sharks.

Prehistory and Archaeology

General and prehistoric

93 **Habitations of the great goddess.**
Cristina Biaggi. Manchester, Connecticut: Knowledge, Ideas and Trends, Inc., 1994. 201p. bibliog.

This very well-illustrated and documented study of the temples of Malta (and of the Scottish islands of Orkney and the Shetlands) focuses on the temple architecture and art dating from the period some 6,000-4,000 years ago. The author adds to previous work on the Maltese temples an analysis specifically concerned with the sites in the context of a theocratic society worshipping a goddess as its main deity. The study provides evidence for the existence across Europe of a goddess religion, which continued nearly a millennium longer in the north Scottish islands than in Malta. It may be seen as renewing the vitality of the thesis of a primordial goddess long associated with Margaret Murray (1920s).

94 **Archaeology and fertility cult in the ancient Mediterranean: papers presented at the first International Conference on Archaeology of the Ancient Mediterranean, the University of Malta.**
Edited by Anthony Bonanno. Amsterdam: B. R. Grüner Publishing Co., 1985. 356p. bibliog.

The 'Prehistory, Malta' section of this collection comprises four papers devoted to aspects of Maltese temples and the sculpture found in them, with a general review of their significance and possible interpretation by Professor Lord (Colin) Renfrew.

95 **An illustrated guide to prehistoric Gozo.**
Anthony Bonanno. Gozo, Malta: Gozo Press, 1986. 48p. map. bibliog.

This useful pocket-guide provides information on twenty-two sites as well as the Gozo Museum and plans of the main temples. The access to each site is described and each is on the map. Thirty-five photographic and other illustrations, plans and charts depict the sites as well as artifacts held in the museum in the Gozo citadel.

96 **Malta an archaeological paradise.**
Anthony Bonanno. Malta: M. J. Publications Ltd., 1987. 62p.
Although brief, the text provides a useful and contemporary description of both the remarkable Neolithic sites and artifacts to be seen in the islands as well as Punic and Roman remains. The excellent coloured photographs by Mario Mintoff are augmented by detailed, scaled plans of the best preserved temples and a chart of radio-carbon dates for each cultural settlement phase. This work is the most accessible, best illustrated and reasonably priced review of some of the greatest buildings of the prehistoric world.

97 **Monuments in an island society: the Maltese context.**
A. Bonanno, T. Gouder, C. Malone, S. Stoddart. *World Archaeology,* vol. 22, no. 2 (1990), p. 190-205. bibliog.
This paper advances an alternative to the assumption that centralized social forces must have been required to mobilize the resources to build these prehistoric temples etc. The authors look to the network theory of social anthropologists and argue that inter-communal rivalry may have determined both the increased complexity of temple construction and then its abandonment in favour of ritual investment in cremation cemeteries and dolmens. Tables and figures are provided to illustrate the paper.

98 **Underwater archaeology: a new turning-point in Maltese archaeology.**
Anthony Bonanno. *Hyphen*, vol. 7, no. 3 (1995), p. 105-10.
Reviews the past and present situation and the potential role of the new Maritime Museum in Birgu (Vittoriosa), which opened to the public in the former Naval Bakery in July 1992.

99 **Research on prehistoric and Roman Gozo: past, present and future.**
Anthony Bonanno. In: *A Focus on Gozo.* Edited by Joseph Farrugia and Lino Briguglio. Victoria, Gozo, Malta: University of Malta Gozo Centre, in collaboration with the Ministry for Gozo and the Foundation for International Studies, 1996, p. 41-57. bibliog.
This chapter by one of Malta's leading authorities on the period, considers the Ġgantija temples, the Għajnsielem huts, and the Xagħra stone circle, together with a look at newly investigated sites. Also reviewed is work on Roman Gozo, with consideration of the written record including inscriptions, and on the physical remains which have escaped destruction in the name of development.

100 **Malta.**
John Davies Evans. London: Thames & Hudson, 1959. 256p. bibliog. (Ancient Peoples and Places).
This authoritative account of Malta's prehistoric past deals with the religion and lives of the earliest people as well as with their temples and tombs. It is well illustrated with figures and photographs, which compensate for the fact that, like Evans's *magnum opus* in Maltese prehistory – *The prehistoric antiquities of the Maltese Islands: a survey* (q.v.) – it predates the introduction of radio-carbon dating techniques.

101 **The prehistoric antiquities of the Maltese Islands: a survey.**
John Davies Evans. London: Athlone Press, 1971. 260p. bibliog.

This is still the most comprehensive review and gazetteer of twenty-four archaeological sites in Malta and six in Gozo, listing the artifacts discovered including complete
pots and those that could be substantially reassembled. It is extensively illustrated
with plans, figures and plates. The bibliography aims to be comprehensive before 1900
and selective thereafter. The book's coverage includes Neolithic and Bronze Age settlements, 'cart tracks', finds of unknown provenance in the National Museum, and
catalogues of sites. The chronology of cultures, however, predates the availability of
radio-carbon dating which has greatly extended the apparent antiquity of these
Maltese sites and their significance for architectural history etc. Three indexes cover
sites, geographical and personal names, and general items.

102 **The prehistoric parish temples of Malta.**
Ian F. G. Ferguson. *Journal of Maltese Studies*, vol. 1, no. 2 (1991),
p. 286-94. bibliog.

Ferguson argues that the development and distribution of the forty-three named temple
sites suggest both demographic growth and local territorialism such as that reflected
today in the monumental parish churches.

103 **Malta's maritime archaeology.**
Alexandra Hildred. In: *St. John's Historical Society Proceedings*.
London: Museum of the Order of St. John, vol. 2 (1988-90), p. 38-46.

This is a general report on the exploratory searches of the Malta Archaeological Project
carried out by the *Mary Rose* Trust. Several sites of different periods are briefly described
as are the sorts of material brought up in the excavation of historic ships lost at sea.

104 **A house for the temple builders: recent investigations on Gozo,
Malta.**
C. Malone, S. Stoddart, D. Trump. *Antiquity*, vol. 62, no. 235 (1988),
p. 297-301. bibliog.

This is a report from new archaeological research into the Neolithic and Copper-Age
monuments of the Maltese Islands. Uniquely, this concerns domestic architecture discovered by Joe Attard, a local amateur archaeologist, in the foundations of a new
house. Figures illustrate the plan of the site and small finds in various materials.

105 **Maltese prehistoric art 5000-2500 B.C.**
Edited by Anthony Pace. Valletta: Fondazzjoni Patrimonju Malti in
association with the National Museum of Archaeology, 1996. 88p.
bibliog.

This is an important publication because it summarizes the results of the recent excavations of the stone circle and hypogeum at Xagħra in Gozo, illustrates these finds with
all the other items in the section forming the catalogue of an exhibition held in Gozo in
April 1996, and provides a comprehensive bibliography of these and other aspects of
prehistoric archaeology in the Maltese Islands. The seven articles preceding the catalogue have good coloured illustrations, which include those painted by von Brockdorff
for the album commissioned by the Duke of Buckingham in 1828. Three of the articles,
by Anthony Pace, David Trump and Anthony Bonanno, are chiefly concerned with

artistic aspects of the artifacts. Two, by Tancred Gouder and Giovanni Bonello, recount the history of Maltese archaeology and the early records of the sites by foreign visitors, through the study of which Joseph Attard rediscovered the site of the Xagħra circle. And another two, by John Evans, and by Caroline Malone and Simon Stoddart, discuss the possible functions of both the temples and the burial chambers. The bibliography includes articles recently published by the authors in a variety of journals.

106   **Cult in an island society: prehistoric Malta in the Tarxien period.**
      Simon Stoddart, Anthony Bonanno, Tancred Gouder, Caroline Malone,
      David Trump.   *Cambridge Archaeological Journal*, vol. 3, no. 1
      (1993), p. 3-19. bibliog.

This article examines the cult practices within the wider context of this type of society and compares the two linked temple and burial sites in Malta and Gozo. Particular attention is given to the relevant finds excavated at the Tarxien temple and the Brochtorff circle mortuary complex, which are illustrated by ten figures. Notable cult items are the twin-seated figurines of mother goddesses and a shaman's bundle of stick figurines etc. The same material was discussed by the same authors in a more general article with an excellent cut-away perspective of the underground burial chambers of the Brochtorff circle: 'The death cults of prehistoric Malta', *Scientific American*, vol. 269, no. 6 (1993), p. 110-17.

107   **Malta: an archaeological guide.**
      D. H. Trump.   London: Faber & Faber, 1972. 171p. bibliog.
      New edition, Malta: Progress Press, 1990.

This excellent guide was one of a series edited by Glyn Daniel and written by an archaeologist and ex-curator of the National Museum of Malta. After a general introduction, the author describes the monuments and sites in six regions of the islands, which are illustrated by clear photographs and precise plans, sections and other line-drawings. Subsequent publications by the author are listed in the bibliographies of recent articles by Bonanno, Malone and Stoddart (q.v.).

108   **Female images of Malta: goddess, giantess, farmeress.**
      Veronica Veen.   Haarlem, the Netherlands: Inannafia Publication,
      1994. 75p. bibliog.

The author associates Malta as the ancient land of the goddess with women's stories about the giantess and the currently threatened existence of the farm woman. The bibliography lists the author's various publications of her interpretation of the Maltese archaeological record.

109   **The cart tracks at San Pawl tat-Tarġa, Naxxar.**
      Frank Ventura, Tony Tanti.   *Melita Historica*, vol. 11, no. 3 (1994),
      p. 219-40. bibliog.

This is an account of the mysterious parallel worn ruts which are to be seen in one of the exposed rock outcrop areas in Malta. The conclusion is that these particular ruts do link fields but this study, which also reviews work on ruts found elsewhere, concedes that there may be alternative explanations in other areas, where the same phenomena are found.

110 **Tarxien temples and Saflieni hypogeum: description.**
Sir Themistocles Żammit with introduction, photographs and drawings
by Karl Mayrhofer.   Malta: Interprint, 1994. 96p.
A useful reprint of the guidebooks originally published by the pioneer of Maltese
archaeology in 1929 and 1935, with Zammit's plans and drawings.

111 **The prehistoric temples of Malta and Gozo: a description by
Professor Sir Themistocles Żammit.**
Sir Themistocles Żammit with additions by Karl Mayrhofer.   Malta:
The Author, 1995. 175p. bibliog.
The text of this pioneer archaeologist's illustrated descriptions of each site have been
augmented by photographs and line-drawings by the editor who has designed it as a
guidebook. It includes plans and sketch-maps and a selected bibliography. The five
original descriptions were published between 1929 and 1935, and this is an accessible
representation of a classic work.

112 **Għar Dalam cave and deposits.**
George Żammit Maempel.   Birkikara, Malta: The Author, 1989. 74p.
bibliog.
This account of the most important site of Pleistocene and subsequent prehistoric
layers in Malta incorporates summaries of various archaeological examinations with
useful plans and photographs of the caves and finds. The latter include tusks and other
bones of dwarf elephants, hippopotami and other animals, some of which were stolen
from the site museum in 1980, indicating the accessibility of Malta to the continental
mainland. The bibliography provides a comprehensive list of publications on the cave
and its excavations.

Phoenician, Greek, Roman, Byzantine

113 **The tradition of an ancient Greek colony in Malta.**
Anthony Bonanno.   *Hyphen*, vol. IV, no. 1 (1983), p. 1-17. bibliog.
The persistent tradition of a Greek colonization of the Maltese Islands in ancient times
was inspired mainly by literary allusions. The tradition seemed to be supported by the
finding in the islands of objects with Greek characteristics or inscriptions. These
include a fragment from a Mycenaean cup, other cups and bell-kraters and a cande-
labrum inscribed in Greek and Punic. However, the assertion that a period of actual
Greek domination prior to the Roman conquest is, it is argued here, untenable.

114 **Malta's role in the Phoenician, Greek and Etruscan trade in the
western Mediterranean.**
Anthony Bonanno.   *Melita Historica*, vol. 10, no. 3 (1990), p. 209-24.
bibliog.
In the light of evidence from various Maltese sites, which are illustrated here, the
author discusses possible trade links.

115　Roman Malta. The archaeological heritage of the Maltese Islands.
Anthony Bonanno, photographs by Maurizio Urso.　Valletta: World
Confederation of Salesian Past Pupils of Don Bosco, with the support
of the Bank of Valletta, 1992. 172p. bibliog.
This beautifully produced work has text in English (p. 13-35), sepia and coloured
drawings and plans (p. 37-60), and eighty-two colour plates (between p. 83 and p.
158). Malta was taken by Rome from Carthage in 218 BC. Roman *Melite* is buried
beneath Mdina close to 'the richest archaeological find of the Roman period in
Malta', the elegant *domus* (house) in what is now Rabat. The main Roman town in
Gozo has not been precisely located but evidently had central functions similar to
Melite – the larger island. Overall, Malta's Roman sites are less well documented
than the prehistoric ones.

116　The Maltese catacombs – characteristics and general
considerations.
Mario Buħaġiar.　In: *Proceedings of History Week, 1983* (1984),
p. 1-26. bibliog.
An analysis of the structural characteristics of the many Maltese hypogea, accompanied by four tables, nine scaled drawings of their plans and artifacts and six
photographic plates. Many have Christian motifs and inscriptions datable to the 5th-
6th centuries AD.

117　The Salina hypogea at St. Paul's Bay.
Mario Buħaġiar.　*Melita Historica*, vol. 9, no. 1 (1984), p. 1-18.
bibliog.
A description of each of the fifteen hypogea in the area with plans of each and sections
and ornamented details of some.

118　Late Roman and Byzantine catacombs and related burial places in
the Maltese Islands: Bar International Series 302.
Mario Buħaġiar.　Oxford: BAR, 1986. 435p. bibliog.
This important book is the primary source of detailed information on the many
Christian and non-Christian catacombs that are a significant feature of late Roman
Malta. After a general analysis of physical characteristics, functions and artifacts associated with these burial places, there is a gazetteer of all known sites in various parts
of the Rabat district, followed by those in each parish of Malta and a few sites in
Gozo. One-hundred-and-twenty pages of figures provide measured drawings of
graffiti, carvings, painting fragments and artifacts as well as plans and sections of each
site. Thirty-one photographic plates provide further information on their structure,
grave typology and ornamentation. The appendices comprise catalogues of: 39 inscriptions with translations provided by Dr Joyce Reynolds; 62 sites with *agape* tables
(circular rock-hewn platforms with a surrounding area possibly for reclining at a
funeral feast); and 102 sites with painted and carved decoration and iconographical
motifs. The book had a limited edition, long exhausted, but the author has published
and extended its data in many different articles, some of which are separately listed in
this volume.

27

119   **Early Christian and Byzantine Malta: some archaeological and textual considerations.**
Mario Buħaġiar.   *Library of Mediterranean History*, vol. 1 (1994), p. 77-125. bibliog.

A useful review of the archaeological, textual and other possible sources of information on the late Roman and Byzantine phase of Christian culture in Malta. It is illustrated with plans of catacombs and photographs and an engraving of relevant artifacts.

120   **The mosaic pavements in the Museum of Roman Antiquities at Rabat, Malta.**
Tancred Gouder.   Malta: Department of Museums, 1983. 11p. bibliog.

A brief but precise description of the discovery, design and materials of these fine Roman town-house mosaics, most of which are substantially intact, although some of the most exquisite in *opus vermiculatum* are only fragments. There are excellent coloured illustrations and rather small plans of the most complete floors.

121   **Malta and the Phoenicians.**
Tancred C. Gouder.   In: *Annual Report, 1991.*   Valletta: Lombard Bank (Malta) Ltd., 1992, p. 3-20. bibliog.

This short article is very well illustrated by photographs of Punic artifacts found at Maltese sites, including the cornice of a building still extant in Żurrieq which was illustrated by Houel in 1785. See J. Houel, *Voyage pittoresque des isles de Sicile, de Malta et de Lipari,* Paris, 1785, vol. 4, p. 97-98, ch. CCLIX.

122   **Malta and the Phoenician World.**
Journal of Maltese Studies, vol. 3, no. 2, part 1 (1993), p. 170-290. bibliog.

Of the eight articles, four are directly related to Malta (one in Italian). One by Michael Heltzer discusses the political evidence contained in a Gozitan Punic inscription. Another by Antonia Ciasca considers the sacrificial precincts at Tas-Silġ (eight figures). A concluding paper by Sabatino Moscati discusses the evidence for Phoenician settlement and trade but an apparent lack of specific connections with Carthage.

123   **Paola: another Punico-Roman settlement?**
George A. Said.   *Hyphen*, vol. 7, no. 1 (1992), p. 1-22. 3 maps. bibliog.

A review of the archaeological sites discovered at various times but especially the Punic rock tombs discussed by J. G. Baldacchino in 1951, with plans and sections based on the latter as well as illustrations of the urns and artifacts found in them.

124   **Ptolemy's Maltese co-ordinates: a reassessment.**
Frank Ventura.   *Hyphen*, vol. V. no. 6 (1988), p. 254-69. bibliog.

In the 2nd century AD Claudius Ptolemaeus calculated the co-ordinates of five sites in the Maltese Islands. These have been applied to Maltese topography mistakenly without correcting for his inevitable errors. Even after doing so the margin-of-error boxes are too great to be used for contemporary site determination.

Mediaeval

125 **Excavations at Ħal Millieri, Malta: a report of the 1977 campaign conducted on behalf of the National Museum and the University of Malta.**
T. F. C. Blagg, A. Bonanno, A. T. Luttrell. Msida, Malta: The University Press, 1990. 152p.

A series of fully illustrated excavation reports followed by longer historical and architectural postscripts and appendices which extend and update the information already published in *Hal Millieri: a Maltese casale, its churches and paintings*, edited by Anthony Luttrell (Valletta: Midsea Books, 1976. 143p. map).

126 **Medieval cave-dwellings and rock-cut churches in Malta.**
Mario Buħaġiar. *Atrium: Mediterranean and Middle East Architectural Construction Review*, no. 3 (1983), p. 17-22. bibliog.

An analysis of these sites in the context of troglodytic settlements in Malta and Sicily and records of their construction from the 13th to the 16th centuries. Clear plans and sections augment photographs of detailed features of the construction and decoration of these churches.

127 **'Ex-votos': a complete study of the stone slabs which are found in the church and at the Museum of Saint Agatha, Rabat.**
Victor Camilleri. Rabat, Malta: Missionary Society of St. Paul, 1994. 40p. bibliog.

Introduces 106 photographs illustrating each of the carved stones, accompanied by the author's notes on them. Some of the stones can be dated to 1504 when they formed part of a church which was replaced by a larger one in 1670.

128 **St. Agatha's Museum, Rabat, Malta G. C.**
Fr. Victor Camilleri. Rabat, Malta: Missionary Society of St. Paul, 1994. 32p.

A well-illustrated catalogue of the items exhibited including geological and palaeontological specimens, archaeological finds, votive and other religious paintings and tablets c.1504. It does not include information on the extensive catacombs excavated by the author.

Conservation

129 **Deterioration of cultural property by airborne pollutants – a case study of a Mediterranean island.**
Anthony Bonanno, JoAnn Cassar.   In: *Airborne particles, their negative effects on the cultural heritage and its environment.*   Edited by D. Moe, S. Hicks.   Rixensart, Belgium: PACT; European Network of Scientific and Technical Cooperation applied to Cultural Heritage, vol. 33 (1991), p. 161-82.

Outlines the sources of pollution in Malta, including the effects of the current and proposed power stations, and the heavy traffic, and examines the susceptibility of local limestones and other materials such as wall-paintings, ironwork and cellulose to these pollutants.

130 **Visitor impact on an underground prehistoric monument: the Hal Saflieni Hypogeum, Malta.**
Antonia Bonnici, JoAnn Cassar, Patrick J. Schembri, Frank Ventura.
In: *Proceedings of the ICOM Committee for Conservation 10th Triennial Meeting.*   Washington, DC: ICOM, August 1993, p. 825-30. bibliog.

Demonstrates the mean monthly air temperature and vapour pressure at various levels of the Hypogeum from June 1986 to May 1989, and the rapid and substantial increase in visitors from 1910-88. Remedial measures will include air conditioning, a limitation of the numbers of visitors allowed entry and a reduction of illumination.

131 **Protective inventory of the Maltese cultural heritage: Żejtun-Marsaxlokk – Marsascala outlying districts 1. Il.-Bidni.**
Edited by Mario Buħaġiar.   Msida, Malta: Malta University Services Ltd. for the Planning Services Division, Works Department, Malta, 1991. 218p. map.

This is the first volume of a potential series of district reviews, recording and assessing the Maltese town and country environment. The classification is a formal listing to assist the deliberation of planning applications in the interests of protecting historic buildings and other amenities. It comprises a copy of the original 109 data-capture cards with descriptions of each site and reasons for protecting it as well as its location and a photograph. A short historical introduction and situation report precedes the classification of all the sites into one of three degrees of protection or one of no protection (i.e. condemnation). Il-Bidni is divided into three sections and cards ordered accordingly.

132 **Protective inventory of the Maltese cultural heritage: Żejtun I.
Ir-Raħal t'Isfel – Villa Cagliares area.**
Edited by Mario Buħaġiar.   Msida, Malta: Malta University Services
Ltd. for the Planning Services Division, Works Department, Malta,
1991. 394p. map.
Comprises a copy of the 197 data-capture cards with descriptions of each site and reasons for its protection, a note on its location and a photograph. A foreword outlines the origins of this prestigious villa and subsequent urban development and five contemporary deleterious effects which are common to the whole island – the mutilation of ground floors to accommodate garages and larger windows; the discarding of timber balconies, doors and windows; the poor design and coarse detailing of accretions and rebuilding; the form of architectural ornament on new buildings; and the abandonment of care for the periphery of settlements. Each site is accorded one of three positive protection classifications or one of no protection. Several buildings were untenanted and liable to dereliction at the time of the survey.

133 **Protective inventory of the Maltese cultural heritage:
Żejtun-Marsaxlokk – Marsascala outlying districts 2. Misraħ
Strejnu area.**
Edited by Mario Buħaġiar.   Msida, Malta: Malta University Services
Ltd. for the Planning Services Division, Works Department, Malta,
1992. 234p. 2 maps.
Comprises a copy of the original 127 data-capture cards with descriptions of each site and reasons for its protection with its location and a photograph. A brief introduction outlines the character of the three zones into which the cards are classified according to three degrees of protection and a fourth of no protection which includes a substantial proportion of this particular list. The comments are therefore an informative guide to current aesthetic values and 'morality' in architectural design.

134 **Past stone restoration methods in the Maltese Islands.**
JoAnn Cassar.   In: *Early advances in conservation*.   Edited by
Vincent Daniels.   London: British Museum, Department of
Conservation, 1988, p. 103-15. bibliog. (British Museum Occasional
Paper no. 65).
Built entirely of local limestone, the prehistoric temples of the Maltese Islands are considered the world's first free-standing monuments in stone. Unfortunately some past restoration measures have been counter-productive. They have now been stopped pending re-evaluation and new approaches by the Stone Research and Conservation Laboratory recently set up within the Museums Department of Malta.

135 **The Hal Saflieni prehistoric hypogeum in Malta. An international effort for the conservation of an underground limestone monument.**
JoAnn Cassar. In: *Conservation of stone and other materials vol. 1. Causes of disorders and diagnosis, Proceedings of the International UNESCO Congress held at UNESCO Headquarters, Paris, with the cooperation of ICCROM, EUREKA/EUROCARE, ICOM, ICOMOS and the Getty Conservation Institute, June 29-July 1993.* Edited by M. J. Thiel. London: E. & F. S. Spon, 1993, p. 287-94. bibliog.
The article summarizes some of the problems of deterioration of this large subterranean Neolithic monument and the various measures being considered for its conservation.

136 **Fr. Manwel Magri's contribution to the conservation of Malta's archaeological heritage.**
Salv. Mallia. *Melita Historica*, vol. 9, no. 2 (1985), p. 145-69.
bibliog. Additional notes are in vol. 9, no. 3 (1986), p. 245-46.
An account of the findings of this pioneer archaeologist in Malta and Gozo at the turn of the century with three illustrations from his photographs.

137 **Factors causing deterioration of frescoes within a medieval church in Malta and a proposed solution.**
Carmen Taliana, JoAnn Cassar, Alfred J. Vella, Frank Ventura. In: *International Symposium on the Conservation of the Relics of Medieval Monumental Architecture, Warsaw-Lednica, 24-26 May, 1994.* Warsaw: ICOM Polish National Committee, Society for the Preservation of Historic Monuments, Museum of the first Piasts in Lednica, 1994, p. 125-34. bibliog.
Reports the results of a study of the wall-paintings at Hal Milieri, Malta, and possible methods for reducing the salt deposits causing their deterioration.

138 **The treatment of a typical soft limestone with different consolidants: a comparative study: treatment tests on the Globigerina limestone used in Maltese architecture.**
Sergio Vannucci, JoAnn Cassar, Gennaro Tampone. *Bollettino Ingegneri*, no. 11, 1985. p. 1-11.
Reports consolidation trials carried out on samples of Globigerina limestone with four commercially available organic products which were applied in two ways. Studies of the effects, including SEM scans and microanalysis, suggested that one of these had excellent properties. The article is illustrated with photographs of the treated samples and graphs.

History

General

139 **Malta. A panoramic history: a narrative history of the islands.**
Joseph S. Abela.   San Ġwann, Malta: Publishers' Enterprises Group
(PEG) Ltd., 1997. 248p.
This is a very accessible overview history aimed at the general reader and written
from a post-colonial perspective. Thirteen 'ages' are identified and discussed in
chronological order: they range from the 'age of the megabuilders', to the 'age of
modern communications'.

140 **Birgu – a Maltese maritime city. Vol. 1. Historical and sociological
aspects.**
Edited by Lino Buġeja, Mario Buħaġiar, Stanley Fiorini.   Malta:
Malta University Services Ltd. for the Central Bank of Malta, 1993.
387p. bibliog.
This and its companion volume, both sumptuously illustrated from the Marquis Cassar
de Sain's photographs, provide a mass of newly documented information on many
aspects of the original harbour stronghold honoured by the Knights of St. John as
Vittoriosa. These first two parts are devoted to six general historical essays ranging from
prehistoric times to the Second World War in their coverage, two of an ethnographic
and demographic nature and two on medical institutions and experiences and a
detailed account of the Order's arsenal. Each is written by a different Maltese scholar.

141 **Birgu – a Maltese maritime city. Vol. 2. Artistic, architectural and ecclesiastical aspects.**
Edited by Lino Buġeja, Mario Buħaġiar, Stanley Fiorini.   Malta:
Malta University Services Ltd. for the Central Bank of Malta, 1993.
869p. bibliog.
The completion of this massive and gorgeously illustrated undertaking consists of two parts. There are six studies of Birgu's built environment, including two studies of local architecture by the late Leonard Mahoney, an account of the development of the Drydocks, and various maps and views of the city. The other four essays are devoted to the diocesan clergy, the Dominicans, other religious orders and the operation of the Inquisition. The bibliographical appendix includes not only printed but manuscript sources of great use to future historians.

142 **Malta: a case study in international cross-currents. Proceedings of the first international colloquium on the history of the Central Mediterranean held at the University of Malta, 13-17 December, 1989.**
Edited by Stanley Fiorini, Victor Mallia-Milanes.   Malta: Malta
University Publications for Malta Historical Society and Foundation
for International Studies, University of Malta, 1991. 300p. bibliog.
Brings together nineteen articles, almost all directly relating to aspects of Maltese history including the 20th century, by Maltese and other historians. All are concerned with Maltese international relations or their cultural influences on aspects of the island's literature and institutions. These include 'Post-Muslim Malta – a case study in artistic and architectural cross-currents' by M. Buħaġiar (p. 13-31); 'Mediaeval Malta: the non-written and the written evidence' by A. Luttrell (p. 32-45); 'Language and demography in Malta: the social foundations of the symbiosis between semitic and romance in standard Maltese' by J. M. Brincat (p. 91-110); 'The development of mathematical education in Malta to 1798' by S. Fiorini (p. 111-45); 'Linguistic and thematic cross-currents in early Maltese literature' by O. Friggieri; and 'The Foreign Office, the Colonial Office and the spy: the Belardinelli affair, Malta, 1934-1935' by B. Collett.

143 **Malta revisited: an appointment with history.**
Eric Gerada-Azzopardi.   Valletta: Progress Press Publications, 1984.
288p. bibliog.
Written as a popular history of Malta, this book can also act as a guide and visual record because it is extensively illustrated with past and contemporary prints, paintings and photographs and numerous line-drawings. It concludes with the closure of the British base in 1979.

144 **Girolamo Manduca and Gian Francesco Abela: tradition and invention in Maltese historiography.**
Anthony T. Luttrell.   *Melita Historica,* vol. 7, no. 2 (1977), p. 105-32.
bibliog.
Given the dearth of information on mediaeval Malta, the few traditional tales are constantly recycled. Many are found for the first time in the history published by Abela

(1582-1655) in 1647. The author discusses the various sources apparently available to Abela, and the unpublished but copied writings of the Maltese Jesuit Manduca (1574-1643) in relation to the developing cult of St. Paul. The appendices provide transcripts of Manduca's writings in Latin and Italian, with an English translation 'concerning the vernacular speech of the Maltese' (p. 129-30).

145 **The making and unmaking of the Maltese Universitas: a supplement to *Heritage*.**
Edited by John Manduca.   Valletta: Midsea Publications, 1993. 29p. bibliog.

Two substantial articles by Charles Dalli and Stanley Fiorini are respectively devoted to the Medieval Commune and to the Municipal Councils from 1530-1800. A third essay by Albert Ganado recounts how the Universitas was wound up by Governor Maitland. (It should be noted that these agencies of local government and taxation have no association with the college of studies or university.)

146 **Maps of Malta in the museum and library of the Order of St. John: a short catalogue.**
Roger Mason, Pamela Willis.   London: The Order of St. John, 1989. 42p. bibliog.

Published in association with an exhibition held at the Museum in St. John's Gate, Clerkenwell, London, this catalogue of 131 items includes maps published between 1536 and 1910 with brief discussion of each. Many of the maps are illustrated but on too small a scale for more than the crudest of comparisons. The exhibition was mounted, in their London headquarters, by The Most Venerable Order of the Hospital of St. John of Jerusalem which was revived in the 19th century as the English branch of the Hospitallers.

147 **Mosta – the heart of Malta.**
Edited by Louis J. Scerri.   Valletta: Midsea Publications (with Vassallo Builders Group), 1996. 165p.

This is a beautifully produced and illustrated collection of papers by Maltese scholars on environmental, social, historical and architectural aspects of one of Malta's oldest towns.

148 **The Malta and Russian connection: a history of diplomatic relations between Malta and Russia (XVII-XIX cc.) based on original Russian documents.**
Guzeppi Schembri.   Malta: Grima Publications, 1990. 99p.

An account of the Russian interest in Malta during the period of expanding French interests in the Mediterranean and Turkey, followed by translations of eight Russian descriptions of Malta, and nine documents relating to Czar Paul I's assumption of the office of grand master of the Sovereign Military Order of Malta in 1798.

Mediaeval (800-1530)

149 **The origin of Franciscanism in late mediaeval Malta.**
George Aquilina, Stanley Fiorini.   Malta: T. A. V. Publications, 1995.
110p. bibliog.
Commemorates the first priory permitted by the Pope in Malta in 1494. It achieved
critical notoriety by challenging the established local history of the Order.
Documentary evidence suggested that the Franciscan Tertiaries working at their hospital in Rabat by 1372 were 'regulars' not laymen. The first part describes the relevant
religious and administrative institutions in Malta in the later Middle Ages, and the
second part the Friars Minor from 1494-1518. Fifteen documents in Latin form one
appendix and the second summarizes the role and position of the Third Order
Regulars.

150 **Mediaeval Inquisition in Malta 1433-1561.**
Alexander Bonnici.   *Hyphen*, vol. VI, no. 2 (1989), p. 62-75.
The inquisition for the suppression of heresy is discussed as well as the influence of
the Sicilian institution and the bishops as pro-inquisitors in Malta before the Roman
Inquisition and Apostolic Delegacy were introduced to the island.

151 **Malta 870-1054. Al-Himyari's account and its linguistic
implications.**
Joseph M. Brincat.   Valletta: Said International, 1995. 52p. bibliog.
Al-Himyari, who died during the 14th or possibly the 15th century AD, left a written
account of the information he gathered about the Maltese Islands – which he never
visited in person. His text consists of three paragraphs on the geographical characteristics, the Arab conquest (870 AD) and subsequent colonization of the islands. Some
already known details are included, such as his reference to the Byzantine attack of
1053-54.

152 **The Maltese toponomy in three ancient Italian Portolans
(1296-1490).**
Arnold Cassola.   *Al-Masaq*, vol. 5 (1992), p. 64-67.
Mediaeval and Renaissance coastal charts often indicate the names of natural features,
such as rocks, headlands, inlets and rivers as well as settlements. The author discusses
the Maltese place-names etc. in these Italian examples.

153 **Santo Spirito Hospital: the early years to 1575.**
Stanley Fiorini.   Malta: Department of Information, 1989. 199p.
bibliog.
The four parts of this study describe the early years of this hospital in Rabat, run under
the auspices of the Franciscans, its services to paupers, foundlings and the sick, its
staff and administration, and its property and accounts. Two appendices include
twenty-two selected documents in their original Latin forms, and a full copy of the
account book for 1494-96. The architecture, equipment, and some documents are illustrated and some admission and financial data tabulated. The hospital buildings
currently accommodate the National Archives of Malta.

154 **The 'Mandati' documents at the Archives of the Mdina Cathedral, Malta, 1473-1539.**
Stanley Fiorini.   Minnesota: The Hill Monastic Library and Mdina; Malta: The Cathedral Museum, 1992. 218p. bibliog.

This substantial volume is introduced by thirty-one pages of introduction to these directives of the *Università* (local government) and the cathedral before the ceding of Malta to the Order of St. John. The bulk of the text lists the persons and services involved and any sum paid for them. Eighteen appendices reproduce some of the documents in full in their original languages. Ten illustrations depict fabric from the mediaeval cathedral which is still extant, some of it in the cathedral museum.

155 **The earliest surviving accounts books of the cathedral procurators: 1461-1499.**
Stanley Fiorini.   In: *Proceedings of History Week 1992.*   Edited by Stanley Fiorini.   Malta: Malta Historical Society, 1994, p. 101-15.

The article outlines the contents of these accounts kept by those responsible for maintaining the structure of Mdina Cathedral, its works of art and the organ. The author suggests the use of these books for evidence of property ownership, data on schoolmasters, craftsmen, clergy and church officials as well as the payment of tithes.

156 **Documentary sources of Maltese history. Part 1: Notarial documents. No. 1. Notary Giacomo Zabbara R494/1 (I): 1486-1488.**
Edited by Stanley Fiorini.   Msida, Malta: University of Malta, 1996. 383p.

This publication, after an introduction in English up to p. xviii, presents a transcription of the first part of register R494/1 which measures 32 x 23 cm. In its bound form it consists of Part I: 156 sheets (1486-88), Part II: 46 sheets (1494-95), Part III: 53 sheets (1495-96), and Part IV: 48 sheets (1496-97). The numbering of the folios is apparently in Żabbara's own hand. The language of the 341 documents is Latin, except for occasional phrases in Sicilian for items – such as house furniture – for which Latin might have been difficult. Each document is accompanied by a brief explanatory abstract in English. These documents provide a unique insight into the social structure of late mediaeval Maltese society. There is a glossary (p. 337-40) and indexes of contracts, personal names, place-names, and subjects (p. 347-83).

157 **Slaves and captives on Malta: 1053/4 and 1091.**
Anthony Luttrell.   *Hyphen*, vol. 7, no. 2 (1992), p. 97-104. bibliog.

A refutation of some of the arguments for Christian continuity in Malta after the Arab conquest, using Muslim and subsequent evidence. This extends the author's discussion within 'Approaches to medieval Malta' in *Medieval Malta: studies on Malta before the Knights*, edited by Anthony T. Luttrell (London: The British School at Rome, 1975, p. 1-70. bibliog.).

158 **Medieval ships and the birth of technological societies vol. 2,**
     The Mediterranean area and European integration.
     Edited by Christiane Villain-Gandossi, Salvino Busuttil, Paul Adam.
     Valletta: SAID International Ltd. for the Foundation for International
     Studies, University of Malta, 1991. 451p. bibliog.

This volume includes two papers on Malta. No. 26, 'Sea craft in the mediaeval Malta:
description and etymology' by Charles Briffa, and 'Maltese ship graffiti' by Joseph
Muscat which includes an appendix of the author's transcriptions of these incisions on
ancient temple, as well as church and chapel, walls which probably originated as *ex
votos* in recognition of graces granted.

159 **Agriculture in Malta in the late Middle Ages.**
     Godfrey Wettinger. *Proceedings of History Week, 1981* (1982),
     p. 1-48. bibliog.

A fully documented account of the variety of agricultural products and animal husbandry underway in the 15th century, types of garden and whereabouts of horses in
the militia lists of 1419-20 and c.1425, as well as references to owners of sheep and
goats. Types of land tenure and the agricultural economy as evidenced by court cases
are exemplified from translated records.

160 **The archives of Palermo and Maltese medieval history: a first**
     report.
     Godfrey Wettinger. *Proceedings of History Week, 1982* (1983),
     p. 59-68. bibliog.

A short account of mediaeval documentary sources of relevance to Malta with an
appendix of two documents concerning the relief of a Muslim siege of the island in
1430.

161 **The Jews of Malta in the late Middle Ages.**
     Godfrey Wettinger. Valletta: Midsea Books, 1985. 352p. bibliog.

A detailed presentation of the sources of information on Maltese Jewry until their
removal under Spanish rule after 1492. Appendices are devoted to the Judaeo-Arabic
language and poetry and a third part to actual documents, mostly taken from notarial
deeds and court proceedings and printed in their original Latin.

162 **The Arabs in Malta.**
     Godfrey Wettinger. In: *Malta: studies of its heritage and history.*
     Valletta: Annual Report of the Mid-Med Bank, 1986, p. 87-104.
     bibliog.

Outlines the sources of evidence on the Arab occupation of the islands, their cultural
predominance, and the lack of evidence for Christianity surviving in Malta when it
was taken by Count Roger in 1090. Although Muslims adhering to their faith were
expelled in 1249, those who accepted Christian baptism were allowed to stay, thereby
continuing the language and use of names which became characterized as Maltese.

The era of the Knights of St. John (1530-1798)

General

163   **The Knights of Malta.**
Joseph Attard.   San Ġwann, Malta: Publishers Enterprises Group
(PEG) Ltd, 1992 (reprinted 1993, 1995). 192p. bibliog.
A readable account of the fortunes of the Order from the 11th century in Palestine to
its present incarnation in an international humanitarian role. There are illustrations
(p. 161-76) and a short list of references (p. 181).

164   **Memorie Melitensi (Maltese memories/records).**
Edited by Gabriele, Maria Teresa Benincasa.   Rome: Vatican Library,
1987. 121p.
This Italian catalogue records documents of the Order of St. John to be found in the
Vatican archive in Rome. It includes a list of grand masters and many illustrations in
colour and black-and-white. Like the Jesuits, the Order had a special relationship with
the papacy, which formally ratified its decrees etc. Many documents were therefore
kept 'on file' at the Vatican which relate to a wide range of the Order's activities as
well as specific correspondence with the papal offices.

165   **The changing landscape of Malta during the rule of the Order of
St. John of Jerusalem 1530-1798.**
Brian W. Blouet.   DPhil thesis, University of Hull, England, 1963.
298p. bibliog.
After three chapters on Malta's physical and historical background and the Order of St.
John, the substantive chapters are devoted to: agriculture; the growth of population; the
evolution of the settlement pattern; industry, trade and finance; and a short conclusion.
Extensive use is made of original maps and plans, aerial photographs, and the author's
own distribution maps of various features. Two appendices list street names in
Valletta and the succession of grand masters of the Order.

166   **The ministers of the Inquisition Tribunal in Malta.**
Alexander Bonnici.   *Hyphen*, vol. V, no. 1 (1986), p. 1-18. bibliog.
This is a study of the retinue and staff of the Inquisitor, who held patents placing them
under his jurisdiction and exempt from various regulations applied to the Maltese by
the Order of St. John.

167 **Non Gode l'Immunità Ecclesiastica.** (Not offering ecclesiastical
sanctuary.)
Frans Ciappara. *Melita Historica*, vol. 9, no. 2 (1985), p. 117-27.
bibliog.
With 327 churches in Malta, the Order of St. John found the consequences of granting
suspected offenders sanctuary an intolerable threat to public order. In 1761 Rome
granted the restriction of this privilege to parish and filial churches in which the Holy
Sacrament was reserved. Notices were fixed to the remaining chapels etc., worded as
in this article's title. A revision of 1762 reduced those losing immunity from 255 to
93. Local immunity was abolished by the British in 1828. An appendix reprints the
edict of 1762 and lists the churches which lost and regained the immunity.

168 **Malta's role in Mediterranean affairs: 1530-1699.**
Domenic Cutajar, Carmel Cassar. *Mid-Med Bank Limited: Report
and Accounts, 1984*, Valletta, Malta, p. 38-71. bibliog.
Primarily an account of the organization and operations of the naval squadron of the
Order of St. John, this includes some discussion of the complex relations with Venice
and the Sublime Porte that extended over 1645-69 and ended with the surrender of
Candia and loss of Crete to the Turks. Demographic data are provided on Maltese set-
tlements from 1590-1740.

169 **Ancient and modern Malta: volume 1.**
Louis de Boisgelin. London: G. & J. Robinson, Paternoster Row,
1804. Reprinted, Valletta: Midsea Books, 1988. 326p.
The first volume of this classic three-volume account (see also following two entries),
first published in London in 1804, was written by a knight of the Order recently
deposed by Napoleon. It includes a description of the islands followed by several chapters on the constitution and finances of the Order, and is illustrated by a splendid
engraved map of the islands and two financial tables of the 1780s. It was re-issued,
with volumes two and three, as Melitensia Book Club No. 7.

170 **Ancient and modern Malta: volume 2.**
Louis de Boisgelin. London: G. & J. Robinson, Paternoster Row,
1804. Reprinted, Valletta: Midsea Books, 1988. 258p.
The second volume of de Boisgelin's publication consists of a ten-chapter history of
the Order from the loss of Rhodes in 1522 until the election of Grand Master de
Rohan in 1775. It is prefaced by a chronological table of principal events in the period
1099-1522. There are two portrait engravings.

171 **Ancient and modern Malta: volume 3.**
Louis de Boisgelin. London: G. & J. Robinson, Paternoster Row,
1804. Reprinted, Valletta: Midsea Books, 1988. 315p.
The final volume of this work on ancient and modern Malta, this concludes the history
of the Order in Malta from the accession of Grand Master de Rohan until the uprising
against the French occupation by the Maltese. The author considered the Russian solution, the restoration of the Order of St. John under the grand mastership of the Czar,
the best because only one-third of the local population could live off the island's own
produce and therefore some form of colonial status would be appropriate because the

Order would need external resources. There are twenty-four appendices including information on the illustrations, Charles V's *Act of Donation*, the possessions of the Order and grand priors of England and Ireland before the Reformation, the Order's primary sites of Hospitaller Dames and their induction ceremony, and significant documents relating to the Order's more recent history principally comprising: the terms of the capitulation of the Order to Napoleon (1798); the articles of the Treaty of Amiens (1804); and Russian Imperial proclamations of 1798 and 1801. These conclude with lists of the commanderies and knights alive in 1788 who belonged to the three Languages (Langues) of Provence, Auvergne and France within the modern state of France and the Bailiffs of Brandenburg from 1327-1762. There is one illustration of Messina.

172 **The history of the Knights of Malta: volume I.**
Mons. l'Abbé de Vertot. London: G. Strahen et al., 1728. Reprinted, Valletta: Midsea Books, 1989. 487p. +155p. of 'Proofs' of books 1-8.

This facsimile was reissued with its second volume (see following entry) as Melitensia Book Club No. 9. Volume one takes this detailed history of the Order down to the loss of Rhodes in 1523. It is illustrated with many engraved maps and portraits of members of the Order.

173 **The history of the Knights of Malta: volume 2.**
Mons. l'Abbé de Vertot. London: G. Strahen et al., 1728. Reprinted, Valletta: Midsea Books, 1989.

The structure of volume two differs from volume one as books 11-15 are separately paginated to include their respective 'proofs' down to 1725, and followed by a dissertation on the ancient and modern government of the Order and the translation of an edition of the old and new statutes of the Order originally printed in 1686 (196p.). This volume is also illustrated with engraved maps and portraits of knights referred to in the text.

174 **Catalogue of the Records of the Order of St. John of Jerusalem in the National Library of Malta: vol. xiii supplement.**
Compiled by Stanley Fiorini, William Żammit. Msida, Malta: University of Malta, 1990. 171p.

This volume, the research for which was supported by the Australian Association of the Sovereign Military Order of Malta, deals with the re-establishment and development of the Order's printing press between 1756 and 1794. The material is divided into three parts – income, expenditure and, in part III (for which William Zammit is responsible) the entries include requests for the printing of certain works. This volume is a supplement to volume XIII in a vast project to catalogue these records since 1964, which are titled in the language of the original but not indexed. Various scholars have been responsible for the different volumes to date as follows:

Volume	Part	Archives	Year	Pages
I		1-72	1964	228
II	1	73-83	1970	168
	2	84-87	1973	164
	3	88-90	1978	148
	4	91-93	1978	196
	5	94-96	1979	326

Volume	Part	Archives	Year	Pages
	6	97-99	1982	198
	7	100	1988	130
	8	101-02	1991	108
III	1	255-60	1965	282
	2	261-67	1966	276
	3	268-79	1966	227
IV		280-315	1964	25
VII		1126-43	1964	251
VIII		1182-99	1967	132
X		1649-1712	1969	110
XI		1713-58	1969	206
XII		1759-1934a	1968	176
XIII		1935-2084b	1967	105
XIII Supplement		2038-71	1990	171

175 **Proceedings of History Week 1994.**
Edited by Stanley Fiorini.   Malta: Malta Historical Society, 1996.
130p. bibliog.

This gives the text of seven of the contributions at the Malta Historical Society's meeting between 26 and 31 October 1994. Such meetings have been held since 1981. The papers in these 1994 'proceedings' are: 'New light on the origins of Franciscanism in the Maltese Islands' (by S. Fiorini and G. Aquilina); 'The warships of the Order of St. John 1530-1798' (J. Muscat), 'The consular network of 18th century Malta' (C. Vassallo); 'Brief note on the black figure in the Mdina St. Paul's polyptych' (G. Bugeja); 'Giuseppe Grech (1755-1787): clarifications on his artistic activity' (K. Sciberras); 'Architectural scenography in 18th century Malta' (C. Thake); and 'In Fronteria Barbarorum: waiting for the Turks on late medieval Malta' (C. Dalli).

176 **The Navy of the Knights of St. John.**
Friends of the Maritime Museum.   Vittoriosa, Malta: The Maritime Museum, 1995. 49p.

Four papers comprise the proceedings of the first seminar organized by the Friends of the Maritime Museum. They are devoted to the building of a Maltese galley, the land-based organization of the Order's Galley Squadron in the 17th century, maritime life in 18th-century Malta, and de la Valette as a naval commander.

177 **An inventory of the manuscript volumes of the 'spoils' (1549-1772) preserved in the archives at the Cathedral Museum, Mdina – Malta.**
Edited by Joseph Galea.   Malta: The Malta Study Center of the Hill Monastic Manuscript Library, St. John's University, Collegeville, Minnesota, 1988. 131p.

A catalogue, with biographical notes, of every member of the Order of St. John whose personal effects were recorded in the absence of any will or testament in one of the sixty-three volumes of these manuscripts. These include both the verdicts and the proceedings of the Order's Commission and an index of the members enlisted. A few later volumes may still be found in the National Archives but most were transferred to the Maltese Diocesan Curia after the eviction of the Order.

178 German Knights of Malta: a gallery of portraits.
Michael Galea.   Malta: Buġelli Publications, 1986. 214p. bibliog.

A useful summary of the activities of seven senior members of the Order between the 16th and the 18th centuries, together with illustrations of their portraits, arms, memorials and buildings with which they were associated. These are: Georg Schilling Von Cannstatt (1490-1550); Christian Osterhausen (1593-1664), Landgrave Cardinal Friedrich von Hessen (1616-82); Wolfgang Philipp von Guttenberg (1647-1733); Heinrich Ludger von Galen (1675-1717); Count Philipp Wilhelm Nesselrode-Reigienstein (1677-1754); and the last grand master in Malta, Ferdinand von Hompesch (1744-1805). The appendix consists of translations of the congratulatory letters sent to the last grand master by the rulers of foreign states. There are lists of the grand masters who ruled in Malta and the grand priors of Germany from 1428-1806.

179 The Knights' State (1530-1798): a regular regime.
Adrianus (Adriannes) Koster.   *Melita Historica*, vol. 8, no. 4 (1983), p. 298-314. bibliog.

A general outline of the organizational structure and institutions of the Order of St. John in Malta. This is particularly useful for the organizational information which indicates the sorts of archives which were kept by these institutions of the Order.

180 Venice and Hospitaller Malta 1530-1798: aspects of a relationship.
Victor Mallia-Milanes.   Marsa, Malta: Publishers Enterprises Group (PEG) Ltd., 1992. 366p. bibliog.

Broadly speaking, the Kingdom of France and Republic of Venice came to an early working relationship with the Ottoman Empire, encouraged by their rivalry with the Kingdom of Spain and the Order of St. John in Malta. But at times some, or all, were in alliance with each other against the Turks or pursuing interests, such as corsairing, with the use of flags of convenience. This substantial monograph, of nine chapters, is the first comprehensive account of the Order's fluctuating relations with the Venetian state throughout its Maltese period which like the Serenissima was ended by Napoleon. The author shows how Venetian interests prevailed when challenged by the activities of the Order in the Levant from the late 16th century. But by the mid-18th century they sufficiently coincided for joint expeditions against the North African ports. Four appendices indicate the sources of income of the Order's grand priory of Venice in 1533, 1583, 1736 and 1776. There are fourteen illustrations from contemporary prints and paintings, some of which are in colour including a photograph of the courtyard of the grand priory in Venice.

181 Hospitaller Malta 1530-1798: studies on early modern Malta and the Order of St. John of Jerusalem.
Edited by Victor Mallia-Milanes.   Msida, Malta: Mireva Publications, 1993. 789p. bibliog.

This extremely useful book consists of sixteen articles by Maltese, British and other scholars, much of whose work has previously been scattered in articles and monographs and is comprehensively reviewed and summarized here. After a Braudelian introduction by Michel Fontenay, Stanley Fiorini provides an extensive account of the Maltese economy, society and demography in the 1530s, Alexander de Grout assesses the continuing Ottoman threat to the Christian states of the Mediterranean, Anthony Luttrell discusses the Order's relations with its Rhodian subjects, and Anne Williams provides a brief description of the Order's constitutional arrangements. Local sources are used by Fiorini to plot the urbanization of the islands in the 17th and 18th centuries, and by Alexander Bonnici to consider aspects of civil society from the cases coming before the Inquisitor's courts. Naval exploits and military projects are analysed by Salvatore Bono and Alison Hoppen, and architectural and artistic development outlined by Quentin Hughes and John Gash, the latter providing a hitherto unobtainable extensive review. Social institutions and socio-medical services are briefly outlined by Carmel Cassar and Paul Cassar. The last articles are fully documented accounts, one by Frans Ciappara on the turbulent relations between a priest who had imbibed the ideas of the Enlightenment and the authorities in Malta, and the other by Alain Bony on French events relating to the Order from 1789 until Napoleon's invasion of Malta in 1798. However, there is no general discussion of relations between the Order and the Maltese priests, nobility and bourgeoisie which would have paralleled some of the earlier contributions. The bibliography is extensive, exemplary and of great value to other scholars. Some illustrations of art and architecture are included as well as demographic and economic tables.

182 **An altar from the galleys of the Order of St. John: the celebration of Mass at sea.**
Joseph Muscat. *The Mariner's Mirror,* vol. 70, no. 4 (1984), p. 389-95.
This altar, in the museum of St. Paul's church at the Wignacourt College in Rabat, is the only known example of a collapsible wooden altar for use in the galleys of the Order of St. John. The author describes its construction as well as its use, at sea or on land.

183 **The warships of the Order of St. John 1530-1798.**
Joseph Muscat. In: *Proceedings of History Week 1994.* Malta: Malta Historical Society, 1996, p. 77-113. bibliog.
This useful article outlines the types of warships powered by oarsmen and the introduction of sailing ships-of-the-line by Grand Master Perellos. The author provides information on the ways in which these vessels were built and on their armament, and line-drawings of fifteen of them are included.

184 **The monks of war: the military religious orders.**
Desmond Seward. London: Penguin Books, 1995. rev. ed. 416p. bibliog.
The last three chapters are mainly devoted to the Order of St. John while it was based in Malta. Five appendices review the different Orders of St. John in the modern world.

185 **The Knights of Malta.**
H. J. A. Sire. London: Yale University Press, 1994. 305p. bibliog.
Although this book has only three of its nineteen chapters devoted to the Order's years in Malta, it provides a well-illustrated and succinct general account of the Order's history in part one, and in part two a map of the commanderies in each of the priories of each of the langues into which the Order was divided. These provided the income and

benefices for the knights whilst based in Malta until sequestration at the Reformation or during the French Revolution and Napoleonic wars. Part three covers the charitable work of the Order and its later history. The three appendices list all the grand masters, the diplomatic representation of the Order today, and its current institutions including national associations with their years of foundation. The coloured illustrations are well chosen from a wide range of sources.

186   **The Navy of the Sovereign Military Order of Malta.**
Robert von Dauber, Antonio Spada.   Brescia, Italy: Grafo Ed., 1992. 111p.

Produced in association with an exhibition mounted in the Genoese hall of the Sovereign Military Order of Malta as part of Genoa's celebration of Christopher Columbus's 500th anniversary, this volume includes an account by von Dauber of the navy's history and organization, its equipment and ship building, its influence on other navies and contribution to exploration and other matters. Antonio Pigafetta, a knight of the Order who sailed with Magellan, dedicated his journal of the voyage to Grand Master Villiers de l'Isle Adam. The thirty-three items – excellently illustrated in colour – include a magnificent group of bird's-eye views of the harbour cities dating from the late 17th century, of which similar versions hang in the Malta Chamber of Commerce and the Wallace Collection in London. Naval engagements of the 17th and 18th centuries are illustrated as well as a manual of signals, a portrait of a galley captain, five ship models, and the Stock and Pilier given to Grand Master de Rohan by Pope Pius VI.

16th century

187   **The Great Siege of Malta, 1565.**
Ernle Bradford.   London: Hodder & Stoughton, 1961. Reprinted, Harmondsworth, England: Penguin Books, 1974. 256p. bibliog.

This readable account has been reprinted by Penguin several times since 1964. It has a useful section of notes and sources used (p. 229-43) and an index.

188   **Jean de la Valette 1495-1568: the man – a siege – a city.**
Edited by Maroma Camilleri.   Malta: The National Library of Malta, 1995. 24p.

Published in association with an exhibition mounted in the Order's current embassy in Valletta's St. John's Cavalier, this book includes: a synopsis of the Grand Master's life; items from the archives of the Order referring to him; engraved portraits; documents, accounts and maps of the Great Siege of 1565; documents relating to the founding and planning of Valletta and 16th-century maps of the city; a section by Joseph C. Sammut on coins and medals of this grand mastership, and by Carmel G. Bonavia on postage stamps depicting de la Valette, the Great Siege etc. in more recent times.

189   **The first decades of the Inquisition 1546-1581.**
Carmel Cassar.   *Hyphen*, vol. IV, no. 6 (1985), p. 208-38. bibliog.

An account of the introduction of this institution to Malta. The four appendices list and date various office-holders, an index of all the people accused before the tribunal, and the charges brought against them.

190 **The Reformation and sixteenth-century Malta.**
Carmel Cassar. *Melita Historica*, vol. 10, no. 1 (1988), p. 51-68.
bibliog.
This paper uses the case brought by the Inquisition against the Flemish master of the Order's mint in 1574 for heresy, to discuss the extent of Lutheranism in Malta and the ownership of books prohibited under the index. The appendix lists all those accused of having perused or owned prohibited books between 1546 and 1580.

191 **The Inquisition Index of Knights Hospitallers of the Order of St. John.**
Carmel Cassar. *Melita Historica*, vol. 11, no. 1 (1993), p. 157-95.
bibliog.
A statistical summary of accusations brought against members of the Order with dated details of each accusation in the appendix.

192 **Psychological and medical aspects of the siege of 1565.**
Paul Cassar. *Melita Historica,* vol. 1, no. 3 (1954), p. 129-40 and no. 4 (1955), p. 193-206.
Despite the limitations of its sources, this article gleans from a range of reports a general picture of medical events and follows civilian reactions to the invasion alarm, hatred of the enemy, resilience, joy of victory and post-war fears.

193 **The Great Siege of Malta (1565) and the Istanbul State Archives.**
Arnold Cassola.   Malta: Said International, 1995. 79p.
This curious little book describes what the author found and, with the help of scholars able to speak Turkish and translate Ottoman, published in English. Too brief an introduction is provided on the State Archives but a series of Ottoman documents offers some account of the siege from the viewpoint of those mounting the offensive. A useful summary of their campaign register forms half the text and provides a gloss to the whole logbook which the author published in weekly instalments in *The Sunday Times,* Malta, 19 June to 13 November 1994.

194 **Malta and the 16th century struggle for the Mediterranean.**
Domenic Cutajar, Carmel Cassar.   *Mid-Med Bank Limited: Report and Accounts 1985*, Valletta, Malta, 1986, p. 22-59. bibliog.
A useful summary of international activity in the region and its effect on Malta and its defences. It is of particular interest for data provided on the demography of Maltese settlements during the century and the coloured illustrations of the murals in the Verdalla Castle depicting stages in the career of Grand Master Hughues de Loubenx Verdalle (d. 1545) from his reception into the Order in 1546 until his investment as a cardinal in 1587.

195 **The Rhodiot community of Birgu, a Maltese city: 1530-c.1550.**
Stanley Fiorini.   *Library of Mediterranean History*, vol. 1 (1994), p. 184-241. bibliog.
When the Order of St. John settled in Malta they were accompanied by about 500 Greek Catholics from Rhodes. From an exhaustive study of three notarial archives,

detailed information is provided on those identified as Rhodiot, their employment, marriage patterns, external contacts, litigation, property and land tenure, slave owner-ship and apprenticeships. The appendix lists all documentary references to individuals by name in alphabetical order.

196   Grand Master Jean Levesque de la Cassière 1572-1581.
Michael Galea.   Malta: PEG Ltd., 1994. 95p.

This illustrated account of this grand mastership covers the construction of most of the Order's primary buildings in Valletta, the attempts made to control both the jealous rivalries and traces of Protestantism within the Order's ranks, the deposition of the Grand Master and his subsequent summons and exoneration by the Pope and reception by his fellow-cardinals prior to his death.

197   The Siege Map of Malta by Francesco de Marchi.
Albert Ganado.   In: *Proceedings of History Week 1984*.   Edited by Stanley Fiorini.   Malta: Malta History Society, 1986, p. 101-39. bibliog.

De Marchi (1504-76) was a servant of the Medici who became engaged in fortifications and wrote a major treatise on the subject which was never published. While working in Flanders in 1565 the Siege of Malta was of much interest to him and its lessons were incorporated in his treatise and illustrated in a map which was pub-lished in 1599 and is reproduced with four others here. The author provides full details on fifty-four other maps of the siege as well as substantial extracts from De Marchi's treatise (in their original Italian) where reference is made to Malta.

198   A study in depth of 143 maps representing the Great Siege of Malta of 1565.
Albert Ganado, Maurice Agius-Vadala.   Valletta: Publishers Enterprises Group (PEG) Ltd., for the Bank of Valletta, 1994 (volume I. 502p.), 1995 (volume II. 369p.). bibliog.

Opulently illustrated (volume II) with photographs (some in colour) of the maps and scenes of the siege, this monumental work must be the definitive publication. Some of the maps considered have never previously been documented. Most of volume I is devoted to detailed description of the maps and of their provenance. An introductory section on the events and people involved in the siege (p. 1-25) is followed by the maps and related illustrations (p. 29-187). The 'Analytical index' by George Mifsud Chircop (p. 203-368) is a major component in itself and there is a 'Key to collec-tions' (p. 487-89) and a bibliography (p. 491-502). This publication, the result of 25 years of research, provides an in-depth study of the 143 siege maps in oils, in manu-script, or in print in 70 libraries, museums, and palaces and in 23 private collections in 16 countries.

17th and 18th centuries

199   **'A parish at sea': spiritual concerns aboard the Order of St. John's galleys in the seventeenth and eighteenth centuries.**
David F. Allen.   In: *The military orders: fighting for the faith and caring for the sick.*   Edited by Malcolm Barber.   Aldershot, England: Variorum, 1994, p. 113-20. bibliog.

This article formed part of a conference held at the Museum of St. John's Gate, Clerkenwell, London in 1992. It discusses the role of conventual chaplains at sea – the advice contained in their confessors' manuals contrasted with that of the Jesuits' mission to mariners which seems to have been less fatalistic.

200   **Upholding tradition: Benedict XIV and the Hospitaller Order of St. John at Malta, 1740-1758.**
David F. Allen.   *The Catholic Historical Review,* vol. 80, no. 1, January (1994), p. 18-35.

This Pope's good relations with members of the French de Tencin family and the Spanish knight who was made a cardinal, Portocarrero, extended to a Crusade Bull, offering dispensations in return for money collected in Malta for the use of the Order of St. John, and diplomatic pressure to dissuade the Bourbon king of Naples from exercising feudal rights in Malta in 1753-54. Several Norman knights proposed colonical ventures to the Order and the Pope supported an Ethiopian scheme which Grand Master Pinto declined to support. This Pope also encouraged P. M. Paciaudi (1710-85), a Theatine enthusiast of the Order, to write a new form of history on the Order as a crusading institution bound by legislation since its earliest days, rather than an heroic chronicle of the hitherto traditional genre.

201   **A 1636 description of Malta by a future Pope.**
Vincent Borġ.   Msida, Malta: Malta University Press, 1990. 24p.

Fabio Chigi, later Pope Alexander VII, was the Inquisitor and Apostolic Delegate in Malta from 1634-39. This paper discusses his description of Malta in a letter of 8 February 1636 and his tour of the island during the carnival period. The appendices describe the carnivals in Malta in the 1630s and include another of Chigi's letters, on the cotton industry, of 2 December 1634.

202   **Marriage in Malta in the late eighteenth century, 1750-1800.**
Frans Ciappara.   Malta: Associated News (M) Ltd., 1988. 144p.

A useful summary and comparison of marriage patterns and irregularities in Malta and Gozo, which also provides some information on child mortality. The material discussed is drawn from a wide range of ecclesiastical parish, court, diocesan and other records.

203   **Private life, religion and enlightenment in Malta in the late eighteenth century.**
Frans Ciappara.   *Revue du Monde Musulman et de la Méditerranée,* no. 71 (1994), p. 109-26. bibliog.

Based on detailed work with church and other local archives, this study looks at marriage, the priesthood and the Enlightenment in Malta. It appears in a collection of fifteen articles – most of them in French – on Malta, *Le Carrefour Maltais* (The Maltese crossroads).

204 **Budgeting in seventeenth century Malta: an insight into the administration of the *Comun Tesoro*.**
Domenic Cutajar, Carmel Cassar. *Mid-Med Bank Limited, Report and Accounts, 1983*, Valletta (Malta), 1984, p. 22-32.

A short account of the *Comun Tesoro*, the officers and institutional establishment through which the finances of the Order of St. John were administered. This includes an outline of the sources of income and fields of expenditure and concludes with a table of the responsions (annual quota in Sicilian currency values) from the twenty priories of the Order in 1670 and a list of the officials responsible for the *Comun Tesoro* 1597-1699.

205 **The Malta quarantine shipping and trade 1654-1694.**
Domenic Cutajar. *Mid-Med Bank Limited: Report and Accounts 1987*, Valletta, Malta (1988), p. 19-66. bibliog.

A study based on the early quarantine registers, this includes maps of places in the Mediterranean where plague was recorded throughout the period, and information on trading links, the types of craft used for commerce and corsairing and taken as prizes, passengers and slaves, and the frequency of different sorts of trade goods from different parts of the Mediterranean and occasionally from Portugal and England. What stands out is the volume and variety of trade with the entire littoral under Turkish rule but no assessment is made of the potential bulk carried in the various types of craft.

206 **The wine trade in Malta in the eighteenth century.**
John Debono. *Melita Historica*, vol. 9, no. 1 (1984), p. 74-92. bibliog.

A well-documented account of the scale, organization and economic consequences of the Maltese wine trade in the 18th century.

207 **The Chamber of Commerce and the cotton trade of Malta in the eighteenth century.**
John Debono. *Melita Historica*, vol. 10, no. 1 (1988), p. 27-50. bibliog.

In 1757 the grand master set up the Chamber of Commerce and a year later a meeting of merchants drew up regulations to govern joint trading ventures. In 1776 the chamber presented a long report on the economic situation and the state of cotton, which was Malta's only exported crop. The Chamber of Commerce was abolished by the grand master in 1781. This report is summarized and discussed. Its full Italian text is printed in an appendix.

208 **The Order of Malta and the Russian Empire.**
Olgerd de Sherbowitz-Wetzor, Cyril Toumanoff. Rome: S.M.O.M., 1969. 131p. bibliog.

Every decade or so, an author returns to the subject of the Order's brief but important relations with Russia during the period 1797-1810 which precipitated its expulsion from Malta. Each adds something new, but this account has many more extensive references to published and other sources as well as illustrations of the leading people involved, and the regalia of the Order received from St. Petersburg. Eight appendices mainly comprise documents in Russian from the registered archives of the Sovereign Military Order of Malta (SMOM) in Rome, seven of which are printed verbatim following an outline of the components of the register.

209 **Bibliography of French rule in Malta, 1798-1800.**
Joseph Galea.   Valletta: Edam Publishing House, 1989. 31p.
This bibliography concludes with relevant original documents of this episode to be found in various Maltese national and private archives, and a list of prominent French prisoners of war at the time of the French capitulation.

210 **Grandmaster Anton Manoel de Vilhena 1722-1736.**
Michael Galea.   Malta: The Author, 1992. 62p. bibliog.
Recounts the story of the Portuguese knight's career and in particular his many buildings, statues and pious legacies. However, the *Cabreo* (register of the Foundation's landed property) of the Manoel Foundation with all the plans and elevations of the properties is not, unfortunately, used for the many illustrations. The *Cabreo* is one of the most informative documents of this type in the National Library, delineating most types of early 18th-century building in the islands as well as ground-plans of land given to the Foundation.

211 **The maintenance of the Order's galley squadron (c. 1600-1650).**
Joseph F. Grima.   *Melita Historica,* vol. 7, no. 2 (1977), p. 145-56. bibliog.
Naval expenditure formed the most substantial element of the Order's budget, but a high proportion of this cost fell on the incumbent captains, who became difficult to recruit. This led Grand Master Lascaris to create a foundation in 1644 for the maintenance of a galley, following the example of other rich knights. There is a brief description of the mode and purposes of this expenditure.

212 **Eighteenth-century Malta: prosperity and problems.**
Anthony Luttrell.   *Hyphen*, vol. 3, no. 2 (1982), p. 37-51. bibliog.
The article is an assessment of what is known of the economic conditions and reputation of the Order in Malta during its later years on the island – in fact almost a century – but lacks much sustained research.

213 **De Scrittione di Malta Anno 1716 – a Venetian account.**
Edited by Victor Mallia-Milanes.   Malta: Bugelli Publications, 1988. 119p.
This extensively annotated document is printed in its original Italian, with an introduction to Maltese-Venetian relations at the time. Appendices include correspondence from the Venetian envoy in Istanbul to the grand master of the Order in 1714, and accounts of Maltese naval engagements from 1706-16 which were recorded in Venetian archives.

214 **The plague of 1676: 11,600 deaths.**
Joseph Micallef. Malta: s.d., 1983. 128p.

The foreword by Mario Buħaġiar and Joseph F. Grima commemorates the contribution of the author to local history. His history describes the spread of the disease first recorded in the Bonnici family in Valletta, the policies and action taken by the civil and medical authorities and the popular and parochial clerical response to the rigours and deprivation brought by the epidemic. Only Mdina and Safi were spared. Several votive paintings, statues and the Sarria chapel in Floriana survive as plague memorials.

215 **The life and times of Grand Master Pinto, 1741-1773.**
Carmel Testa.   Valletta: Midsea Books, 1989. 350p. bibliog.

One of the most important works of original research in recent years, this account of events during one of the longest grand masterships in Malta is impeccably referenced and constitutes a comprehensive source-book for those with more specialized research interests. The large and well-selected set of illustrations include twenty-six in colour. Early 18th-century Malta and the external relations of the Order need no longer be restricted to the scanty recycled outlines to which the history of this period has tended to be reduced.

216 **Malta and the Czars: diplomatic relations between the Order of St. John and Russia 1607-1802.**
Andrew P. Vella.   Msida, Malta: Malta University Press, 1972. 79p.
bibliog.

A fully documented account of the tortuous negotiations that culminated in Czar Paul I assuming the grand mastership of the Order, with illustrations of the church of St. John and the palace that served as the grand priory in St. Petersburg. There follow transcripts, in their original languages and English translation, of the congratulations sent by the European heads of state to Grand Master Ferdinand de Hompesch on his election in 1797.

217 **Documents relating to Maltese history in the State Archives of Naples.**
Anthony Żammit Gabarretta.   *Proceedings of History Week, 1983*
(1984), p. 65-71.

A brief outline of the fifty-one bundles of Bourbon foreign affairs papers from 1735-1860, within which may be found letters relating to the Order, to the Maltese rising against the French occupation in 1798-1800, and from the Neapolitan Consul in British Malta to his foreign ministry. Reference numbers are provided for several interesting examples.

19th and 20th centuries

General

218 Governors of Malta.
A. E. Abela.   Valletta: Progress Press, 1991. 167p.

An attractively produced and illustrated account, distinguishing governors and civil commissioners (part one, p. 1-119) and lieutenant governors and chief secretaries (part two, p. 123-43).

219 The genesis of freemasonry in Malta (1730-1843).
A. J. Agius.   Malta, 1993. 92p.

This rather untidy but short account aims to provide the scanty information available on masonic activity under parts of the Order and the French lodge, and in particular on the work of Walter Rodwell Wright (1775-1826) for Maltese freemasonry in the years 1814-26. An illustration of Wright's gravestone is included. Unfortunately it does not surpass *The history of freemasonry in the district of Malta from the year 1800 up to the present time* (q.v.) published by A. M. Broadley in 1880, which is relatively inaccessible.

220 New light on Malta during the Peace of Amiens, 1801-1803.
D. F. Allen.   *The British Library Journal*, vol. 20, no. 2 (Autumn 1994), p. 173-83. bibliog.

Sir Charles William Pasley (1780-1861) became a renowned military engineer and Inspector General of Railways, but he spent time in Malta from 1801-04 as a young lieutenant of the Malta Garrison. He established good relations with several of the Maltese *periti* (architects) and his impressions of the situation in Malta form an interesting prelude to those of General Sir George Whitmore KCH after 1812.

221 Britain and Malta: the story of an era.
Joseph Attard.   Marsa, Malta: Publishers Enterprises Group (PEG) Ltd., 1988. 222p.

An accessible account of 180 years of British colonial and military presence concluding with the withdrawal of the last UK forces on 31 March 1979. Sources are not indicated but there is an index (p. 215-22). There are thirty-six illustrations.

222 Description of Malta and Gozo.
George Percy Badger.   Malta, 1838. Reprinted in facsimile, Valletta: Melitensia Editions, Valletta Publishing, 1989. 317p. 2 maps.

The author worked for the Church Missionary Society in Malta and learnt Maltese followed by Arabic of which he produced an authoritative lexicon. This description is in four parts. The first comprises a short history of the islands and the second a review of their geography, culture and administration of justice. The third part takes the form of a guided tour of the towns and other places of interest in Malta, and the fourth a similar tour of Gozo. Engraved illustrations delineate costumes and buildings in Malta. It is one of the earliest guidebooks devoted solely to Malta.

223 **British colonial budgeting in Malta: the first formative decades 1800-1838.**
Paul Bartolo. *Melita Historica*, vol. 8, no. 1 (1980), p. 1-22. bibliog.

Governor Maitland introduced a centralized system of public accounts in 1814 and was critical of the state of affairs in the management of public property and the *Università* corn monopoly which could not be audited. This article discusses the various funds under the first two governors, including Hastings's extensive expenditure on repairing the governor's palaces and charitable institutions. The Maltese criticized the expenditure on British officials, with which the Austin and Lewis Commission of 1836 concurred on the grounds that their jobs were actually performed by Maltese subordinates.

224 **Malta picture postcards 1898-1906.**
Giovanni Bonello, Graham Sheed. Malta: The Authors (printed by Interprint), 1985. Reprinted with corrections, 1986. 101p.

Two major functions are served by this book. The first is to give an impression of the way in which Malta was represented, largely one presumes for the foreign recipients, many of whom could have been the families of British service personnel but also Maltese abroad. A limited number of major buildings and views around Valletta, Mosta and the harbour area predominate, with the route to Mdina, and various costumes and occupations typical of Maltese life, including goats. The second function, which forms the text, catalogues the postcards produced by forty-two photographers, printers and publishers – local, British, Italian, German, Viennese and Swiss. In each case the function of the card, mode of printing, and type of subject are listed as well as the likely date of publication.

225 **Maltese in Spain during the Napoleonic Age.**
Giovanni Bonello. *The P. S. M. Magazine (Malta),* vol. 19, no. 3 (1990), p. 5-20.

Using the evidence of twenty-nine original letters to, from, or relating to, Maltese settlers in Spain between 1792 and 1818, the writer aims to demonstrate something of the commercial activity of the time. Italian is used in the great majority of cases, plus some French. Some are illustrated.

226 **Malta then and now: Dari u llum.**
Joseph Bonnici, Michael Cassar. Malta: The Authors, (3 vols.), 1987, 1989, 1993. each 64p.

Each of the three volumes provides sixty-four comparative photographs of past and present views of the harbours and fortifications, street scenes and rural views. Although there are descriptive captions they seldom include even the approximate dates of each pair. The collections provide an evocative glimpse of change in both town and country and the way of life of people in the islands. In some cases, e.g. Sliema, buildings appear to have been reconstructed at least twice since the earliest photograph published in these volumes, which indicates the pace of change in some, once residential, as well as in the new built-up rural areas.

227 **The history of freemasonry in the district of Malta from the year 1800 up to the present time.**
A. M. Broadley.   London: George Kenning, 1880. 122p.

Outlines the little that is known of freemasonry under the Knights of St. John and concentrates on developments in the first three-quarters of the 19th century. 'There is, probably, no part of the world in which Freemasonry has so greatly prospered during the present century as in Malta', says the author who goes on to detail the reasons for this, including 'the floating nature of its military and civil populations . . .' (p. 1). A chapter on Walter Rodwell Wright is followed by others on individual lodges and there are discussions of Masonic developments in general in Malta and nearby areas.

228 **John Hookham Frere in Malta (1821-1846): a link with our social and cultural past.**
Paul Cassar.   *Melita Historica*, vol. 9, no. 1 (1984), p. 49-73. bibliog.

A useful summary of information on this significant British resident and some of his many local cultural activities as well as the circle of Maltese and some others with whom he was in contact. The Villa Frere in Pietà and its garden architecture are described but not illustrated, with the text of an inscription that its creator placed in it. An appendix lists classical works from Frere's library given to local libraries.

229 **British temperance reformers and the island of Malta 1815-1914.**
N. D. Denny.   *Melita Historica*, vol. 9, no. 4 (1987), p. 329-45. bibliog.

Teetotalism was a major part of the Methodist programme of John Laverack, which was also taken up by the Scottish Church minister George Wisely. But British governors did not encourage it as a wider social movement and extension to Maltese society.

230 **The British in the Mediterranean.**
Peter Dietz.   London: Brassey's (UK) Ltd, 1994. 228p. bibliog.

A useful general account of the region, with many references to Malta, and a section containing illustrations. It mainly covers the 19th and 20th centuries. The annexe provides a short guide for travellers.

231 **Sir Alexander John Ball and Malta: the beginning of an era.**
Michael Galea.   Marsa, Malta: Publishers Enterprises Group (PEG) Ltd., 1990. 235p. bibliog.

Ball (1756-1809) commanded the British blockade of the French in Malta from 1798, was invited to preside over the National Congress that co-ordinated the Maltese insurrection against the French occupation, and became Britain's Civil Commissioner of the islands. Half of the book is devoted to the military and diplomatic vicissitudes which culminated in Britain's retention of Malta despite the Treaty of Amiens in 1802, and the rest to chapters on Ball's relations with the Maltese, the British government and Samuel Taylor Coleridge, his civil secretary in 1805, and to the memorial constructed in his honour in the Lower Barracca gardens. The appendices include the *Articles of capitulation of the French garrison* in 1800, Ball's *Memorandum on Malta* of 1801, and *Article ten of the Treaty of Amiens* of 1802. A summary of Ball's Maltese career with much more extensive coloured illustrations of relevant people and places was published as 'Sir Alexander Ball and Malta 1798-1809' in *Mid-Med Bank Limited: report and accounts 1990* (1991), p. I-XX.

232 Malta, Britain and the European Powers 1793-1815.
Desmond Gregory. London: Associated University Presses, 1996.
370p. 4 maps. bibliog.

The twenty chapters comprising this important book provide the first comprehensive recent analysis of the French, British, Sicilian and Russian interests in Malta during the French Revolutionary and Napoleonic Wars. By retaining Malta after the Treaty of Amiens, Britain provided one of the pretexts for the resumption of the war in 1803, and at its end in 1814 was still in possession despite protests. Malta had been formally annexed the year before. Almost half the book discusses the British modes of administration, the economy of the island, its public health, church/state relations, and the establishment of the naval and military base. The appendices outline the British project to garrison Lampedusa, abandoned after a survey visit by Governor Maitland and Col. George Whitmore in 1814, a chronological table of relevant events from 1793-1814, and some of the grand masters of the Order of St. John. In addition to his ability to incorporate much published research, the author has paid exhaustive attention to official documentary sources and his extensive knowledge of the situation relating to other Mediterranean and Atlantic islands during this period. Two prints of the harbours and four portraits of British commanders/governors are illustrated.

233 Troubled lives: John and Sarah Austin.
Lotte Hamburger, Joseph Hamburger. Toronto, Buffalo; London: University of Toronto Press, 1983. 261p. bibliog.

John Austin (1790-1859) was a major English legal philosopher who taught at the University of London. His wife Sarah (1793-1867) was a writer best known for translating German works. Both were close to the utilitarians although John became more conservative after 1848. They came to Malta in October 1836 and stayed for twenty months during John's appointment as the leading member of a commission to inquire into affairs in the Crown Colony. Chapter 5 (p. 95-118) recounts the Austins' activities in Malta, John's clash with the Chief Justice Sir John Stoddart, who wished to introduce English law and procedures, the abolition of the post of treasurer, the introduction of a press-freedom law, and the attack on John Austin's work by ex-Lord Chancellor Brougham in the House of Lords, London.

234 A history of Malta during the period of the French and British occupations, 1798-1815.
William Hardman, edited and introduced by J. Holland Rose.
London: Longmans, Green, & Co., 1909. Facsimile edition, Valletta: Midsea Books Ltd. (Melitensia Book Club Issue 10), 1994. 657p.
2 maps. bibliog.

A most useful source of documents on the whole period with a historical commentary comprising twenty-four chapters. Appendices include a note on the financial condition of the Order in 1798, a report on the revenue of Malta c.1800, and extensive extracts in French from General Vaubois' *Journal du Siège de Malte* (Journal of the Siege of Malta).

235 **The Knights of St. John in the British Realm, being the official history of the Most Venerable Order of the Hospital of St. John of Jerusalem.**
Col. Sir Edwin King, Sir Harry Luke.   London: St. John's Gate, 1967. 307p.

Although focused on the restoration of the Grand Priory in England since the mid-19th century and its pre-reformation presence, this work includes accounts of the Order's history in the Mediterranean including Malta, the functions of the Venerable Order, and appendices of charters and other significant documents.

236 **The Maltese Protestant College.**
Salv. Mallia.   *Melita Historica*, vol. 10, no. 3 (1990), p. 257-82.

This missionary college, first proposed by Governor Hastings twenty years before, functioned from 1846-65. The article, making extensive use of documentary quotations, outlines its functions and activities.

237 **The British colonial experience 1800-1964: the impact on Maltese society.**
Edited by Victor Mallia-Milanes.   Malta: Mireva Publications under the auspices of The Free University, Amsterdam, 1988. 422p. 2 maps. bibliog.

The sixteen historical essays in this work are devoted to ecclesiastical, cultural and political relations as well as to the development of the economy and Maltese nationalism. Fifty half-tone reproductions illustrate aspects of Maltese social and political life as well as its architecture and painting. In 'The nature of Maltese politics, c. 870-1964', Godfrey Wettinger questions the use of the term 'colonial' to cover the millennia of domination by a succession of cultures, states and dynasties. Joseph Bezzina and Adrianus (Adriannes) Koster provide 'Church and state in an island colony' and 'Regular and secular clergy in British Malta'. Arthur Clare outlines 'Features of an island economy' in the 19th century. Aspects of Maltese behaviour and identity are discussed in relation to British colonial experience and Jeremy Boissevain explodes the myth that *festa* band club rivalry was fostered by colonial policy. A mass of data on 'Maltese art 1800-1964' is provided by Domenic Cutajar and Emmanuel Fiorentino. Oliver Friggieri discusses 'The search for a national identity in Maltese literature' and Denis de Lucca looks at 'British influence on Maltese architecture and fortifications'. Stephen Howe analyses both theories of, and local political responses to, 'British decolonization and Malta's imperial role'. Each article has its own references and the book has its own substantial bibliography.

238 **Antique Malta 1842-1885: a topographical and historical catalogue of engravings and articles as depicted in the major English magazines of the eventful period.**
Edited by A. Nicholas.   Valletta: Nicholas Books, 1982. 114p.

Albert Ganado's short introduction provides the context for this large collection of reproductions of engraved illustrations from *The Illustrated London News* and *The Graphic*. These remarkably clear images present a British view of life in Malta in chronological order, but no specific source references are provided to the actual issues of either journal, which reduces its easy use for historical purposes. However, the original text which accompanies each engraving appears to be complete.

Second World War

239 The Battle of Malta: an epic true story of suffering and bravery.
Joseph Attard.   Valletta: Progress Press, 1994. 252p. Previously
published, London: William Kimber, 1980. Reprinted, London:
Hamlyn Publishing Co., 1982.

Written in the first person, this is a Maltese perspective on the Battle for Malta, 1940-
43, using contemporary sources (such as *The Times of Malta*). The writer stresses the
honour due to the Maltese, British, and others involved in the conflict.

240 Siege: Malta 1940-1943.
Ernle Bradford.   London: Hamish Hamilton, 1985. 247p. bibliog.

The author of *The Great Siege of Malta, 1565* (q.v.), and other works on the Maltese
Islands, Bradford details events from when he served in the Mediterranean in the
Royal Navy. Bradford later lived in Malta. A Penguin version of the 1985 volume
appeared in 1987 and a large-print edition a year later.

241 Malta George Cross. Victory in the air.
Richard J. Caruana.   Valletta: Modelaid International Publications,
1996. 255p.

This work is in two main parts. The first deals with the air war centred on Malta which
culminated in the invasion of Sicily in July 1943. The second presents the two main
phases of the offensive against Malta by Germany's *Luftwaffe* and Italy's *Regia
Aeronautica* up to October 1942. The photographs and military detail give a vivid and
compelling picture of the conflict but there is also much about the impact of the hostilities on the islands and their people.

242 The epic of Malta: a pictorial survey of Malta during the Second
World War: facsimile edition.
Introduced by Henry Frendo.   Valletta: Melitensia Editions, Valletta
Publishing & Promotion Co. Ltd., 1990. 128p. bibliog.

Reprints the extensively illustrated book first published by Odhams Press, London,
shortly after Malta was awarded the George Cross in April 1942. Frendo provides a short
introduction and his bibliography provides a useful list of books on the war in Malta.

243 Malta and the Second World War. A bibliography.
Joseph Galea.   *Melita Historica,* vol. 1, no. 1 (1952), p. 33-51.

Lists over 250 books, chapters, articles and pamphlets. All but a few (in Italian or
Maltese) are in English and there is an index of writers involved (p. 50-51). The main
categories are narrative, descriptive, political, and miscellaneous. This very comprehensive list covers the period 1939 to 1950.

244 Malta: diary of a war (June 1940-August 1945).
Michael Galea.   Marsa, Malta: Publishers Enterprises Group (PEG),
1992. 307p.

This is a chronological account, by a Maltese, of momentous events as they affected
the lives of the inhabitants and garrison of the islands.

245 **Malta: the triumphant years, 1940-43.**
George Hogan. Valletta: Progress Press, 1988. 208p. Originally
published, London: Robert Hale, 1978.

This is an illustrated account of hostilities in the siege years and their impact on the
everyday lives of civilians and armed forces personnel. Based on the author's recol-
lections of the conflict, the work also draws on war-time accounts.

246 **Besieged: the World War II ordeal of Malta, 1940-1942.**
Charles A. Jellison. Hanover, New Hampshire: University Press of
New England, 1984. 288p. maps. bibliog.

A well-researched, illustrated study showing aspects of the impact of the conflict on
the islands and their people – social history against the backdrop of military action.

247 **'The Med'. The Royal Navy in the Mediterranean 1939-45.**
Rowland Langmaid. London: Batchworth Press, 1948. 130p.

An often personal history of this theatre of war, copiously illustrated by half-tone
reproductions of the author's pictures. Langmaid was Official Admiralty Artist
appointed by the Commander-in-Chief Admiral Viscount Cunningham. The illustrations depict engagements off Malta as well as many depictions of ships that used the
facilities of the island.

248 **Malta: the thorn in Rommel's side: six months that turned the**
war.
Laddie Lucas. London: Stanley Paul, 1992. 205p. Also published,
London: Penguin, 1993. 311p.

A personal account of the 1942 Battle for Malta set in the wider context of the Second
World War in the Mediterranean.

249 **The Air Battle of Malta: the official account of the R. A. F. in**
Malta, June 1940 to November 1942.
Prepared for the Air Ministry by the Ministry of Information.
London: HMSO, 1944. 97p.

An extensively illustrated account of the campaign, with descriptions of the assault on
HMS *Illustrious*, the 'Santa Maria' August convoy and the offensive against
Rommel's supply routes.

250 **Malta: the hurricane years, 1940-41.**
Christopher Shores, Brian Cull, with Nicola Malizia. London: Grub
Street, 1987. 457p. bibliog.

The writers provide an extremely detailed day-by-day account of the ferocious air battles over land and sea during 1940 and 1941 from the bases at Hal Far, Luqa, and
Ta'Qali (Takali) in Malta. This is an impressive piece of historical record.

251 **Pedestal: the Malta convoy of August 1942.**
Peter C. Smith.   London: William Kimber, 1970. 208p. 9 maps.
bibliog.
This remains one of the best accounts of the critical sea war centred on Malta and the
ways in which supplies were maintained to sustain the blockaded and bombed islands.

252 **Faith, hope and Malta G.C.: ground and air heroes of the George
Cross island.**
Tony Spooner.   Swindon, England: Newton, 1992. 166p.
Vividly describes the interlinked sagas of aircrew who flew the combat missions and
the ground crews who kept the planes airworthy. This book is written by the author of
Warburton's war: the life of Wing Commander Adrian Warburton (London: William
Kimber, 1987. 222p.) and illustrated from contemporary photographs.

253 **Supreme gallantry. Malta's role in the Allied victory 1939-1945.**
Tony Spooner.   London: John Murray, 1996. 358p.
A vivid account of the air war from 1940-43 waged over the central Mediterranean
from the Royal Air Force bases in Malta. The author, a participant himself, recounts
exploits of heroes and documents the role of intelligence in the conflict and the run-up
to the invasion of Italy. The book says a lot about the impact of the air war on Malta
and the Maltese. Photographs are contained between p. 134 and p. 135.

254 **Malta: blitzed but not beaten.**
Philip Vella.   Malta: Progress Press for the National War Museum
Association, 1985. 332p.
A comprehensive account, extensively illustrated from contemporary photographs, of
various aspects of Malta's experience of the Battle for Malta, 1940-42 – military,
social and economic. Separate chapters are devoted to particular episodes such as the
deportations, Pisani's trial for serving the enemy, the visit of King George VI in June
1943 and highlights of this most recent siege. A third of the text consists of statistical
and other appendices and the Roll of Honour of Maltese and UK personnel who lost
their lives in the conflict (p. 265-322).

Other military history

255 **The Malta Grand Harbour and some of its visitors: a pictorial
review l879-1979.**
Joseph Bonnici, Michael Cassar.   Luqa, Malta: Tecnografica Design
Centre Co. Ltd., 1985. 179p.
A volume of reproductions of ships, mostly of the Royal Navy, which were recorded
by an unspecified photographer on original negatives in the author's possession.
There are four parts covering 1879-1919, 1920-39, 1945-59 and 1960-79, with an
index of ships' names. The photographs have been selected to show changes in the
design, size and function of warships and also indicate the modification of the Grand
Harbour to accommodate them. The type, building date, tonnage, horsepower and
speed of each ship is usually given as well as the date of its photograph.

256   **The Royal Navy in Malta. A photographic record.**
Joseph Bonnici, Michael Cassar.   Malta: The Authors (distributed by
Miller Distributors Ltd., Valletta; printed by Interprint Ltd.), 1989. 104p.
An imposing collection of black-and-white photographs of ships in Malta's harbours,
each picture accompanied by an explanatory caption.

257   **The Malta Grand Harbour and its dockyard.**
Joseph Bonnici, Michael Cassar.   Malta: The Authors (printed by the
Gutenberg Press, Żabbar, Malta), 1994. 480p. bibliog.
This imposing study of the harbour, and in particular its dockyard, is copiously illustrated with contemporary plans, prints, photographs and chronologies and pays
attention to both the architecture and its technical functions. Twelve chapters cover
the history of the main subject from 1530-1994, followed by thirty-six specific aspects
– though not including the splendid model designed by Lt. Col. Clarke to demonstrate
his proposals in 1865 for the expansion of the dockyard.

258   **Salute to Maltese infantrymen.**
C. L. Borġ.   Valletta: Valletta Publishing, 1990. 166p.
An account of the Maltese infantry who served in the King's Own Malta Rifles in Malta
and elsewhere during the Second World War and subsequently. It is mainly based on the
personal experience of Lt. Col. Borġ who commanded the regiment from 1959-62.

259   **Historical records of the Maltese Corps of the British Army.**
A. G. Chesney (Maj.).   London: William Clowes & Sons, 1897.
Reprinted facsimile edition, Valletta: Midsea Books Ltd. (Melitensia
Book Club Issue 6), 1986. 210p.
This study of the records from 1815 offers brief sketches, with appendices detailing
establishments, pay rates, etc. Fourteen of the illustrations of uniforms in this reprint
edition are in colour. The corps was one of the several local military units raised in the
British colonies and was ultimately succeeded by other local units that were amalga-
mated to form the armed forces of Malta in 1972.

260   **The Royal Dockyards 1690-1850: architecture and engineering
works of the sailing navy.**
Jonathan G. Coad.   Aldershot, England: Scholar Press; Brookfield,
Vermont: Gower Publishing, for the Royal Commission on the
Historical Monuments of England, 1989. 399p. bibliog.
This important book reviews these establishments of the Royal Navy at home and
overseas. Chapter 16 on Malta (p. 341-54) includes fully documented information on
the period from 1800, when the British took over the naval base of the Knights of St.
John from the French, with special reference to new and adapted installations, vict-
ualling, and hospital provision for the Royal Navy.

261   **The cross and the ensign: a naval history of Malta, 1798-1979.**
Peter Elliott.   Cambridge, England: Patrick Stephens, 1980. 217p.
The author traces the ways in which the fortunes of Malta and Britain were linked by
the Royal Navy's presence in the islands.

262   The Royal Navy at Malta. Vol. 1, The Victorian era, 1865-1906. Vol. 2, 1907-1939.

Richard Ellis, Ben Warlow.   Liskeard, England: Maritime Books, vol. 1, 1989. 132p. vol. 2, 1990. 144p.

Comprises black-and-white photographs of vessels of the Royal Navy and harbour scenes in Malta, accompanied by annotations. Photographs taken by the Ellis family firm were a regular feature of a ship's service in Malta. These two volumes provide a comprehensive record of these types of warship up until the outbreak of the Second World War.

263   Military aviation in Malta G.C., 1915-1993: a comprehensive history.

John F. Hamlin.   Peterborough, England: G. M. S. Enterprises, 1994. 254p.

Starting from descriptions of the early flying boats, the establishment of an airfield, and flying practices of the 1930s, this well-illustrated and detail-packed account covers the events of 1940, the peak 'Siege' years of the assault on Malta (1941-42), and the islands' vital part in the invasion of Sicily. Via the Suez campaign of 1956, the account records the strong post-war presence of the (British) Fleet Air Arm and then looks at the declining strategic role of Malta. This, the definitive work on its subject, ends with an account of the development of the air element of the Maltese forces.

264   Gallipoli: the Malta connection.

John A. Mizzi.   Luqa, Malta: Tecnografica Publications, 1990. 186p. 3 maps. bibliog.

The thirteen chapters and ten appendices contained in this book are devoted to an account of the Dardanelles campaign and its associations with Malta. These included the islands' role as a primary naval base and as a point of ANZAC and other embarkation for the war front. Maltese combatants had direct experience of the campaign and the islands acted as 'the nurse of the Mediterranean'. The whole book is extensively illustrated with photographs of the period.

265   Malta G.C.

Winston G. Ramsey.   In: *After the Battle, No. 10.*   London: Battle of Britain Prints International Ltd., 1975, p. 1-41.

The format of this series of Second World War publications is the juxtaposition of war-time photographs and similarly posed contemporary photographs of the same scenes. Volume no. 10 is mostly (41p. out of 54p.) devoted to Malta – to the airfields and air battles, the bombing of the cities, the King's visit in 1943, the Italian naval attack on the Grand Harbour in 1941 and the Italian Naval surrender in 1943, the RAF Gladiator *Faith* and the preservation of items in Valletta's National War Museum, whose association distributes this useful pictorial publication.

266   The history of the King's Own Malta Regiment and the armed forces of the Order of St. John.

Captain J. M. Wismayer.   Valletta: Said International Ltd., 1989. 376p.

An extensively illustrated account of this Maltese regiment with separate chapters on the Maltese militia that preceded it and the Royal Malta Artillery. The regiment was disbanded in 1972 when the Armed Forces of Malta were unified.

Heraldry, Orders and Decorations

267 **The Order of St. Michael and St. George in Malta and the Maltese Knights of the British Realm.**
A. E. Abela. Malta: Progress Press, 1988. 206p.

Instituted by Letters Patent in 1818, at the behest of Governor Maitland, this Order was intended to replace that of St. John and be of especial use to those residing in the Maltese and Ionian Islands. The insignia, some members, and the hall of the Order are illustrated in colour, and biographical notes are provided on many Maltese members, the last of whom was appointed in 1960. All of the latter are included in an appendix.

268 **Maltese George Cross and war gallantry awards.**
A. E. Abela. Valletta: Progress Press Co. Ltd., 1989. 100p. bibliog.

This book has two parts. The first is devoted to the George Cross award and Maltese recipients of the George Medal as well as the Albert Medal. The second details Maltese recipients of the DSO, DSC, MC, DSM, Military Medal, and the DFC. The appendix lists Maltese recipients of other British honours and awards during both world wars. There are many illustrations of the recipients of, or events associated with, the awards, including the image of each type of award.

269 **The nobles of Malta as at present existing.**
George Crispo-Barbaro. Valletta: Victoria Press, 1987. 66p. + 16p.

This essentially contains lists of: those nobles recognized by the committee of privileges; their children; members of the Assembly of Maltese Nobility; and cadets of noble families. Appendices are also included on the holders of other orders and on extinct families and titles. The additional sixteen pages reprint the 1887 directory of the Maltese nobility.

270 **The genealogy and heraldry of the noble families of Malta.**
Charles A. Gauci. Valletta: Gulf Publishing Ltd., 1981. 309p.
bibliog.

The first of two volumes (see also item no. 274), this is divided into three parts.
Section one introduces the feudal lords and then the nobility of Malta. The second part
lists the marquises, counts and barons alphabetically with their coats of arms and
genealogies. All of the appendices relate to aspects of the latter section, and they
include a map of the principal fiefs in Malta and Gozo. Part three deals with some
technical aspects of heraldry. The Labour Government of Don Mintoff had withdrawn
official recognition of these titles in the Republic of Malta. This publication sought to
keep their knowledge and interest alive.

271 **The Palaeologo family: a genealogical review.**
Charles A. Gauci, Peter Mallat. Malta: PEG Publications, 1985. 125p.

As well as being mentioned in the New Testament, as the location of St. Paul's shipwreck, Malta claims direct descent from the Palaeologos, the last Byzantine imperial
family, for two of its noble houses. These, and twenty-six other lines of male and
female descent – one of which is the House of Trebizond – are printed here in detail
with illustrations of past and present scions of the dynasty.

272 **A guide to the Maltese nobility.**
Charles A. Gauci. Marsa, Malta: Publishers Enterprises Group (PEG)
Ltd., 1986. 100p.

This guide amends previous publications by the author and includes more genealogical data. It lists titles in order of precedence as well as the current holders of titles,
their heirs and widows. The full blazons for their coats of arms are described but not
illustrated.

273 **A key to Maltese coats of arms.**
Charles A. Gauci. Marsa, Malta: Publishers Enterprises Group (PEG)
Ltd., 1988. 131p.

The two parts of this handbook provide an index of the charges (symbols) held by different Maltese families and of the families holding a variety of different charges. Two
appendices provide some alternative spellings of Maltese surnames, and the symbolic
meaning of many of the charges in Italian heraldry. Black-and-white illustrations
exemplify many of the charges listed.

274 **The genealogy and heraldry of the noble families of Malta.**
Volume two.
Charles A. Gauci. Marsa, Malta: Publishers Enterprises Group (PEG)
Ltd., 1992. 505p. bibliog.

The six parts of this second volume (see item no. 270 for the first) comprise: titles
revived since 1981; extinct magistral titles; papal titles granted to Maltese citizens;
royal connections of the Maltese nobility, mostly in the remote past; some families of
historical interest; and foreign titles in Malta. Coats of arms and genealogies illustrate
most entries. Three appendices comprise a list of the coats of arms of foreign families
and two Italian decrees of 1926 and 1943.

275 **An illustrated collection of the coats of arms of Maltese families (Stemmi Maltesi).**
Charles A. Gauci.   Marsa, Malta: Publishers Enterprises Group (PEG) Ltd., 1996. 214p. bibliog.

A short essay on the rules of blazon introducing 802 heraldically coloured coats of arms of different families in alphabetical order. It therefore complements the other books by this author which have no coloured plates, in particular *A key to Maltese coats of arms* (q.v.).

276 **Malta's nobility and the winds of change 1888-1988: an analytical study of the rules and regulations governing the 'Assembly of Nobles' and the 'Committee of Privileges' of the Maltese nobility.**
Stephen D. G. Giles Ash.   Marsa, Malta: Printed by Publishers Enterprises Group (PEG) Ltd., 1988. 108p.

This consists of reprinted sections for the Standing Orders of 1888 which were adapted from those of the English House of Lords, the articles governing the Assembly of the Maltese Nobility of 1889, and an edited discussion of the correspondence that was presented to both Houses of Parliament from 1886, including the characteristically animated interventions of the Count della Catena, Lord Strickland, who had just resigned from the Maltese Committee of Privileges. The final part consists of observations by the author on the current situation, but no reference is made to the derecognition of noble titles by the Maltese legislature during Dom Mintoff's prime ministership.

277 **The nobility of Malta: an analytical study and reappraisal of the Royal Commission of 1877.**
Stephen D. G. Giles Ash.   Marsa, Malta: Printed by Publishers Enterprises Group (PEG) Ltd., 1988. 141p.

The primary value of this book is its reprinted text of the report of the Royal Commission which was appointed to investigate the claims of the Maltese nobility, presented on 10 December 1877. The author has added some further information and his own opinions.

278 **A look at Maltese insignia.**
Adrian Strickland.   Balzan, Malta: Cyan Ltd., 1992. 87p. bibliog.

Provides 192 coloured illustrations of the wide range of insignia to be found in modern Malta including flags and standards, orders and decorations. Strickland covers the armed forces and other services, some civic and corporate and ecclesiastical heraldry, and some badges etc. associated with Malta's history and Maltese associations in other countries.

Population

Demography

279   **Census '85. Vol. I – A demographic profile of Malta and Gozo.**
Valletta: Central Office of Statistics, 1986. 319p.
Chapters on historical and organizational background, demographic characteristics, socio-economic characteristics, housing, and future trends are followed by statistical tables (from p. 135 onwards). See also volume III (item no. 280). Volume II was not published.

280   **Census '85. Vol. III – A computer-drawn demographic atlas of Malta and Gozo.**
Valletta: Central Office of Statistics, 1987. 48p.
This volume of forty-eight pages of maps and accompanying text was produced in collaboration with the Department of Geography at the University of Keele in England. The atlas is divided into six sections. Reference maps of census regions, localities and the built-up area are followed by data on demographic characteristics, education and literacy, economic status, housing characteristics and domestic amenities.

281   **Census of population and housing, 1995: preliminary report.**
Valletta: Central Office of Statistics, March 1996. 64p.
A text which summarizes the methods of the census and its principal findings is followed (p. 25-64) by statistical tables. These show that the total population had gone up by nearly 31,000 since 1985 to 376,335, with the highest population growth rates in the outer harbour region – though inner-harbour localities registered a substantial population loss.

282 **Demographic review of the Maltese Islands, 1995.**
Valletta: Central Office of Statistics, 1996. 77p.
Forty-seven tables of data are preceded by a brief descriptive introduction (p. 1-3).
Annual volumes in this series, which have been very similar in format to the 1995
issue for over fifteen years, are available dating back to 1960.

283 **Status Animarum I: a unique source for seventeenth and
eighteenth century Maltese demography.**
Stanley Fiorini. *Melita Historica*, vol. 8, no. 4 (1983), p. 325-43.
bibliog.
This article, with its appendix of eighteen tables, is designed to introduce and demonstrate the sorts of demographic data that can be gained from the regular records of the
Roman Catholic Church in Malta, and more occasional survivals such as militia lists.

284 **Status Animarum II: a census of 1687.**
Stanley Fiorini. *Proceedings of History Week, 1984* (1986), p. 41-100.
bibliog.
The second of two papers (see also item no. 283), this makes use of the first almost
complete set of these ecclesiastical 'census' records, that of 1687. Discussion of the
local returns is followed by statistics of the population in each locality, place and
street names, the priest-population ratio and foreign surnames. All examples of the
latter are tabulated by locality and frequency in each place. The records were compiled annually at the Easter parochial visitations and submitted to the Bishop of Malta.
Many examples survive but few years are so well covered across the islands.

285 **Malta: the 1985 census.**
Douglas G. Lockhart, Keith T. Mason. *Geography,* vol. 73, part 3,
no. 320 (1988), p. 261-65. maps.
Comments on the results of Malta's fourteenth Census of Population and Housing
taken on 16 November 1985. The article stresses *inter alia* that the rate of population
growth, although little higher than the European average, is contributing to considerable problems of suburban sprawl and loss of agricultural land.

286 **The population of the Maltese Islands. Census 1995.**
M. Markwick. *Geography*, no. 355, vol. 82, part 2 (1997), p. 179-82.
2 maps.
With the help of two maps, this brief comment notes that the population is ageing as
well as growing and that the decline in numbers in the inner-harbour areas, centred on
Valletta, is continuing. Recent policy changes are likely to restrict further blurring of
distinctions between rural and urban settlement.

287 **The hierarchy of Maltese towns.**
André Żammit. *Hyphen*, vol. VI, no. 4 (1990), p. 191-96.
An application of the Rank Size Rule to thirty-six Maltese and ten Gozitan localities
according to the censuses of 1931, 1957 and 1985 with a discussion of particularity
despite contiguity.

Settlement and migration

288 Early Maltese emigration 1900-1914.
Lawrence E. Attard.   Valletta: Gulf Publishing Ltd., 1983. 58p.
bibliog. (Man and Means Series, no. 1).

Reviews the economic and colonial context in the first years of the 20th century when emigration was seen as the solution to problems of over-population and unemployment as perceived at the time (p. 1-19). There then follow chapters on the Brazilian venture (1912-13), the 'American dream', 'Canada: the second choice', and 'The call of Australia'.

289 The great exodus (1918-1939).
Lawrence E. Attard.   Marsa, Malta: Publishers' Enterprises Group (PEG) Ltd., 1989. 141p. (Man and Means Series, no. 2).

The second volume of the author's study of Maltese emigration (see also item no. 288), this illustrated account of the policies, practice and experience of migration continues the story in the Mediterranean, America, Canada and, at greater length, in Australia where Maltese workers in the Queensland cane fields continue to influence village life today.

290 Rural settlement in Malta.
Brian W. Blouet.   *Geography*, vol. 56, part 2 (1971), p. 12-18.

A discussion of how, in the 15th century, a period of marked insecurity, there was very little tendency for settlements to agglomerate. However, in the 16th and 17th centuries, with growth in population and in the economy, many smaller rural settlements declined and some larger villages, each with thousands of inhabitants, emerged.

291 The impact of armed conflict on the rural settlement pattern of Malta (A.D. 1400-1800).
Brian W. Blouet.   *Institute of British Geographers, Transactions* (New Series), vol. 3, no. 3 (1978), p. 367-80.

It appears that warfare played a part in the contraction in the pattern of villages between 1400 and 1530 by bringing about a decline in population numbers which was reflected in the distribution of settlements. Between 1530 and 1800 village desertion continued but at a slower rate and in locations which suggest that armed conflict was not the major cause of abandonment. This study uses, *inter alia*, data assembled by G. Wettinger in *Medieval Malta: studies on Malta before the Knights,* edited by A. T. Luttrell (London: British School at Rome, 1975. 232p.).

292 Return migration to the Maltese Islands in the postwar years.
E. P. Delia.   *Hyphen*, vol. 3, no. 1 (1981), p. 1-8.

Assesses return migration between 1945 and 1974 when official data showed low incidences. Delia comments on migration statistics for Malta and derives an estimate of the net return flow, and identifies some implications for planning.

293 **Modern emigration from Malta: a liability?**
E. P. Delia. *Hyphen*, vol. 3, no. 4 (1981-83), p. 141-64.
Emigration was one solution to demographic and economic problems in Malta for more than a century but it was only after 1945 that it was officially encouraged and even subsidized. The writer argues that emigration during the three decades after 1945 was not a liability for Malta. It was not unduly skill selective and benefited from liberal policies in receiving countries which encouraged family – as distinct from labour – migration.

294 **The determinants of modern Maltese emigration.**
E. P. Delia. *International Migration*, vol. xx, nos. 1-2 (1982), p. 11-26.
This study of cross-sectional data for the intercensal years 1957-67 stresses the importance of economic factors – represented by a locality's index of unemployment – in stimulating emigration. A similar conclusion emerges from time-series analysis. However, the pattern of emigration by destination seems to have been primarily conditioned by the size of the Maltese population abroad.

295 **Some considerations on postwar migration from the Maltese Islands.**
E. P. Delia. In: *Issues.* Edited by Ernest Azzopardi and Louis J. Scerri. Malta: The New Economic Society, 1984, p. 15-24.
A useful review of the emigration policies of successive governments, the deficiencies of official statistics at certain periods, and the opportunities offered by the freedom to emigrate.

296 **Maltese in London. A case-study in the erosion of ethnic consciousness.**
Geoff Dench. London: Routledge and Kegan Paul for the Institute of Community Studies, 1975. 302p.
This first detailed study of the main Maltese settlement in Britain assesses the contradictory images of immigrants from Malta and Gozo as anything from quiet and unassuming people to pimps. The author suggests that, although assimilation of Maltese was rapid it was not the smooth process assumed by the traditional liberal model. There is a valuable review of this book, by C. J. M. R. Gullick, in *New Community. Journal of the Community Relations Commission*, vol. 4, no. 3 (1975), p. 404-07.

297 **Marginal Mediterraneans: foreign settlers in Malta: their participation in society and their contribution to development.**
Loek Esmeijer. Amsterdam: University of Amsterdam, 1984. 137p. map. bibliog. (Papers in European and Mediterranean Societies, no. 18).
Prepared as a 1982 doctoral thesis in social anthropology, this illustrated study has three core sections – context, impressions and evaluations – within which the writer assesses 'the unique milieu' which attracts settlers (who have a wide choice of settlement locations). He views the 3,000 settlers as agents of socio-economic change and finds their contribution 'considerable'.

298 **The resettlement of Gozo after 1551.**
Stanley Fiorini. *Melita Historica*, vol. 9, no. 3 (1986), p. 203-44.
bibliog.
Gozo was largely depopulated after the Turkish raid of Dragut (Turgut Reis) in 1551.
The article discusses the sources and presents evidence for slow repopulation. Six
appendices detail the evidence and provide the Latin texts of two documents.

299 **Reciprocal migration: a Mediterranean example.**
C. J. M. R. Gullick. *Journal of the Faculty of Arts* (University of
Malta), vol. 4, no. 4 (1977), p. 31-41.
The writer contends that reciprocal migration – the movement of groups from A to B
and B to A – is important in the study of inter-ethnic relations. The two places
exchanging migrants in this article are Malta and Britain.

300 **The design and initial analysis of an ethnohistorical project of
West Indian and Maltese migration.**
C. J. M. R. Gullick. *The Journal of the Durham University
Anthropological Society*, no. 7 (1983), p. 84-94.
This paper discusses the experience of Maltese migrants to the West Indies. It com-
pares attitudes to migration of Maltese and West Indians and comments on studies of
other communities of Maltese in the light of the evidence from the West Indies.

301 **Modern emigration from Malta.**
Huw R. Jones. *Institute of British Geographers, Transactions*, no. 60
(1973), p. 101-19. bibliog.
In this paper Maltese emigration is used as a case-study to illustrate the range of factors which have influenced the level, direction and composition of international
migration in recent years. The importance of government involvement at both origin
and destination is emphasized and the problems arising from Malta's active emigration programme are assessed. The spatial pattern of emigration by Maltese localities is
related to the island's social and economic geography by multiple regression analysis.
Jones concludes that emigration seems to have been influenced more by socio-demo-
graphic, than by economic, factors.

302 **The Maltese migration cycle: an archival survey.**
Russell King. *Area*, vol. 11, no. 3 (1979), p. 245-49.
In response to the dearth of longitudinal migration studies that trace migrants' move-
ments through to their return home, this article reports on an archival survey of
Maltese migrants returning in 1976.

303 **Boomerangs on a small island: Maltese who returned from
Australia.**
Constance Lever-Tracy. *Economic and Social Studies*, vol. 4 (1987-
88), p. 70-102. bibliog.
Some 35,000 fewer Maltese were found in the 1987 Australian Census than immigra-
tion data and previous censuses suggested. The study of return-migration did not

suggest that it was on quite this scale, but that it was, including children, much greater than the authorities assumed. The rest of the study is based on twenty-two long open-ended interviews and letters in response to a Maltese newspaper request for information, as well as a survey of returned parents of children in five secondary schools. The implications for Australia's policies are discussed.

304 **Malta and the Maltese: a study in nineteenth century migration.**
Charles A. Price. Melbourne: Georgian House, 1954. Reprinted,
New York: AMS Press, 1977; Gozo, Malta: Gozo Press, 1989. 272p.
bibliog.

A facsimile reproduction of this classic analysis of the various planned and independent patterns of emigration from the island. It is an important source of information on the response to population pressure. Appendices include tables of economic, population and migration data as well as an estimate of numbers of Maltese abroad. The bibliography is extensive (p. 237-63).

305 **The Maltese in Australia.**
Barry York. Melbourne: A. E. Press, 1986. 161p. (Australian Ethnic
Heritage Series).

This work is based on many personal accounts, mainly of the inter-war years, of Maltese immigrants. Like the author's 1990 *Empire and race: the Maltese in Australia 1881-1949* (q.v.), this was written with an Australian readership in mind. The author's father was the first Maltese-born mayor of an Australian municipality (Brunswick, 1972 and 1977).

306 **Empire and race: the Maltese in Australia 1881-1949.**
Barry York. Kensington, New South Wales, Australia: New South
Wales University Press, 1990. 229p. bibliog.

This important book, by an author who publishes much on the subject, has twelve chapters tracing the establishment of Maltese emigration to Australia before the First World War, the attractions of this source to the White Australia policy, the difficult experiences of Maltese in the country between the wars, and the introduction of the assisted-passage scheme in 1949. Throughout the text, British, Maltese and Australian policies are outlined and discussed. There is a substantial section of photographs of Maltese Australians and three tables of migration and census data form the appendices. York examines the forces which supported, and those which opposed, Maltese and Australian migration policies and analyses the Maltese struggle for acceptance in Australia. The book ends when the assisted-passage agreement (which lasted until the early 1970s) opened the doors of Australia to large numbers. This work has a broader coverage of its topic than the author's *The Maltese in Australia* (q.v.), but both were written very much with an Australian readership in mind.

307 **Maltese settlers in Australia: spatial distribution 1954, 1961, 1966 and 1971.**
Barry York.   Canberra, Australia: Australian National University,
Centre for Immigration and Multicultural Studies, 1995. 50p.
(Maltese-Australian Studies Series, no. 12).

An introductory text (p. 1-6) is followed by tables showing localities with 'more than 99 Malta-born persons' (distinguishing men and women). As Local Government Areas with fewer than ninety-nine Malta-born persons have been excluded, grand total populations for each Division do not always add up. See other titles in this series.

Language

Dictionaries and learning aids

308 Maltese-English dictionary.

Joseph Aquilina.   Valletta: Midsea Books, 1987 (vol. 1, A-L, p. i-xliii, 1-764), 1990 (vol. 2, M-Z, p. 765-1,673).

This is the definitive Maltese-English dictionary. It is the culmination of a lifetime study by the foremost specialist on Maltese. The two volumes give the origins of both main word groups, the Semitic and the European (principally Sicilian/Italian). There is a particularly useful bibliography of dictionaries, grammars, and other works on Maltese (p. xxv-xxxvi). No dictionary hitherto has offered the range and etymological coverage of this one. Words of Semitic origin – the basis of Maltese – are entered under their main verbal and nominal roots together with all their derivatives, each of which is also cross-referenced. Words of Romance or English origin are similarly given with their derivatives and cognate formations which are themselves cross-listed. These, and other presentational details, are clearly set out in a 'Guide to the dictionary' (vol. 1, p. vii-xvi) which is itself a valuable brief snap-shot of the main features of the Maltese language. It is difficult to accept Joseph Aquilina's modest proposition that he has 'exposed [himself] to many sins of omission and commission' (vol. 1, p. xviii).

309 Maltese. A complete guide for beginners.

Joseph Aquilina.   London: Hodder & Stoughton, 1995. rev. ed. 240p. (Teach Yourself Books); Chicago: NTC Publishing Group, 1995.

First published in 1965, this remains the best self-teach volume for English-speaking readers. A short section on sounds and letters is followed by major sections on grammar and verbs.

310   **The Biblioteca Vallicelliana.** *Regole per la lingua Maltese.* (The
      Vallicelliana Library. Maltese grammar.)
      Edited by Arnold Cassola.   Valletta: Said International, 1992. 190p.
Dating back to the early 18th century, this is the earliest extant grammar and dictionary of the Maltese language, with an 'Introduction' (p. ix-xlviii) by the editor. There
are some 1,700 entries. The original bound volume is in the Roman Library indicated
in the title.

311   **Learn Maltese: why not?**
      Joseph Vella.   Valletta: Valletta Publishing, 1993. 215p.
This is a teach-yourself course of twenty-four lessons, each of which introduces a
specific piece of grammar and new vocabulary. There are exercises based on each
lesson. An associated *Workbook* was published in 1995 (139p.).

Linguistics

312   **Morphological alternatives in the Gozitan dialects of Maltese.**
      Dionisius A. Agius.   In: *Matériaux arabes et sudarabiques:*
      publications du Groupe d'Etude de Linguistique et de Littérature
      Arabes et Sudarabiques.   Paris: University of Paris, Association
      Gellas, 1992, p. 111-61. bibliog.
This is a geographical linguistic survey of nouns, adjectives, and verbs eliciting morphological variations of seventeen items. There are maps of the frequency and
distribution of morphological alternatives, with isoglosses to mark boundaries (p. 140-
58), and there is a bibliography (p. 158-61).

313   **A survey of the constituent elements of Maltese.**
      Joseph Aquilina.   *Orbis. Bulletin International de Documentation*
      Linguistique, vol. 7, no. 1 (1958), p. 65-78.
The writer stresses that Maltese is a distinct language with Sicilian and other
European elements grafted onto a Semitic base. It is thus a blend rather than a case of
linguistic corruption or decay.

314   **The structure of Maltese: a study in mixed grammar and**
      vocabulary.
      Joseph Aquilina.   Msida, Malta: University of Malta Press, 1973.
      358p. bibliog.
Provides a detailed phonological analysis emphasizing the mixed origins of the language, with a Semitic (Arabic) base and substantial Siculo-Italian additions – plus
some words from English and other languages.

73

315 **A survey of contemporary dialectical Maltese: report on the results of field work undertaken during the years 1964-71 on behalf of the Department of Maltese and Oriental languages in the Old University of Malta and the Department of Semitic Studies in the University of Leeds. Volume 1: Gozo.**
Directed by Joseph Aquilina and B. S. J. Isserlin. Leeds, England: B. S. J. Isserlin (printed by Leeds University Printing Service), 1981. 222p. maps.
Part one consists of chapters on the study of Maltese dialects in the past (by E. Fenech) and of the comparative linguistic background of Maltese (B. S. J. Isserlin). Part two has chapters on the phonetic analysis of Gozitan dialectical Maltese (P. J. Roach) and on its phonology (J. Aquilina, E. Fenech and B. S. J. Isserlin).

316 **Papers in Maltese linguistics.**
Joseph Aquilina. Msida, Malta: University of Malta, 1994. 240p.
This is a facsimile reproduction of the 1970 printing which includes corrections from the 1960 edition: both were also published at the University of Malta. The volume offers a range of scholarly studies of enduring value on Maltese semantics, lexicography, phonetics, orthography, and links with Semitic and Romance languages.

317 **To be or not to be a copula in Maltese.**
Albert Borġ. *Journal of Maltese Studies*, nos. 17-18 (1987-88), p. 54-71. bibliog.
Discusses, with examples, this aspect of Maltese usage and grammar.

318 **The Maltese noun phrase meets typology: EUROTYP working papers: theme 7, noun phrase structure working paper no. 25.**
Edited by Albert Borġ and Frans Plank. Konstanz, Germany: EUROTYP Programme in Language Typology. European Science Foundation, 1995. 309p. bibliog.
The thirteen papers comprising the proceedings of this conference are by Maltese and foreign scholars and represent the most intensive scrutiny of this vital component of the language. The papers include the structure of the noun phrase, collective nouns and other aspects of quantification and enumeration, possessive noun phrases, definitive pronouns and the Maltese article.

319 **Some Maltese toponyms in historical and comparative perspective.**
Alexander Borġ. In: *Studia linguistica et orientalia memoriae Haim Blanc dedicata.* (Oriental and linguistic studies dedicated to the memory of Haim Blanc.) Edited by Paul Wexler, Alexander Borġ, Sasson Somekh. Wiesbaden, FRG: Otto Harrassowithz, 1989, p. 62-85. bibliog.
This article comments on one noun-phrase structure commonly encountered in both old and contemporary orthographical representations of certain Maltese toponyms displaying the form [Noun + il + Adjective]. There is an extensive bibliography on p. 80-85. In

1978 this author completed a PhD dissertation on 'A historical and comparative phonology and morphology of Maltese' at The Hebrew University, Jerusalem, p. 425.

320 **Object diffuseness in Maltese.**
A. J. Borġ, B. Comrie. In: *Objects: towards a theory of grammatical relations.* Edited by Frans Plank. London: Academic Press, 1984, p. 109-26. bibliog.
Aims to show that Maltese has a grammatical relation of direct object on the basis of: a number of independent language-internal tests; and comparability with direct objects in other languages.

321 **White dipping sails.**
Charles Briffa. *Journal of Maltese Studies*, nos. 19-20 (1989-90), p. 62-70. bibliog.
A linguistic survey of sail terminology in English, Maltese and Italian.

322 **Languages of the Mediterranean: substrata – the islands – Malta: proceedings of the conference held in Malta 26-29 September 1991.**
Edited by Joseph M. Brincat. Msida, Malta: Institute of Linguistics, University of Malta, 1994. 323p. bibliog.
The third part of these proceedings comprises twelve articles by Maltese and other linguists on aspects of the Maltese language. Eleven of the articles are in English (p. 209-323). Among them are Ray Fabri's 'The syntax of numerals in Maltese' (p. 228-39) and 'The weak-final conjugation of the Semitic component of Maltese' by Manwel Mifsud (p. 244-65). These, and the other contributions, have their own bibliographies and offer a valuable entrée to specialized literature on Maltese.

323 **A mixed orthography of the Maltese language: the Latin-Arabic alphabet.**
Arnold Cassola. In: *Collected papers, contributed by members of the academic staff of the University of Malta.* Edited by Roger Ellul-Micallef, Stanley Fiorini. Msida, Malta: University of Malta, 1992, p. 203-19. bibliog.
Outlines the development of the mixed alphabet which was used by some writers from the 17th to the 19th centuries. The author argues that, in the 19th century, Azzopardi, Trapani, Casolani, and other writers used no more than six Arabic characters but, during the 18th century, up to twelve such characters were combined with Latin letters – see, for example, the works by De Guignard and Thezan, and *Regole per la lingua Maltese* (q.v.). There is a bibliography (p. 217-19).

324 **The tense and aspect system in Maltese.**
Ray Fabri. In: *Tense systems in European languages II.* Edited by Rolf Thieroff. Tübingen, Germany: Max Niemeyer Verlag, 1995, p. 327-43. bibliog.
Outlines this system in the Maltese language and several questions that remain open such as the exact syntactic and semantic status of tense markers.

325 **Contemporary journalistic Maltese: an analytical and comparative study.**
Edward Fenech.   Leiden, the Netherlands: E. J. Brill, 1978. 251p.
(Studies in Semitic Languages and Linguistics, edited by G. F. Pijper, no. 8).

The author argues that traditional grammarians have started from the language 'fossilized' by the influence of Latin, Italian, Hebrew, and Arabic grammar. So he adopts a 'non-normative' approach to the Maltese used in newspapers. This is the main work in this field. It is based on a detailed study of the three Maltese-language dailies in publication in August 1973 and covers phonology, orthography, morphology, syntax, lexical and phraseological aspects, and style.

326 **A survey of Maltese nicknames, I: the nicknames of Naxxar, 1832.**
Stanley Fiorini.   *Journal of Maltese Studies*, no. 16 (1986), p. 62-93.

Nicknames have traditionally been important in Malta, having a socially integrative and class-distinctive function and playing a part in social control. They also constitute a vehicle for social satire. The *Libri Status Animarum* covering 1680-1832 – especially vol. XXIVb.N.17 (1832) – lists almost every nickname in the parish of Naxxar for the period. This article is a case-study of the 1832 list, showing the types and distribution of nicknames and their intersection with several surnames.

327 **Sicilian connections of some medieval Maltese surnames.**
Stanley Fiorini.   *Journal of Maltese Studies*, nos. 17-18 (1987-88), p. 104-38. bibliog.

Discusses the roots of different surnames and their apparent association with the much larger neighbouring island of Sicily with which Malta was most closely associated before 1530.

328 **A bibliography of Maltese (1953-1973).**
Giovanni Mangion.   *Melita Historica,* vol. 6, no. 3 (1974), p. 279-306.

This annotated series of entries was designed to update P. P. Saydon's 'Bibliographical aids to the study of Maltese', published in the *Journal of Near Eastern Studies* in 1953. It covers publications in all languages on the Maltese language. The author has subsequently published a sequel to this bibliography (see item no. 329).

329 **A bibliography of Maltese (1974-1984).**
Giovanni Mangion.   *Studi Magrebini,* vol. 21 (1989), p. 143-79.

Updates the author's previous bibliography (see item no. 328) and represents an important source on the development of Maltese linguistic studies. The sixty-five entries provide annotations on these publications in various languages on the subject of the Maltese language and its use, etc.

330   **Loan verbs in Maltese. A descriptive and comparative study.**
Manwel Mifsud.   Leiden, the Netherlands: E. J. Brill, 1995.
339p. bibliog.

An impressive linguistic analysis of the processes by which Sicilian, Italian, and later, English loan verbs have been integrated to varying degrees into the Arabic structure of Maltese morphology. It proposes a typological classification of borrowed verbs in a continuum from fully integrated types to largely 'undigested' loans. The interest to scholars is heightened by the apparent incongruence between the languages involved, the long period of contact, and the small area in which it occurred. There is an outline account of the development of language in Malta in its historical context (p. 20-31). Three appendices are devoted to inflexional paradigms, corpora, and the historical development of weak-final verbs in Semitic Maltese. There is a substantial bibliography (p. 319-25).

331   **The emergence of standard Maltese: the Arabic factor.**
Mathias Hubertus Prevaes.   Nijmegen, the Netherlands: Catholic
University of Nijmegen, 1996. 121p. bibliog.

This doctoral thesis for the College of Deacons of the Catholic University of Nijmegen attributes the origin of Maltese to the Arabic brought by settlers from Sicily in the 11th century. Christian rule, from the 12th century, brought the Siculo-Italian Romance component. Inevitably, this major study of linguistic change includes much on the demographic and social trends among the inhabitants of the islands.

332   **History of the Maltese Bible.**
P. P. Saydon.   *Melita Theologica*, vol. X (1957), p. 1-15.

Traces the Maltese translation of the Bible in three periods. From 1822 to 1847 the key trends were the literary development of Maltese and Protestant missionary work. In the years up to 1917 there were first attempts to use a Maltese Bible among local Catholics. Since about 1917 the writing of Maltese has been consolidated and there has been a full translation from original tongues.

333   **Peter Caxaro's 'Cantilena': a poem in medieval Maltese.**
Godfrey Wettinger, Michael Fsadni.   Ħamrun, Malta: Lux Press,
1968. 52p. bibliog.

The discovery of this text in September 1966 revolutionized assumptions about the first writing of Maltese, pushing the date back from the late 17th century to the third quarter of the 15th century. The authors discuss the cultural life and place of the Maltese language at this time. Caxaro, a judge and jurat resident in Mdina, wrote his poem in three stanzas of six, four and ten lines. It is presented here as a transcription of the manuscript and as transliterated into the modern Maltese alphabet, followed by a detailed analysis of the text, which only resorts to the Arabic when no apparent current Maltese word is available. Appendices include the proceedings of the Town Council in 1479 where Peter Caxaro played a dominant role, the alphabet used by his descendant in whose notarial records the poem was written, and a genealogy of the Caxaro family.

334 **Some grammatical characteristics of the place-names of Malta and Gozo in early times.**
Godfrey Wettinger. *Journal of Maltese Studies*, no. 15 (1983), p. 31-67.

The article provides many place-names, which are translated as well as given in their original sources. The latter were usually written in Italian so that the Maltese names stand out as would not be the case with Italian names, or Arabic names written in Arabic.

Language and society

335 **The study of Arabic in Malta 1632-1915.**
Dionisius Agius, translated by Vincenz P. Borġ and edited with revisions by Francine Geraci. Louvain, Belgium: Peeters, 1990. 52p. bibliog.

A revised English edition of that first published in Maltese in 1980. The three chapters recount the foundations for the study of Arabic in Malta, its teaching at the University from 1795-1915, and Arabic works in Maltese collections and local literature. An important resource is the fully classified list of Arabic, Turkish and Persian manuscripts in various archives and libraries of Malta, mostly dating from the 17th and 18th centuries, and the publications of the Arabic Press in Malta, 1821-44, which was run by the Church Missionary Society. Six relevant documents are reproduced in their original Latin in the appendices and three Arabic texts written by slaves are illustrated.

336 **Crosslinguistic influence in a bilingual classroom: the example of Maltese and English.**
Antoinette Camilleri. In: *Edinburgh working papers in applied linguistics, no. 2.* Edited by Tony Lynch. Edinburgh: University of Edinburgh, 1991, p. 101-11. bibliog.

Using a continuum model of cross-linguistic influence, the paper analyses recorded transcripts from classroom teaching and discusses: the different extent to which English words may be assimilated, tag and code switching, and the developing patterns of Maltese English.

337 **Bilingualism in education: the Maltese experience – Sammlung Gross 53.**
Antoinette Camilleri. Heidelberg, Germany: Julius Gross, Verlag, 1995. 259p. bibliog.

A very thorough analysis of the mixed use of Maltese and English by Maltese teachers in secondary-school classrooms. The taxonomic and quantitative analysis of code-switching is evidenced and illustrated by twenty-six figures and thirty-three tables based on transcripts of recordings. The book concludes with a consideration of its implications for language planning.

338   **Mikiel Anton Vassalli: a preliminary survey.**
Frans Ciappara.   *Melita Historica*, vol. 10, no. 2 (1989), p. 145-56.
bibliog.
Outlines events in the life of this significant scholar of the Maltese language up to his
imprisonment for leading a revolt against the Order of St. John in 1797 and the subsequent suspicions placed on him by the Church. Vassalli's petition to the Pope at the time
of his application to lecture at the Sapienza University in Rome in 1788 is illustrated.

339   **A case study in bilingualism: code-switching between parents and
their pre-school children in Malta.**
Sonia Ellul.   Cambridge, England: Huntingdon Publishers Ltd., 1978.
33p. bibliog.
A study of the words spoken by parents to their children drawn from fifty-one families
with a variety of educational and social backgrounds. These were analysed according
to their Maltese/English components and the situations in which people shifted from
one to the other in a flow of speech. Where children differed from their parents, it was
towards a greater use of Maltese, by then established as the language of the courts,
religious observance, broadcasting and the medium of primary-school instruction.

340   **Italy and Britain in Maltese colonial nationalism.**
Henry Frendo.   *History of European Ideas*, vol. 15, nos. 4-6 (1992),
p. 733-39. bibliog.
A general introduction to the political implications of the language question in Malta
with emphasis on the period of self-government between the two world wars.

341   **Essays on Mikiel Anton Vassalli.**
Edited by Oliver Friggieri.   *Journal of Maltese Studies*, nos. 23-24
(1993). 236p. bibliog.
This special number of the *Journal of Maltese Studies* was published at the time of the
University of Malta's quartercentenary to commemorate the contribution of Vassalli
(1764-1829) to Maltese self-consciousness as expressed in both national sentiment
and the mother tongue. Sixteen authors have contributed to the volume in Maltese,
Italian, and French, but the material is mainly in English to which reference is made
here. Most of the essays are short. Frans Ciappara provides six on Vassalli's earlier
years, Karm Sant two on his sojourn in Rome and his scholarly reputation, and Guzè
Cassar Pullicino four on his troubled time in Malta in the last years of the Order and
on some of Vassalli's writings. A series of essays follow on Vassalli's commercial
activity, his various publications, his political ideas, his 1796 plan for Maltese in primary education, and his possible place of burial. Carmel Bonavia provides a
bibliography of Vassalli's own publications and works about him as well as a pictorial
biography, with many reproductions of original documents and buildings associated
with him, culminating in the new monuments erected before the De Rohan gate to
Żebbuġ and at the University.

342 **Language and sentiment in Malta.**
Charles J. M. R. Gullick. *New Community, Journal of the Community Relations Commission*, vol. 3, nos. 1-2 (1974), p. 92-103.
Examines the changing attitudes, over time, of Maltese to their own language and compares its status with that of English and Italian in the context of society and identity in the islands.

343 **The Malta language question: a case study in cultural imperialism.**
Geoffrey Hull. Valletta: Said International Ltd., 1993. 418p. bibliog.
Language education in Malta has for the last century and a half been a major bone of political contention because of its role in forming and expressing national identity and allegiance to foreign states. The British, in order to reduce Maltese cultural affinity with Italy, favoured the development of the Maltese language alongside a predominant reliance on English. It was a colonial policy that, assisted by the Italian bombing of the island in the Second World War, was ultimately totally successful, not least because of its appeal to the Maltese working class who did not share the interests of the local intelligentsia. An alternative thesis, espoused by the author, was that of Italo-Maltese nationalism, which despised the local language as a bastard that should not thrive, and argued that this cultural aspiration was done to death by colonialist lackeys. The book is replete with condemnatory adjectives which make it an interesting component of, rather than commentary on, the struggle. Part one aims to provide an up-to-date overview but omits consideration of the British Council's role in developing English teaching in Malta in the 1970s. Parts two and three describe the fate of Italian under British, and Maltese, rule. Part four and the four appendices argue for Malta's socio-racial Italianity and its lost place in the Italian state 'in which Maltese would have been set on a course of gradual extinction' (p. 358). Numerous photographic portraits of the dramatis personae are included.

344 **Language maintenance and language shift of the Maltese migrants in Canada.**
Lydia Sciriha. *Journal of Maltese Studies*, nos. 19-20 (1989-90), p. 34-41. bibliog.
A study of the languages spoken by three generations in a Maltese-Canadian quarter of Toronto with its own church, shops, band club (social club constituted around a brass band) and park, prophesying the death of the Maltese language within twenty to thirty years.

345 **Plurilingualism and cultural change in medieval Malta.**
Godfrey Wettinger. *Mediterranean Language Review*, nos. 6-7, 1990-93. Edited by Alexander Borġ, Marcel Erdac. Wiesbaden, Germany: Harrossowitz Verlag (1993), p. 144-60. bibliog.
The article discusses the languages used in ancient Malta, the sort of Arabic that was introduced and manner in which Maltese is transliterated in local Sicilian records where no exact Sicilian or Latin equivalent seemed available. There is considerable evidence for Maltese having been spoken to explain contracts etc. and for the existence of a local form of Judaeo-Arabic at this time. The table gives the references for all mentions of the Maltese language in Malta's public records from the 15th-17th centuries as well as in G. F. Abela's *Descrittione* of 1647.

Religion and the Church

346 Social consciousness of the Church in Malta, 1891-1921: the impact of the *Rerum Novarum*.
Emanuel Agius. Malta: The Author, 1991. 182p. bibliog.
The book discusses attitudes of the Catholic Church in the context of social conditions during the period covered. A prominent theme is that of social awakening among the Maltese laity and the involvement of the local church. Another is the impact of the papal encyclical *Rerum Novarum* on social, political, and trade-union groups. There is an extensive bibliography (p. 176-82).

347 Archives of the Cathedral of Malta Misc. 32A: 1313-1529. The study and text of an eighteenth-century index of transcripts.
Edited by John Azzopardi. Malta: The Malta Study Center of the Hill Monastic Manuscript Library, St. John's University, Collegeville, Minnesota, 1977. 98p.
This volume includes the text of the first of a three-volume chronological *Index Notitiarum*, transcripts of documents in the cathedral archives from 1313-1767. This one covers the later mediaeval period until the arrival of the Knights of St. John and was compiled by Canon G. G. Borġ. It is prefaced by two essays. The first, by the editor, describes the formation of the cathedral archives and the purpose of this index in the 18th century. The second, by Dr Anthony Luttrell, discusses the fourteen earliest documents that are transcribed in this collection, from 1316-72, indicating their origins, the current location of these originals if known, and the significance of the documents. These throw light on the relations between Malta and Sicily, the involvement of several prominent Sicilian aristocratic families in the islands and the establishment of some of those who were to become leading landowners and nobles in Malta.

348　**St. Paul's Grotto, Church and Museum at Rabat, Malta.**
Edited by John Azzopardi.　Rabat, Malta: The Friends of the Museum
of St. Paul's Collegiate Church, 1990. 558p. bibliog.

This substantial book of essays by twenty-one Maltese scholars was produced for the
papal visit in 1990 which also marked the jubilee of the reunification of the grotto
with the adjacent parish church. The grotto and its history during the era of the
Knights of St. John is a good example of ecclesiastical politics induced by religious
and economic enthusiasm, some of which is described here although more attention is
given to the wide variety of artistic and architectural features of this complex of
ancient and early modern sites, which are illustrated from 560 photographs, 30 of
which are full-page colour reproductions. The two essays in part one describe the
social characteristics of the population in the late Middle Ages, and in later centuries.
Part two consists of seven essays on the sequence of buildings dedicated to St. Paul
and the development of the sites as a place of pilgrimage, followed by three on the
reputation and representation of various aspects of the grotto, and appendices of the
clergy holding responsible office over the church and the grotto since 1418. Part three
consists of nine essays on the Wignacourt College in Rabat which was built to accommodate the Order's chaplains appointed to officiate at the grotto. The college is now
the Museum of St. Paul's Church, and displays many different types of objects: paintings; an archaeological collection of classical pottery from Maltese sites; maps; the
unique example of a portable altar used in the galleys of the Order and *ex voto* offerings depicting ships; a probably 17th-century copy of the Holy Shroud of Turin; and
representations of St. Paul's shipwreck in Maltese and other countries' art.

349　**Religion and politics in a Crown Colony: the Gozo-Malta story
1798-1864.**
Joseph Bezzina.　Malta: Bugelli Publications, 1985. 384p.

A primary focus here is the pressure leading to the establishment of an independent
bishopric in Gozo in 1864. Some of the background to these developments is presented with a social survey of the clerical and lay populations of Gozo and a series of
appendices on various categories of presiding officials.

350　**The Bishop's archives, Gozo: a descriptive hand-list, including a
chronological list of bishops and provicars.**
Joseph Bezzina.　Victoria, Gozo, Malta: Lumen Christi, 1992. 48p.

This brief but informative booklet provides a handy list of documents in the Gozo
archives (*Archivum Episcopale Gaudisiense*). Many of these papers have only recently
been sorted and listed – including those constituting the *Acta Originalia* beginning in
1561. Information is provided on access to the archives.

351　**Play and identity: ritual change in a Maltese village.**
Jeremy Boissevain.　In: *Revitalizing European rituals.*　Edited by
J. Boissevain.　London: Routledge, 1992, p. 137-54. bibliog.

Contrary to the author's expectations in the 1970s, succeeding decades have seen a
remarkable increase in some Maltese celebrations, in particular the elaboration of
Holy Week and parish and other neighbourhood patron saints. But the celebration of
secondary saints and of the Eucharist has declined along with the confraternities that
sponsored them. Such *festa* (festival) celebrations stimulate local bonds as well as
boundaries but tourism has helped to make them more socially acceptable locally. The

significance of the ludic elements are stressed. Two photographs illustrate the types of celebration discussed.

352 Saints and fireworks: religion and politics in rural Malta.

Jeremy Boissevain. Valletta: Progress Press, 1993. 178p. bibliog.

This is the second amended edition of this now classic analysis of the relations between the Maltese church, state and politics reflected in leadership and rivalry between different *festa* (festival) supporters in the village of Kirkop. First published in 1965, postscripts were added by the author in 1968 and 1993, of which the latter records the development of pageantry and conspicuous consumption which now accompanies *festas*, encouraged by the attention of the government's mass media as well as tourism but still as a celebration of locality and community elements, intensively discussed by Huizinga in relation to the declining Middle Ages. Appendices include a list of titular and secondary feasts in Maltese parishes and their associated band clubs, extracts from the Malta Labour Party's *Manifesto* of 1962, and a bibliography of the author's publications on Malta.

353 The reform of the Council of Trent in Malta and Gozo.

Anthony Joseph Borġ. Malta: 'Il-Hajja' Press, 1975. 83p.

An abridged version of the author's DD thesis for the University of Malta. The four parts describe: relations between the Order of St. John, the Council and the Maltese, church and laity; the general application of the Tridentine decrees; their application to, and implementation by, the Maltese clergy; and the effect of the Council's decrees on lay practices, including the foundation of charitable institutions, for which a brief subsequent history is provided. The Council of Trent (initiated in December 1545) dealt with canons of a dogmatic nature and decrees of a disciplinary character. For their part the Knights in Malta sent a representative to the Council. In 1566 Pope Pius V confirmed the privileges of the Order but stressed that the jurisdiction of the local bishop was to be safeguarded as laid down at Trent.

354 The Seminary of Malta and the ecclesiastical benefices of the Maltese Islands.

Vincent Borġ. Malta: The Author, 1965. 57p.

A summary of the author's DD thesis, this describes the post-Tridentine provisions for the erection of a seminary in Malta, the Jesuits' largely successful struggle to obtain the benefices to support their own college and their subsequent redemption for the support of a diocesan seminary in the early 18th century. In 1890 the finances of the seminary were secured after the governor's visit to the Vatican. Appendices list the various benefices in the gift of the Order, of the *Università*, and under British royal patronage and the Seminary.

355 Ecclesiastical immunity and the powers of the Inquisitor in Malta (1777-1785).

Annetto Depasquale. Malta: Pontifica Universitas Lateranesis, 1968. 171p.

This canon-law thesis outlines the history of these rights before 1777 and the particular position of patentees between 1777 and 1785, as well as the powers of the Inquisitor by virtue of his office and that of the Apostolic Delegate in Malta. Appendices include three papal documents.

356   **The Collegiate Church and Pro-Cathedral of Saint Paul the
       Apostle, Valletta, Malta.**
       C. E. de Wolff.   Malta: Progress Press, 1960. 28p.
This account of the primary Church of England in Malta contains long quotations
from Queen Adelaide's letter to Queen Victoria proposing its foundation, from *The
Harlequin* of 20 March 1939 describing the Queen Dowager laying the foundation
stone, and the Malta Government Ordinances of 1876 and 1895 under which the
church was subsequently run. There is a brief description of the fabric and appendices
of office-holders in the church and diocese.

357   **The Maltese Cardinal: Fabrizio Sceberras Testaferrata.**
       Robert Farrugia Randon.   Malta: The Author, 1988. 108p. bibliog.
For all its devotion to the Holy See, Malta has only achieved one Prince of the Roman
Church whose long life (1757-1843) was spent abroad in its service, whilst his
brother, Camillo, became a major Maltese nationalist against British colonial rule.
After holding offices in the Papal States, Fabrizio was appointed nuncio to
Switzerland from 1802-15, and one of the thirty-one new cardinals appointed in 1816,
with the Bishopric of Senigallia to follow in 1818 where he resided as a pastoral and
civil ruler. His silver plate was bequeathed to Mdina cathedral chapter.

358   **Minding their own business: British diplomacy and the conflict
       between Italy and the Vatican during the pontificate of Leo XIII,
       1878-1903.**
       Dominic Fenech.   *Journal of Anglo-Italian Studies*, vol. 4 (1995),
       p. 76-104. bibliog.
Britain had interests in the new Italian state but also in the Vatican because of the con-
tinuous conflict in Ireland. The Pope seriously considered asylum in Malta as well as
Spain and Austria. This paper discusses the policies and negotiations by successive
British governments. Crispi's indication that the Pope was free to go but would not be
permitted to return terminated these negotiations.

359   **Descrizione storica delle chiese di Malta e Gozo.** (An historical
       account of the churches of Malta and Gozo.)
       Achille Ferris.   Reprinted, Valletta: Midsea Books Ltd., 1985. 702p.
       (Melitensia Book Club no. 3).
Ferris (1838-1907) was a prominent educationist, a student of the Maltese language
and compiled this important classic work on Maltese parishes, churches and chapels
which was first published in 1866. Its five parts, in Italian, comprise brief biographies
of the bishops of Malta, a concise history of the Church in Malta, parish histories of
Malta and Gozo with notes on their filial churches and chapels, a history of local
houses of the religious orders, and a list of the churches included in Mons. Dusina's
apostolic visitation in 1575. Lists of the grand priors of St. John's, the superiors of the
various religious orders and the rectors of St. Paul's Grotto in Rabat are provided.

360 **St. Paul's Grotto and its visitors. Pilgrims, knights, scholars, and sceptics, from the Middle Ages to the nineteenth century.**
Thomas Freller. Valletta: Valletta Publishing Ltd., 1995. 312p. bibliog.

This study of the Pauline cult in Malta and the development of its international reputation is thoroughly documented. The eight chapters describe the cult and its devotees and their different records, thirty-seven of which are printed in their original languages. There are bibliographies of 'Travelogues and diaries' (p. 265-75), 'Treatises and works with references to St. Paul's Grotto and the Pauline tradition in Malta' (p. 277-87), 'Modern literature' (p. 289-96), an 'Index of persons' (p. 299-304) and an 'Index of places' (p. 305-08). The cult in Malta resulted from St. Paul's shipwreck there in AD 60 (Acts of the Apostles, Chaps. 27 and 28). St. Paul's Grotto is located in Rabat, Malta. Ninety-seven illustrations, documents and portraits are reproduced throughout the text.

361 **St. Paul in Malta: a compendium of Pauline Studies.**
Edited by Michael Galea, John Ciarlò. Żabbar, Malta: Veritas Press, 1992. 132p.

This publication was provoked by Dr Heinz Warnecke's doctoral thesis discarding the belief that St. Paul set foot in Malta after his shipwreck. Two papers are concerned with commenting on this and a third deals with new perspectives on the historicity of the event recounted in the Acts of the Apostles. The fourth, by Joseph Cassar Pullicino, outlines the Pauline traditions in Malta itself which have played an active role in public devotions.

362 **The Kappillani: the changing position of the parish priest in Malta.**
Adrianus (Adriannes) Koster. In: *Religion, power and protest in local communities: the northern shore of the Mediterranean*. Edited by Eric R. Wolf. Berlin: Mouton, 1984, p. 185-211. bibliog.

The position of the parish priest before and after independence in 1964 is examined. The influence of the Second Vatican Council is then considered as is the attitude of the Church to Labour Party policies and personalities. The relations between government and bishops and clergy are seen to be changing and certainly as being more difficult than under British rule.

363 **Prelates and politicians in Malta: changing power-balances between Church and State in a Mediterranean island fortress (1800-1976).**
Adrianus (Adriannes) Koster. Assen, the Netherlands: Van Gorcum & Co., 1984. 312p. bibliog.

The eleven chapters of this important book map the church's involvement in political affairs and its relations with the British colonial authorities, Maltese politicians and, in particular, the struggle between Archbishop Gonzi and Labour leader Dom Mintoff. Appendices provide background information and the results of Maltese general elections. There are many photographic illustrations of the personalities referred to in the text. This is a revised and updated version of the author's 1981 doctoral thesis at the Free University of Amsterdam. The thesis had the same title except that the period covered was given as 1530-1976. The book preserves the three-part structure of the thesis.

The first part reviews the formation of the Church in Malta and Gozo from 1530 to 1921 – i.e. under the Knights of St. John and the British. Between 1921 and 1964 the Church is seen as having been challenged by the emergence of a political party system, home rule, war (1939-45) and the conflict between Government and Church in the run-up to independence in 1964. Part three sees 'a Church on the wane . . .' in post-1964 Malta. There is a substantial bibliography (p. 297-307).

364 **Church and State intervention in feasts and rituals in independent Malta.**
Adrianus (Adriannes) Koster. *Economic and Social Studies*, vol. 4 (1987-88), p. 1-28. bibliog.
Primarily concerned with Vatican, Maltese clerical, and Mintoffian, interventions and disputes, this article updates Boissevain's book of 1965 (see item no. 352) in this respect. It also describes some of the secular community rites instituted by Maltese governments.

365 **A moment with Christ: the importance of feelings in the analysis of belief.**
Jon P. Mitchell. *The Journal of the Royal Anthropological Institute,* vol. 3, no. 1 (1997), p. 79-94. bibliog.
In Malta, religious explanations of uncanny experiences present themselves as being particularly convincing. Powerful feelings become sedimented as memories for the believer and serve as reference points for subsequent strange experiences. The writer contends that feelings are both produced by, and give meaning to, religious belief. Though he is here concerned generally with the anthropology of feelings, this article is based innovatively on the significance of components of social memory in the reproduction of religious belief in Malta.

366 **Priestly vocations in the Maltese ecclesiastical province 1911-1964.**
Fortunato P. Mizzi. Malta: Pastoral Research Services, Centre for Social Studies, 1966. 50p.
A tabulated series of comparative data on diocesan priests and those in religious orders and the Maltese population according to census districts, with an introductory commentary.

367 **Religious vocations (nuns and sisters) in the Maltese ecclesiastical province, 1911-1966.**
Fortunato P. Mizzi. Malta: Pastoral Research Services, Centre for Social Studies, 1970. 26p.
The sequel to the volume on priestly vocations by the same author (see item no. 366), with some comparable tables and more information on the work done by these women in schools and hospitals etc.

368 **From lordship to stewardship: religion and social change in Malta.**
Mario Vassallo. The Hague: Mouton Publishers, 1979. 270p. bibliog.
The six chapters of this book are devoted to: an outline of the social and economic changes in modern Malta; the significant place of religion and the Roman Catholic

Church in Maltese society; and the social and educational characteristics of the diocesan clergy and their perception of their position and identity as well as of their ministry and the contemporary role of the Church and its priesthood. Appendices include information on the main ecclesiastical bodies and institutions and the various questions asked of the diocesan clergy, priests with only one year's ministry, and seminary students.

369 **Diocese of Gozo directory.**
Edited by Jimmy Xerri. Victoria, Gozo, Malta: Bishop's Curia, 1991. 4th ed. 146p.
A directory of clerical offices, residences, parish and other ecclesiastical addresses, and those of institutes, agencies, services and associations run by, or affiliated to, the Roman Catholic Church in Gozo. The whole archdiocese of Malta is covered by a publication in Maltese.

Society and Anthropology

Society

370 **Transmitting values in European Malta. A study in the contemporary values of modern society.**
Anthony M. Abela. Valletta: Jesuit Publications, published jointly in Rome by Editrice Pontificia Università Gregoriana, 1991. 340p. bibliog.

The author asks which values unite and distinguish the Maltese today from each other *and* from other systems. What happens to their traditional system as they experience new work opportunities, education, leisure, media, overseas travel and mass tourism? An analysis of survey data from the European Value Systems Study Group and a follow-up participant observation in religious organizations in Malta provide the basis for the study.

371 **Changing youth culture in Malta.**
Anthony M. Abela. Valletta: Jesuit Publications, 1992. 104p. (Social Values Studies).

This is a report, reflecting concern about the increasing secularization and alienation of youth, of a survey under the auspices of the Diocesan Youth Commission (set up in 1989). The survey took the names of 33,000 unmarried people in the 18-25 age bracket (from census sources), identified 8 representative clusters and then selected 500 names – 428 of whom were actually interviewed. Questions covered youth culture, leisure, permissiveness, church attendance, and the impact of tourism on Maltese youth. The questionnaire is included on p. 78-104.

372 **Shifting family values in Malta: a Western European perspective.**
Anthony M. Abela.   Floriana, Malta: Discern – Institute for Research
on the Signs of the Times, 1994. 85p. bibliog.

Reports the results of attitudinal surveys carried out in 1983 and 1991 by the European
Value Systems Study Group. The study charts the shift from traditional, to more individual, values with reference to the expectations of marriage and its termination, the
upbringing of children and the roles of mothers, and the difference between the values
held and hopes for personal changes in life experience. The questionnaire in the
appendix includes the frequencies for different responses in both of the surveys.

373 **Introducing social studies (revised edition).**
Godfrey Baldacchino.   Marsa, Malta: Publishers Enterprises Group
(PEG) Ltd., 1991. 242p. bibliog.

A text in five sections written as a comprehensive course for Maltese students studying for the 'O' level Matriculation Course in Social Studies. Each essay within these
sections is written from both an international and local perspective and followed by a
series of questions. Appendices reproduce the syllabus and a specimen paper.
Photographic illustrations are provided as well as some figures and numerical tables.

374 **Social class in Malta: insights into a homegrown relationship with
special reference to education.**
Godfrey Baldacchino.   *Education: the Journal of the Faculty of
Education*, University of Malta, vol. 5, no. 1 (1993), p. 23-32. bibliog.

A rare discussion of the concept of social class and its application to the classification
of occupations in Malta, and the role of education as a means of conserving social differentiation despite its apparent use as a means to social mobility.

375 **Friends of friends: networks, manipulators and coalitions.**
Jeremy Boissevain.   Oxford: Blackwell, 1974. 285p. bibliog.
(Pavilion Series).

This book is a contribution to the development of sociology, specifically the analysis
of social networks as a means of understanding the creation and use of social capital.
It is also a detailed account, through specific case-studies, of the ways in which men in
Malta may establish their position through gaining influential contacts which may be
used in various political and personal ways. The author relates these processes and
structures to local and national rivalry and political activity.

376 **A village in Malta (fieldwork edition).**
Jeremy Boissevain, edited by George and Louise Spindler.   New
York; London: Holt, Rinehart & Winston, 1980. 136p. bibliog. (Case
Studies in Cultural Anthropology).

First published as *Hal-Farruġ* in 1969, this new edition incorporates as chapter nine
the author's methodological description of *Fieldwork in Malta* (first published in
1970), and as chapter ten his short *1979 Epilogue*. Through the case-study of this
small, once agricultural, village, the author analyses the patterns of kinship and marriage, social differentiation, religion and its expressive forms, and the articulation of
local and national politics. There are relevant illustrations of the village (Kirkop) and
its people.

377 **Ritual escalation in Malta.**
Jeremy Boissevain. In: *Religion, power and protest in local communities: the northern shore of the Mediterranean.* Edited by Eric R. Wolf. New York: Houston, 1984, p. 163-83. bibliog.

The first of a series of articles in which the author discussed the ways in which parish celebrations had increased in Malta since 1961. His attempts to understand and explain these phenomena continued until his publication in 1992 – *Revitalizing European rituals* (q.v.) – which placed Maltese rituals in a European context.

378 **Residential inversion: the changing use of social space in Malta.**
Jeremy Boissevain. *Hyphen*, vol. 5, no. 2 (1986), p. 53-71. bibliog.

A provocative case-study of the ways in which the pattern of village suburbanization has transformed not only the size of Naxxar village since 1964, but also its physical layout and social focus. New roads, the style of outward-looking residences initially introduced for foreign settlers who wanted gardens, and the influx of internal migrants from other parts of the island, have opened up the closed parochial centre and dispersed this concentration of shops and high-status residents. Domestic TV and private cars reduced communal life even more and the countryside has ceased to be associated with poverty and deprivation.

379 **Changing betrothal and marriage ceremonies in Malta, 1960-1986.**
Jeremy Boissevain. *Ethnologia Europea*, vol. 17 (1988), p. 129-34. bibliog.

This points to the escalation of betrothal and marriage celebrations by comparing the weddings of two working-class couples.

380 **Why do the Maltese ask so few questions?**
Jeremy Boissevain, Alfred Sant, C. J. Farrugia, Joe Friggieri, Peter Serracino Inglott. *Education*, vol. 3, no. 4 (1990), p. 16-23.

Reprints the talk given by the first author to a teachers' refresher course in 1968 with the recent responses of four Maltese university educators and the author's subsequent reflections.

381 **What's in a name? The social prestige of residential areas in Malta as perceived by their inhabitants.**
David M. Boswell. In: *The urban context: ethnicity, social networks and situational analysis.* Edited by Alisdair Rogers, Steven Vertovec. Oxford: Berg Publishers (1995), p. 287-334. bibliog.

This article analyses the results of a sample survey carried out in 1979 in four socially different residential areas. All the relevant statistical techniques of data analysis pointed to a distinct pattern in the overall gradient in householders' responses as well as the significance of particular clusters of socially similar places. These are discussed with reference to social stratification and internal migration in Malta.

382 **Time allocation and urban adjustment: a Maltese case study.**
Stefan Cornelius Goodwin. DPhil thesis in Anthropology,
Northwestern University, Evanston, Illinois, 1974. 253p. bibliog.
Reports and discusses an extended study of seventy-nine Maltese households in
Floriana, Senglea and Siġġiewi, the former pair being totally urban and the last the
most agriculturally based village area in Malta. This study of what people did with
their time was extended to those in various kinds of institution, namely: the seminary;
a monastery; the nuns and residents of a home for aged people; and the national
prison. Appendices detail the apparatus used for codifying the results and the author's
own timetable of data collection from May to October 1973.

383 **Issues in the anthropology of Maltese society.**
Journal of Maltese Studies, vol. 3, no. 2, part 2 (1993), p. 291-381.
bibliog.
Five articles comprise this collection including: a review of the history of anthropological and folkloric research in Malta, and a paper on representations of Malta in the
19th century, both by Paul Sant-Cassia; 'Witchcraft beliefs and social control in seventeenth century Malta' by Carmel Cassar; 'The wounding song: honour, politics and
rhetoric in Maltese *għana*' by Ranier Fsadni; and 'Far from the tourist gaze', in which
Patrick Fenech introduces twelve photographs taken in various Maltese social settings.

384 **The quality of life in Malta and Gozo.**
Douglas G. Lockhart. *Hyphen*, vol. VI, no. 1 (1989), p. 1-7.
Based on the information collected for the 1985 Census, the author constructed an
index based on thirty-four socio-economic and demographic variables, the scores of
which are used to rank the localities according to their levels of living and explain the
movement of the affluent to the urban periphery.

385 **Gender politics and ritual in the construction of social identities:
the case of *San Pawl*, Valletta, Malta.**
Jon P. Mitchell. PhD dissertation, University of Edinburgh, 1996.
287p. bibliog.
This dissertation in social anthropology is framed in terms of an analysis of ritual to
explore issues of gender and politics (local and Malta-wide) and patron-client relationships. It is being prepared for publication in book form.

386 **Women in Senglea: the changing role of urban, working-class
women in Malta.**
Sibyl O'Reilly Mizzi. PhD thesis in Anthropology, State University
of New York, Stony Brook, New York. Available from Ann Arbor,
Michigan: University Microfilms International, 1981. 306p. 3 maps.
bibliog.
This thesis reports one of the few social research studies carried out in Malta. It is
based on a social survey administered in 1973 and subsequent field visits up to 1979.
Data were collected from documentary sources, by informants, and structured interviews with 4 age cohorts of a total of 158 women. The questions are provided in
an appendix. Chapters discuss the constraints and options open to women, family

91

organization and relationships, courtship and marriage, and the women's role in reproduction, household management and the larger community. Appendices include lists
of women who have stood in Parliamentary elections from 1941-71 and the Church
directives for confessors on 'the relations of married people'.

387 **Research on Malta. A German perspective.**
Edited by Horst Reimann. Augsburg, Germany: Lehrstuhl für
Soziologie und Kommunikationswissenschaft, University of Augsburg,
1991. 194p. bibliog.

Aims to acquaint readers of English with the results of the work, over several years, of a
German research group including some fifteen scholars. (Five doctoral dissertations on
Malta were published in the University of Augsburg's series 'Augsburger Schriften zur
Wirtschaftssoziologie'; four other publications appeared in *ABAKUS.)* The present
volume includes, in English, Horst Reiman's 'Malta survey: a German perspective', p. 3-
23; Anita Bestler's 'Political participation of women in Malta', p. 24-26; Manfred Kopp's
'The Maltese electoral system', p. 24-65; Petra Simmoleit's 'Tourism and its prospects',
p. 106-18; Ulricke Brosthaus's 'Tourism in Gozo', p. 119-29; Helga Reimann's 'Aspects
of Maltese identity', p. 130-34, 'Maltese fireworks and their baroque antecedents',
p. 144-54; Heike Bartholy's 'Language and cultural identity in Malta', p. 155-69; and
Brigit Bosch's 'Malta: the Republic's image in the German press (1974-1988)', p. 170-
83. There is also a list of German-language studies on Malta (p. 184-92).

388 **Love relationships and gender differences over time.**
Alexandra Scicluna Calleja. DEd thesis, Department of Counselling
Psychology of the Faculty of Graduate Studies, University of British
Columbia, Vancouver, 1992. 431p. bibliog.

This thesis presents the results of research in which a mixed qualitative and quantitative design was selected, consisting of open-style interviews before and after a
Q-sorting exercise with five Maltese couples. The aim was to construct both individual
and common stories of these marriages, focusing on differences as well as harmony.
There were common factors related to gender as well as individual factors associated
with the previous life history, personality, gender and culture of the respondents. The
results are discussed in their relation to counselling as well as future research. The
appendices include the research apparatus and questions as well as the component
loading of lifetime events for each respondent.

389 **Sociological perspectives on class in Malta.**
Ronald G. Sultana. *Economic and Social Studies*, vol. 5 (1988-90),
p. 1-24. bibliog.

An outline of different models of social class and their application to the little information on it available in Malta.

390 **Maltese society: a sociological inquiry.**
Edited by Ronald G. Sultana and Godfrey Baldacchino. Msida,
Malta: Mireva Publications, 1994. 729p. bibliog.

This is the most important and substantial sociological study of Malta to have been
published since 1985. Professor Anthony Giddens provides the foreword to thirty-six
chapter articles written by thirty different authors, all of whom have studied and/or

taught at the University of Malta. These are presented in six parts entitled: 'Dependence and social stratification'; 'Distinction and differentiation', including the relationship of language and residence to social stratification; 'Continuity and change', including changes in family practices and values, in parochial rivalries and secularization, and in response to TV and tourism; 'Control and resistance', including gossip, labour and political relations and the use of mass media; 'Work and production relations', including several case-studies of topical disputes; and 'Deviance and social problems'. Relevant tables, charts, diagrams and maps illustrate several of the articles which all have their own bibliographical references.

391 **The secularization of the family in changing Malta.**
Carmel Tabone. Malta: Dominican Publication, 1987. 268p. bibliog.
The book is in three parts. Part one reviews sociological research into the family and the concepts of social change and secularization. The second part has five chapters on aspects of the secularization of the Maltese family. Part three comprises a discussion of six different factors associated with social change and their impact on the family, namely economic development, politics, religion, education, mass media, and migration and tourism, followed by a general conclusion. An appendix outlines the sampling procedure, and contains the text of the questionnaire and ten of the tables used.

392 **Maltese families in transition: a sociological investigation.**
Carmel Tabone. Beltissebh, Malta: Ministry for Social Development, 1995. 222p. bibliog.
Reporting on a social survey carried out in 1993, this study followed up that of 1983 which the author used for a previous publication. The seven chapters analyse the methodological implications of the survey, the economic condition of Maltese families, family stability, life problems, and the trend to secular family life and a symmetrical role for both spouses, concluding that there has been a shift in fundamental values and development of different types of family. Twenty-six tables (six of them comparative) and five figures augment the text, and ninety tables, mostly simple frequencies, are contained in an appendix. Another appendix reproduces the questionnaire which can be applied to all areas of Malta and Gozo.

393 **Malta trends 1993: the signs of the times.**
Benjamin Tonna. Blata l-Bajda, Malta: The Institute for Research on the Signs of the Times, 1993. 172p. bibliog.
Professionally interested in the collection and digest of social and religious statistics, the author has revived their publication after retiring from the archpresbytery of Rabat. In the absence of officially published analyses and discussion of locally published data, this is a useful substitute, covering the period c.1985-92. Following his review of socio-economic, demographic and political trends, the author provides his own analysis of cultural, ethical and spiritual values and likely future developments.

394 **Honour and shame in late fifteenth century Malta.**
Godfrey Wettinger. *Melita Historica*, vol. 8, no. 1 (1980), p. 65-77. bibliog.
Discusses the details of some marital and murder cases and the evidence they provide of codes of family honour and relations between different orders of society in these aspects of behaviour.

Folklore and customs

395 Lexical material in Maltese folklore.
J. Aquilina, J. Cassar Pullicino. *Journal of the Faculty of Arts* (Royal University of Malta), vol. 1, no. 1 (1957), p. 1-36.

Reports on a range of archaic or obsolete words collected from old Maltese proverbs, plus some from the everyday conversation of villagers.

396 A comparative dictionary of Maltese proverbs.
Joseph Aquilina. Valletta: G. Muscat for the Royal University of Malta, 1972. 694p. bibliog.

This is a collection of 4,630 proverbs, from both written and oral sources, arranged under 45 headings covering epigrams, riddles, puns, etc. The work also deals with the structure of proverbs and the link between them and folk verse. There are indexes of etymology, topics, and key words.

397 Realms of fantasy: folk tales from Gozo.
George Camilleri. Marsa, Malta: Publishers Enterprises Group (PEG) Ltd., 1991. 128p. map.

Introduces and recounts twenty Gozitan folk-tales, accompanied by sixteen illustrations (most in colour) of places on the island

398 Maltese children's rhymes and poetry.
J. Cassar Pullicino. *Journal of Maltese Studies*, no. 15 (1983), p. 69-86. bibliog.

Discusses aspects of the form and content of both nursery and children's rhymes in the context of comparable Mediterranean examples.

399 Some Maltese traditions about the sea.
Joseph Cassar Pullicino. In: *The Mediterranean man and the sea (L'homme Méditerranéen et la mer): proceedings of the Third International Congress of Studies of the Western Mediterranean (Jerba, April 1981).* Tunis: Les Éditions Salammbô for the Association International d'Étude de Civilisations Méditerranéennes (AIECM) and Institut National d'Archéologie et d'Art de Tunis (INAA), 1985, p. 443-55.

Presents folk beliefs and traditions connected with the origins of Malta and Gozo and with their people. Some stories evoke echoes of other places and of ancient times, for example, the eye painted on Maltese fishing boats. Among prominent legends are some connected with the dolphin who is said to protect men – but not women.

400 **Some parallels between Maltese and Arabic folklore.**
Joseph Cassar Pullicino. *Acta Ethnographica*, vol. 34, nos. 1-4
(1986-88), p. 143-75. bibliog.
Aims to demonstrate that there are parallels and relationships with Arab folklore
which complement the much better documented ties between Maltese folklore and
that of Sicily. Examples of rhymes, folk-tales, proverbs, and beliefs and practices are
provided.

401 **Studies in Maltese folklore.**
Joseph Cassar Pullicino. Msida, Malta: The University of Malta
Press, 1992. 271p. bibliog.
A revised and enlarged edition of the author's essays, first published in 1976, including thirty-one illustrations of past and present folkloric events etc. as well as details of
folklorists of Malta. Children's rhymes, religious festival customs, riddles, nicknames, animals, and birth and infancy beliefs and customs are the main topics covered
in this study aimed at an anglophone readership. There is an extensive bibliography
(p. 249-58).

402 **The folklore of Maltese fossils.**
George Żammit Maempel. Valletta: Midsea Books, 1989. 29p.
bibliog. (Papers in Mediterranean Social Studies, no. 1).
This is the first attempt at a survey of the folklore associated with Malta's prehistoric
vegetable and animal remains embedded in rocks. It has a bibliography (p. 26-29) and
illustrations.

Social Conditions, Health and Welfare

Epidemiology

403   **A safe place in the sun? Health precautions, behaviours and health problems of British tourists in Malta.**
Nicola Clark, Stephen Clift, Stephen Page.   Canterbury, England:
Canterbury Christ Church College, 1993. 44p. (Travel, Lifestyles and Health, Paper no. 1).

In a study of health issues and tourism, in March 1993, 785 British tourists in Malta were interviewed using a structured questionnaire. The limitations of this survey are discussed and suggestions for future research on the social and psychological dimensions of health risks associated with travel and tourism are explored.

404   **A survey of congenital anomalies in Malta.**
Alfred Cuschieri.   In: *Collected papers, contributed by members of the academic staff of the University of Malta.*   Edited by Roger Ellul-Micallef, Stanley Fiorini.   Msida, Malta: University of Malta, 1992, p. 221-44. bibliog.

This register of all cases of congenital anomalies recorded at birth between 1983 and 1991 provides accurate prevalence and incidence figures and constitutes a source for the ascertainment of hereditary anomalies with their inherent risks which are important for genetic counselling.

405 **Proceedings of the European study group on social aspects of human reproduction: 5th annual meeting, Malta, September 1987.**
Edited by E. S. Grech, C. Savona-Ventura. Malta: The Editors, 1987. 159p.

Includes several epidemiological papers on Malta, dealing with teenage pregnancies, risk factors in elderly patients, and trends of maternal mortality and morbidity – all written by the editors. The other papers in the report do not refer to Malta.

406 **Changing patterns in contraceptive use in Malta.**
Robin G. Milne, Robert E. Wright. *Economic and Social Studies: Journal of the Faculty of Economics, Management and Accountancy, University of Malta*, vol. 7 (1993-94), p. 1-7. bibliog.

The 1985 Census demonstrated the scale of the reduction in family size and the speed of ageing in the population. This paper compares the extent and modes of contraception in use at the time of two surveys in 1971 and 1993, which were carried out with the assistance of family doctors and married women. Whilst the extent was little different, there had been a marked shift from other methods to the use of condoms and then oral contraceptives. The appendix reproduces the short questionnaire used.

407 **Cancer in Malta: trends in mortality and incidence rates of lung and breast cancer.**
Yana Mintoff. *Economic and Social Studies*, vol. 5 (1989-90), p. 38-63. bibliog.

By 1986 the cancer death rate in Malta approached that of highly industrialized countries and was a greater risk in each age group although most of the people affected died in later life. The available data are graphically displayed and possible carcinogens discussed.

408 **Endometrial adenocarcinoma in the Maltese population: an epidemiological study.**
C. Savona-Ventura, E. S. Grech. *European Journal of Gynaecology and Oncology*, vol. VII, no. 3 (1986), p. 209-17. bibliog.

The Maltese population has a high incidence of this disorder compared to other European countries. It is correlated with a high prevalence of abnormal glucose metabolism as well as a high dietary fat intake.

409 **Infant feeding in Malta.**
C. Savona-Ventura, E. S. Grech. *Journal of Psychosomatic Obstetrics and Gynaecology*, vol. 11 (1990), p. 107-17. bibliog.

Presents data collected from a questionnaire sample survey of patients delivering at St. Luke's Hospital, revealing that only a quarter of mothers were breast-feeding on leaving the hospital in 1981 compared with a rise to over two-thirds after an educational campaign five years later. The reasons for discontinuing or not breast-feeding are outlined.

410   **Reproductive performance on the Maltese Islands during the Second World War.**
C. Savona-Ventura.   *Medical History*, vol. 34 (1990), p. 164-77. bibliog.

So great was the social disruption and economic hardship of the Maltese during the Second World War that birth rates fell dramatically, to rise even more so after the end of local hostilities. The data is compared with the experience of other countries over this period.

411   **Caesarean Section in the Maltese Islands.**
C. Savona-Ventura.   *Medical History*, vol. 37 (1993), p. 37-55. bibliog.

A graphic indication of the decline in maternal and infant death rates and the rise in Caesarean deliveries without any necessary association between them.

412   **Reproductive performance on the Maltese Islands during the First World War.**
C. Savona-Ventura.   *Journal of the Royal Army Medical Corps*, vol. 141 (1995), p. 107-11.

Presents graphic data on birth, marriage, still birth and various mortality rates together with a discussion of the decrease in birth rates and slight increase in maternal mortality rates during the First World War, and the founding in 1919 of a Mothers and Infants' Health Association.

413   **Diabetes in Malta in the '80s.**
Antoine G. Schranz.   Malta: Maltese Diabetics Association, 1989. 15p. bibliog.

Summarizes epidemiological research into this highly prevalent disorder, offering comparative international figures.

414   **Collected papers on diabetes in Malta and its cardio-vascular complications and some other cardiological problems.**
J. V. Żammit Maempel.   Msida, Malta: University of Malta, 1979. 93p. bibliog.

Twenty-two papers, all but three in English, are reprinted in two parts. Part I consists of eleven papers on diabetes dating from 1965-78, and part II has eight entries on heart disease (1960-74). Two annexes comprise two further papers on diabetes (1981) and a 1984 paper on brucellosis. Some of the papers are illustrated and each carries references.

History of medicine

415 **Why Malta: an autobiography.**
Stanley Barnes.   Marsa, Malta: Publishers Enterprises Group (PEG)
Ltd., 1987. 131p. bibliog.
The author (born 1908) came to Malta in 1938 to set up a milk scheme for the
Government, two years after having the call to Moral Re-armament. Eight chapters
recount his experiences in Malta which included his marriage, and the construction of
the goats-milk centre and delivery scheme to replace the itinerant carriers of undulant
fever. Barnes joined the RAF on the island in 1941 and remained until 1944. In later
years he was active in the 200 Million Hungry Children Project. The book is illustrated with personal and official photographs.

416 **The economics of imperialism and health: Malta's experience.**
Yana Bland.   *International Journal of Health Services,* vol. 24, no. 3
(1994), p. 549-66.
This article is concerned with comparative mortality rates in Malta since 1927. There
was no decline in Maltese infant mortality rates until the later years of the Second
World War, although even then they exceeded those of Italy and Cyprus and were
three times as high as rates in the UK. Despite the small size of the population and
therefore the low levels of expenditure required, the colonial government failed to
invest in basic preventive measures such as mass radiography and pasteurization of
milk for general consumption. The reduction of TB and undulant fever was thus
delayed until the 1950s, following the election of a Labour government led by the
author's father, Dom Mintoff.

417 **The blue epidemic cholera: some aspects of treatment in the mid
nineteenth century.**
W. Bonnici.   *Journal of the Royal Army Medical Corps*, no. 139
(1993), p. 76-78.
Cholera was the epidemic scourge of the 19th century and an entrepot like Malta was
especially vulnerable. This account adds to the many published descriptions of
responses to the disease and its pre-biochemical treatment.

418 **The Ophthalmic Institute of Malta: the Manché's philanthropic
strategy to combat the spread of trachoma in Malta.**
Louis Borġ Manché.   Malta: The Author, 1993. 32p. bibliog.
A short account of the role of physicians of the Manché family in setting up and maintaining the Institute from 1908, with illustrations of contemporary documents and doctors.

419 **Occupational therapy: origins and development in Malta and
Gozo.**
Joseph Busuttil.   Malta: Prosan Ltd., 1986. 58p. bibliog.
Introduces the subject and outlines the various psychiatric, general and other hospitals
in which forms of occupational therapy (OT) have been practised. Some tabulated data
is provided as well as many photographs of current OT in practice.

Social Conditions, Health and Welfare. History of medicine

420 **Medical votive offerings in the Maltese Islands.**
Paul Cassar. *Journal of the Royal Anthropological Institute*, vol. 94, no. 1 (1963), p. 23-31.
Several churches in Malta display offerings promised in response to answered prayers. These include naive paintings of the disaster or suffering from which the donor was saved, wax and plaster casts of the limbs or other diseased organs, crutches and other aids, and other items. They date from all periods and remain a feature of popular religion today.

421 **Historical development of the concept of diabetes in Malta.**
Paul Cassar. Malta: Ministry of Health, 1982. 27p. bibliog.
The high prevalence of this disorder in Malta makes this historical study of topical interest. It outlines the awareness of the condition and application of treatment etc. in the islands. Photographs of the leading physicians are reproduced.

422 **The ophthalmic surgeon Joseph Barth 1746-1818.**
Paul Cassar. Msida, Malta: The University Press, 1982. 38p. bibliog.
This founder of the School of Ophthalmology at the University of Vienna from 1773 was born in Malta and a student at the Order's Holy Infirmary in Valletta before going to study in Rome where he was recruited by an Austrian member of the Order and taken to Vienna. Barth had a fine collection of classical antiquities which were later acquired by the Holy Roman Emperor and the British Museum.

423 **Three medical biographies: Joseph Żammit, Gabriele Henin, Joseph Edward Debono.**
Paul Cassar. Msida, Malta: The University Press, 1984. 48p. bibliog.
Contains short accounts, with references and lists of publications, of: Joseph Żammit, the first director of the School of Anatomy and Surgery in Malta; Gabriele Henin, the first surgeon to hold the Chair at the Holy Infirmary; and Edward Debono, a celebrated 20th-century physician whose family have subsequently achieved equal eminence.

424 **The John Hookham Frere Memorial Medical Library and the origins of the Malta Medical School Library.**
Paul Cassar. Malta: The University Press, 1985. 37p. bibliog.
Hookham Frere is renowned in Malta for his contribution to the actual establishment of the National Library and his chairmanship of the University Council from 1824-33, after which he donated a collection of thirty-three contemporary medical books (eighty-five volumes). These are listed by subject with an appendix on the authors and the books' significance at that time.

425 **The availability of medical records in Malta.**
Paul Cassar. In: *Economy in health care: proceedings of the 6th European Conference on Health Records, Malta, May 5-7, 1986.* Edited by C. O. Köhler, R. Z. Wick, U. Hoffmann. Heidelberg, FRG: Ecomed, 1986. 16p. bibliog.
Lists the general and special hospitals of Malta and outlines the records available from various starting dates in the 19th century and the sorts of information to be obtained

from them. Appendices list the surviving archives for each hospital and some examples from them. The author published what is still the only outline, *Medical history of Malta* (London: Wellcome Historical Library, 1964. 586p. 2 maps. bibliog.).

426   **A tour of the Lazzaretto buildings.**
Paul Cassar.   *Melita Historica,* vol. 9, no. 4 (1987), p. 369-80.
bibliog.
A description of the *Lazzaretto* (quarantine station) on Manoel Island in Marsamxett Harbour, the quarantine system operated by the Order of St. John and in the earlier years of British rule, the different cemeteries used and memorial and other inscriptions to be found there.

427   **Malta's role in maritime health under the auspices of the Order of St. John in the eighteenth century.**
Paul Cassar.   Lombard Bank (Malta) Ltd.   *Annual Report 89,*
Valletta, 1990, p. 1-25.
This well-illustrated account provides a wide range of information on various aspects of the Order's use of quarantine, the *barriera* on the Valletta Marina and the *Lazzaretto* on Fort Manoel.

428   **Saint Luke's Hospital foundation and progress 1930-1990.**
Paul Cassar.   Malta: Parliamentary Secretary for Health, 1990. 19p.
map. bibliog.
A short account of Malta's large teaching hospital with a summary of developments since 1963 and a series of aerial and other photographs of the site.

429   **The Holy Infirmary of the Knights of St. John 'La Sacra Infermeria'.**
Paul Cassar.   Valletta: The Mediterranean Conference Centre, 1994.
2nd ed. 87p. bibliog.
Revised, enlarged and better illustrated than its 1983 edition, this book provides a general account of the role and practices of the hospital through the use of specific examples. It covers the organization of the hospital and goes on to review its use by the British and its restoration as a conference centre which opened in 1979 only to be burnt down and reopened a decade later.

430   **St. Vincent de Paule's residence for the elderly: the medico-social record.**
Paul Cassar.   Malta: Parliamentary Secretariat for the Care of the
Elderly, 1994. 31p. bibliog.
A short, illustrated outline of the various institutions for the care of old people founded during the era of the Order, followed by a more detailed account of the protracted plans to build one of the type proposed by the British Poor Law from 1848-88 at Mġieret near the new public cemeteries. Contrary to popular local belief, Malta in the 1980s had a much larger and younger proportion of its increasingly elderly population in this and private church-run institutions than Britain. So the significance of such establishments is great. Unfortunately, few statistics are provided.

431 **Milestones in the evolution of pathology in Malta.**
Paul Cassar. Msida, Malta: University of Malta, Department of
Pathology, 1996. 36p. bibliog.
This is useful for the names of individuals and accounts of medical activities in Malta
it provides, and for its thirty-one references (p. 31-34).

432 **The Corps Disease: Brucellosis and its historical association with
the Royal Army Medical Corps.**
D. J. Vassallo. *Journal of the Royal Army Medical Corps*, vol. 138
(1992), p. 140-50. bibliog.
Outlines the role of members of the corps in the discovery of Malta Fever's vector,
discovered by Dr Themistocles Zammit when local goats were being used as experimental animals because of a shortage of monkeys. The bibliography lists all relevant
works published in the RAMC journal as well as other publications.

Social policy and welfare

433 **Youth, religion and community care in Malta.**
Anthony M. Abela. *Social Compass*, vol. 42, no. 1 (1995), p. 59-67.
This article, which is based on a comparative analysis of the European Values Surveys
conducted in Malta in 1983 and 1991, seeks to assess the impact of social and economic development on the religious and social values of youth in Malta. It examines
the change in religiosity of young people over the past decade and explores whether
there is any relation between this and community care in Malta relative to other western European countries.

434 **Food and health in Malta: a situation analysis and proposals for
action: the Malta case study for the FAO/WHO International
Conference on Nutrition, Rome 1992.**
Edited by Mary Bellizzi, Hugo Agius Muscat, Gauden Galea. Malta:
Department of Health and Ministry for Home Affairs and Social
Development, 1993. 93p. bibliog.
The five chapters of this study review the outcomes of the Department of Health's
plans and identify critical trends, dealing with the health of the nation, the Maltese
diet, nutrition education, and various aspects of food availability. Many tables, graphs
and diagrams provide the evidence for each chapter.

435 **A study on the aged: based on a census, a survey and official statistics.**
Edited by Victor F. Buhagiar, E. P. Delia. Valletta: Centre for Social
Research (Social Action Movement), 1982. 98p. bibliog.
A general introduction and essay on the characteristics and life-style of aged people
precedes a large number of frequency tables based on data collected from a randomly

selected sample of Maltese aged over sixty years, relating to their education, economic circumstances, life-style, health and home conditions. The projected distribution of the elderly population is discussed and further tabulated data are provided on the sample's aggregate social conditions and the regional distribution of many variables within the islands.

436 **Maltese youths in the European Union: a study report on the impact of Malta's membership of the European Union on Maltese youths.**
Simon Busuttil, Joanna Drake.   Floriana, Malta: National Youth Council (Malta), 1994. 239p. bibliog.

The twelve chapters of this volume aim to outline aspects of the rights, regulations, policies and ways of life in the European Union and their implications for young people in Malta. In many cases these appear to apply to any citizen and this handbook is relevant to everyone. It is about the formal aspects of life in the EU rather than the experience of being young in it.

437 **Adolescent drug use in Malta: a survey.**
Caritas Malta.   Floriana, Malta: Caritas Malta, 1993. 208p. bibliog.

A report prepared by DISCERN (Institute for Research on the Signs of the Times), of a survey conducted in November 1991, with the technical assistance of PRIDE (National Parents' Resource Institute for Drug Education, USA) International. A PRIDE questionnaire was used for the survey of the use and effects of drugs (including tobacco and alcohol), in which 10,297 males and 9,133 females aged 11-17 were questioned. It emerged that 4.7 per cent had come into contact with illicit drugs and almost 4 in every 5 had 'reached the gateway' through drinking alcohol. The final, seventh chapter presents these findings and the response of Caritas to them. For tables of findings see p. 147-89.

438 **Young people in Europe: Malta 1994.**
Edited by Charles Cini.   Malta: Polisportive Giovanili Salesiane, 1994. 188p.

Within the context of the European Games for Salesian Youth, half of this book (eight papers) is devoted to aspects of young people's education, values and behaviour in Malta and Gozo.

439 **National report on women in Malta in preparation for the United Nations Fourth World Conference on Women, Beijing, 1995.**
Malta: Commission for the Advancement of Women, 1994. 67p.

The bulk of this report discusses the evidence for change, since the early 1980s, in ten different fields and then future strategic goals and objectives in seven of these fields: decision-making, national machinery, legislation, education, employment, health, and violence against women.

Social Conditions, Health and Welfare. Social policy and welfare

440 **Health Vision 2000: a national health policy.**
Department of Health Policy and Planning. Malta: Health Division,
Ministry for Social Development, 1996. 127p.

This document sets the scene and in three substantive chapters outlines the current health status of the Maltese population, the sorts of reforms proposed for the development of the various departments of the Health Division, and key areas and targets for treating ill health, health promotion and developments in health service organization. There is a summary of conclusions and recommendations and three annexes outlining a strategy against drug and alcohol abuse, national nutrition policy, and areas of concern with reference to consultative processes.

441 **National policy on Mental Health Service.**
Department of Health Policy and Planning with the Scientific Board –
Mental Health Reform and the National Commission for Mental Health
Reform. Malta: Ministry for Home Affairs and Social Development,
1995. 80p.

This document combines a review of the current epidemiology and community and hospital services for those with a mental disorder, with a mission statement and objectives for reforming the Mental Health Service. It considers mental health promotion, implementing and monitoring policy, resources and other requirements and strategies, the role of other government departments and non-governmental organizations, and relevant legislation.

442 **Health services development plan, Malta 1986-1990.**
Valletta: Department of Health, 1986. 179p.

This illustrated study was produced in collaboration with the Copenhagen office of the World Health Organization (WHO).

443 **Malta human development report 1996.**
Edited by Joe Inguanez. Malta: UNDP, Media Centre Print, 1996.
114p. bibliog.

A valuable source of information and commentary on social and economic conditions and policies in contemporary Malta with reference to the concept of human development, compiled by staff of the University of Malta. The first two chapters are devoted to an outline of the concept and its statistical indicators, with a summary of conclusions and recommendations in the final chapter. The other nine chapters are devoted to: the system and outcomes of education; the labour market, labour relations and changes in work culture; the economy, income distribution and the welfare budget; legislative changes, the courts and human rights and liberties; citizenship, participation in voluntary work and values with reference to social policy; the inequitable predicament of women; caring for, and curing, elderly people; the natural environment, tourism and energy; and housing policies and practices and the need to conserve land. These chapters are extensively illustrated by statistical boxes, figures, tables and two maps, mostly drawn from a wide range of official sources, which are listed.

104

444 **Public housing initiatives in Malta since 1955.**
Douglas G. Lockhart. *Scottish Geographical Magazine*, vol. 103,
no. 1 (1987), p. 33-43. bibliog.
This article discusses policy, with particular emphasis on home ownership schemes
and building development areas. It examines the roles played by political parties and
the Housing Authority.

445 **A social and economic atlas of Malta and Gozo.**
D. G. Lockhart, K. T. Mason. Keele, England: University of Keele,
Department of Geography, 1989. 89p. bibliog. (Occasional Paper no. 16).
This informative study arose from a collaborative project between the authors and the
Central Office of Statistics in Valletta (which led to the publication, in 1987, of a computer-drawn atlas of the results of the 1985 Census). The present work contains
thirty-four maps of Malta and Gozo showing distributions, by locality, of aspects of
population, economic activity, and housing and household amenities. The central
theme of the study is concern with levels of living and the 'quality of life'. There is a
bibliography (p. 68-70).

446 **International comparisons of nursing manpower and nursing
officers' opinions of their work in Malta: Nursing Research Study
Part 1.**
Audrey Miller, Gillian Tipping. Msida, Malta: Institute for Health
Care, University of Malta, 1991. 80p. bibliog.
The research for this report arose from continual complaints about the shortage of
nursing staff in Malta and the discovery of eight largely ignored reports originally
requested from foreign advisers between 1972 and 1990. Changes proposed to the
education of nurses were seen as feasible but suggested amendments to nursing practice and nurse management were set aside. The first part of this report comprises a
review of expenditure on health care, hospital beds and their management, the labour
force, and nurse training, recruitment and rates of qualification. The survey of nursing
officers' perceptions of their work is divided into staff issues, the adequacy of facilities for patients and staff, perceptions of the quality of care, and administration and
management. Appendices include tables on Maltese expenditure and hospital bed and
patient statistics as well as a copy of the questionnaire. Other tabulated data are distributed through the text. The report begins with a page of eight recommendations.

447 **Full participation and equality of the disabled: myth or reality:
the situation of the disabled in Malta.**
Joseph Troisi. Valletta: Studia Editions, Social Action Movement,
1992. 226p. bibliog.
This report by the director of the Research Team of the Centre for Social Research
was part of a study co-ordinated by Oasi Maria Santissima's *Città Aperta* project in
Troina, Sicily. It reviews the responses to the three survey schedules printed in the
appendices which were administered to disabled people, their parents or legal
guardians, and members of the general public. The six chapters outline the framework
of the inquiry, the situation and experience of disabled people, the attitudes of those
responsible for them as well as female and male members of the public, and the implications of the findings for various aspects of social policy.

448   **Too late for too many . . . special education in Malta.**
      Mario Vassallo, Victoria Farrugia Sant' Angelo, Lydia Sciriha.
      Malta: Media Centre, 1994. 123p. bibliog.
This book is drawn from the mass of basic data and assessments of children in Maltese
special schools by staff of the University's Department of Social Studies and the
Institute of Health Care which were published separately from 1990-93 in twelve volumes. The categories and education of handicapped children are introduced, followed
by a summary of their social and other characteristics, their language abilities, and a
discussion of the adequacy of current services, etc.

Politics

Pre-Independence (-1964)

449 **Mabel Strickland.**
Joan Alexander.   Valletta: Progress Press, 1996. 354p.
This biography, by Lady Carnwath, of a formidable figure in Malta's 20th-century journalism and politics, sheds some new light on social and political trends in the islands. Mabel Strickland (1899-1988), daughter of Gerald Strickland, Prime Minister of Malta from 1927 to 1932, was no stranger to controversy whether with the government of Dom Mintoff or with the church under Archbishop Gonzi. She will be best remembered as editor and proprietor of *The Times of Malta*. This volume includes more than forty photographs, some previously unpublished. There is a foreword by HRH the Duke of Edinburgh.

450 **Malta and the end of empire.**
Dennis Austin.   London: Frank Cass, 1971. 132p. bibliog.
This account of events leading up to independence in 1964 pays special attention to the 1955 proposal for the integration of Malta within the United Kingdom. There is a valuable section of notes (p. 112-28), a short bibliography (p. 129-30) and four pages of photographs.

451 **Maltese administrators and reserved matters 1921-1933.**
Joseph D. Buġeja.   *Hyphen*, vol. IV, no. 3 (1984), p. 80-118. bibliog.
The 1921 Constitution introduced a diarchy with certain matters reserved for the colonial government in London. The Nationalist government clashed over emigration policies but the Strickland administration appealed for reform of the constitution to strengthen its own hand and then became embroiled in a dispute with the church that inevitably affected British relations with the Vatican.

452   **The St. John's Co-Cathedral affair – a study of a dispute between Church and State over property rights.**
Mario Buħaġiar.   *Melita Historica*, vol. 10, no. 4 (1991), p. 359-74. bibliog.

A brief survey of past disputes introduces an account of the major quarrel that arose in 1957 when the Labour Government placed the two works by Caravaggio in the National Museum instead of St. John's after their return from restoration in Rome. After mediation they were ultimately returned to the Church and its Oratory a year later.

453   **The Left within the Maltese labour movement.**
John Chircop.   Malta: Mireva Publications, 1991. 237p. bibliog.

The Malta Labour Party was the child of the Dockyard Workers' Union but, like its British counterpart, the labour movement had various radical components. There were supporters of Manwel Dimech (1860-1921) who died in exile after campaigning for a national, secular and semi-socialist alternative to clerico-colonialism. They were succeeded in the 1920s by members of the Socialist League, to whom the Roman Catholic Church, the Nationalist Party, and the imperialist Constitutional Party were equally opposed. Its members had links with the Communist International and also sent for the literature of the Rationalist Press Association. Following an ordinance against seditious propaganda, six Socialist League activists were put on trial in 1933 and their continued employment in the RN Dockyard barred. There is an extensive bibliography on p. 220-27.

454   **Malta's road to Independence.**
Edith Dobie.   Norman, Oklahoma: University of Oklahoma Press, 1967. 286p.

This book reviews events in, and options open to, Malta in the years up to 1964. Issues such as the influence of the Roman Catholic Church in the island and the nature of the link with Britain are examined.

455   **Polluted politics: background to the deportation of Maltese nationals in 1942.**
Carmel Farrugia.   Valletta: Midsea Books Ltd., 1995. 124p. bibliog.

Another short account of the detention and deportation of Maltese who were considered a political danger to the colonial state after Italy entered the Second World War. Appendices include a chronicle of events, a list of those deported as well as examples of the warrants of internment, the text of the ordinance empowering deportation, and the Maltese Prime Minister's speech to the Council of Government on 9 February 1942.

456   **Camillo Sceberras: his life and times.**
Robert Farrugia Randon.   Malta: The Author, 1991. 169p.

A useful account of the life and times (1772-1855) of one of the founders of the *Comitato Patriotico Maltese* in 1836, this provides information on other members of the influential Sceberras family and their involvement in Italian affairs as well as Maltese politics, and the activities of George Mitrovich, another Maltese patriot. The *Comitato* was an assembly claiming to represent the Maltese in their problematic constitutional dealings with the British authorities.

457   **Malta's quest for Independence: reflections on the course of Maltese history.**
Henry Frendo.   Valletta: Publishing and Promotion Co. Ltd., 1989.
282p.
A personally opinionated but not populist review of the island's political history, a third of which comprises an excellent photographic archive of political personalities and events.

458   **Party politics in a fortress colony: the Maltese experience.**
Henry Frendo.   Valletta: Midsea Books, 1991. 2nd ed. 243p. bibliog.
(Maltese Social Studies, no. 5).
The first edition of this pioneering work on Maltese historiography appeared in 1979. Based on work for a DPhil thesis at Oxford University, this is a discussion of the place of politics in colonial Maltese society with emphasis on the search for national identity. Five of the seven chapters deal with the emergence of nationalism and moves towards more representative government in the later 19th century. The focus of the sixth chapter is the development of political parties and more local responsibility, while the final chapter looks at the transition to a two-party system within an increasingly assertive national culture. There are thirty-two pages of photographs (between p. 116 and 117) and a valuable bibliography (p. 225-32).

459   **Intra-colonial nationalism: the case of Malta 1922-1927.**
Henry Frendo.   *Melita Historica*, vol. 11, no. 1 (1992), p. 79-93.
bibliog.
Outlines the disputes and policies of the various Maltese political parties in government during the period.

460   **Maltese political development 1798-1964: a documentary history.**
Edited by Henry Frendo.   Malta: Printed by Interprint Ltd., 1993.
921p. bibliog.
This publication of ninety-two constitutional and political documents in their original languages (mostly English and some in Italian or Maltese) provides an important array of source material introduced and annotated by the author. It is divided into eight parts, starting with the brief period of French occupation, 1798-99, and thereafter tracing the constitutional vicissitudes during British rule until political independence in 1964. As well as some official notices, the bulk of the documents consist of remonstrances and formal appeals, programmes and policies, speeches, press reports, testimonies and evidence to royal commissions, governor's addresses, Round Table Conference proceedings and extracts from the 1964 Independence Constitution.

461   **Britain's European Mediterranean: language, religion and politics in Lord Strickland's Malta (1927-1930).**
Henry Frendo.   *History of European Ideas*, vol. 21, no. 1 (1995),
p. 47-65. bibliog.
Strickland's election to power in the Lower House but not the Senate paved the way for the crisis which led to the suspension of the 1921 Constitution. The issues related to his policy of Anglicization to which both the *professionisti* and the church were

opposed, and which was noted in Fascist Italy, which had its own designs on Malta. This article inquires into the contest between assimilation (or imperial uniformity) and resistance (or local autonomy) in Malta as one part of the colonial 'periphery'. Frendo asks how cultural politics, signalled from a metropolis – Britain – penetrated internal relations.

462 **Fortress colony: the final act 1945-64, vol. 1, 1945-54.**
Joseph M. Pirotta.   Valletta: Studia Publications, The Social Action
Movement, 1987. 444p. bibliog.

Section one presents the prelude to the restoration of responsible government, from the aftermath of the 1939-45 war, the rise of trade unionism and of the Labour Party, and the inauguration of the National Assembly (1945). Section two assesses the economic difficulties facing political progress under Boffa and Dom Mintoff. Section three assesses two other leaders, Edgar Mizzi and George Borġ Olivier, and the continuing political instability in the context of uncertainties about Malta's future relationship with Britain.

463 **Fortress colony: the final act 1945-64, vol. 2, 1955-58.**
Joseph M. Pirotta.   Valletta: Studia Productions, The Social Action
Movement, 1991. 533p. bibliog.

This is the second of two volumes (see previous item), to which one hopes others will soon be added. It provides by far the best analysis of the political, social and economic causes of the changes that brought Malta to independent statehood and the political, religious and trade-union leaders who influenced this process. After so many partial accounts this one is easily the most exhaustively researched in British and Maltese archives. The cumulative bibliographies are themselves of great value and the appendices document Malta's constitutional negotiations, etc.

464 **Record of proceedings in the Privy Council, on appeal from Her
Majesty's Court of Appeal for the Island of Malta and its
Dependencies, between the Marchese Felicissimo Apap (appellant)
and the Noble Luisa Strickland, widow of Captain Walter
Strickland, R.N., and Gerald Strickland (respondents).**
London: HM Privy Council, 1879. 264p.

This is a translation of all the original acts and documents originally drawn up in Italian as a record of the proceedings in the Maltese courts which were printed for the consideration of the case on appeal to the Privy Council in London. It includes a series of death, marriage and christening certificates of the Bologna, Strickland and other related families as well as genealogies, deeds of grant, petitions, judgements and other procedural documents related to this important case, the winning of which secured the right of Lord Strickland, Count della Catena, to the Villa Bologna and that family's inheritance in Malta. This established his wealth and noble position in the island which was to provide the springboard for his influential entry into local affairs, as a senior civil servant and party politician successively.

465 **Malta and me.**
Eric Shepherd.   London: Selwyn & Blount Ltd., 1926. 292p.
A fascinating autobiographical memoir by a British lecturer in English literature, appointed in 1920 for three years and pitchforked into the turmoil of local autonomy politics, an experience with several subsequent parallels at the University of Malta. As the author says, this 'does not profess to be an exhaustive account of the island and its institutions, but rather a semi-autobiographical record . . .'. The volume does, however, contain much descriptive writing about the islands' people and landscapes.

466 **Lord Strickland: servant of the crown. Vol. 1 parts 1 and 2.**
Harrison Smith, revised and edited by Adrianus (Adriannes) Koster.
Valletta: Progress Press, 1984. 402p.
Smith's authorized biography was withheld from publication until Koster received the consent of Lord Strickland's daughter, Mabel Strickland, to his revision of it. Part one is devoted to the portrayal of Strickland as a young colonial servant (1861-1902) and part two to his service to the Crown as governor of the Leeward Islands and then a succession of Australian states from 1902-17.

467 **Lord Strickland: servant of the crown. Vol. 2 part 3.**
Harrison Smith, revised and edited by Adrianus (Adriannes) Koster.
Malta: Progress Press, 1986. 672p.
Subtitled, 'The people's servant in Parliament (1917-40)', this volume is devoted to Strickland's turbulent return to the Maltese political arena, his breach with the Church as well as Nationalist Party politicians, and his pursuit of his own objectives for Malta in the British legislature as a member of the House of Lords. Nine appendices document Strickland's and others' political proposals as well as Maltese election results under the 1921 and 1939 Constitutions.

468 **The King's guests in Uganda: from internment to independence 1939-1964.**
Edgar Soler.   Malta: Lux Press, 1986. 302p.
A detailed autobiographical memoir of one of the younger Maltese Nationalists who was detained and deported from Malta to Uganda from 1941-45, where he married a Viennese detainee. Prior to independence in 1964, he was elected to the Maltese Parliament after a career in private industry and then running the Trade Fair.

469 **Malta Round Table Conference, 1955: report.**
United Kingdom Government.   London: HM Stationery Office
(Command 9657), 1955. 38p.
The emphasis in this official statement is on the views for and against Malta becoming independent and their implications.

Post-Independence (1964-)

470 **Nothing but the truth: an illustrated autobiography.**
Alfred J. Bencini. Malta: The Author, 1987. 283p.

An account by a former Commissioner of Police and co-founder of the Malta Police Federation, who ran the 100 metres for Malta at the 1936 Berlin Olympics. It is largely devoted to a description of his experience of Dom Mintoff's two periods as prime minister (1955-58 and 1971-84) which culminated in Bencini's resignation from the force in 1973. The years 1957-70 are omitted.

471 **A politician and his audience: Malta's Dom Mintoff.**
Jeremy Boissevain. In: *Maltese society. A sociological inquiry.*
Edited by Ronald G. Sultana and Godfrey Baldacchino. Msida,
Malta: Mireva Publications, 1994, p. 409-20.

This chapter presents a portrait of one of Malta's outstanding figures in the era of transition to political independence. It analyses his rhetorical style from an examination of his 1976 'Milk them, Ġuż, milk them' speech in Qormi and discusses the basis of his 'big-man' image.

472 **Patron-client relations in the Mediterranean with special reference to the changing political situation in Malta.**
David M. Boswell. *Mediterranean Studies,* vol. 2, no. 1 (1980),
p. 22-41.

Malta's political independence did not reduce its dependence on foreign economic support, but it altered the position of the Church as its focus of national identity. In the 1970s Prime Minister Mintoff's foreign policy claimed such support abroad and at home that the pattern of clientelism continued. Traditionally based on the clients of local professionals – doctors, lawyers, architects as well as some businessmen – the Malta Labour Party (MLP) relied on the General Workers' Union. But during its first decade in power, Mintoff centralized the power of the party in government and some of his ministers established their office-based clientele, based on the public housing allocations, planning permission and import licences in their 'gift'. Holding onto office therefore became of even greater personal interest and the author predicted the sorts of manoeuvre which permitted the MLP to preserve its majority in the 1981 elections despite the Nationalists winning the majority of the votes in a proportional system of representation.

473 **Clientelism, patronage and accusations of corruption in Malta in the 1970s and 1980s.**
David M. Boswell. In: *Distorting democracy: political corruption in Spain, Italy and Malta.* Edited by Paul Heywood. Bristol, England: Centre for Mediterranean Studies, University of Bristol, 1994,
p. 27-39. bibliog. (Occasional Paper no. 10).

This paper combines an analysis of the climate of opinion within which corruption is assumed and discussed and the particular pattern of political corruption that actually surfaced in public during the period of Malta Labour Party government from 1971-87.

474   **The 1987 Maltese election: between Europe and the Mediterranean.**
Dominic Fenech.   *West European Politics*, vol. 11, no. 1 (1988), p. 133-38.

A useful summary of the political scene at the time of the election with a comparative table of the percentage of votes cast for the 2 major parties and the high turnout of 96.1 per cent, with a review of the economic and other issues facing the incoming Nationalist Government after 16 years in opposition and, in particular, its relations with the European Community.

475   **Malta.**
Dominic Fenech.   *European Journal of Political Research*, vol. 22, no. 4 (1992), p. 471-73. bibliog.

This is the first of a series of annual reviews by the author in the journal's *Special Issue: Political Data Yearbook*, edited by Ruud Koole and Peter Nair. It includes electoral and political party data as well as a list of cabinet members and a brief review of the political issues of the previous year.

476   **The 1992 Maltese election.**
Dominic Fenech.   *West European Politics*, vol. 15, no. 4 (1992), p. 189-95.

A comparative table of votes cast for major parties including the Alternativa Demokratika (AD) for the first time, whose small but notable vote shocked both established parties. In common with other European socialist parties, the Malta Labour Party had to find a new way and elected a new leader. There is a brief discussion of the Maltese economy.

477   **Explaining near-universal turnout: the case of Malta.**
Wolfgang Hirczy.   *European Journal of Political Research*, vol. 27 (1995), p. 255-72. bibliog.

Although voting is not compulsory, Malta has the highest turnout of all democratic nations. The author highlights the following factors: intense partisanship, power concentration in one elective institution, single party governments despite proportional representation, the impact of the voting system on a single ballot, and intense campaigning by competing candidates within, as well as between, parties to maximize and mobilize committed voters.

478   **Malta.**
Michael Hodges.   In: *Political parties in Europe. Albania – Norway.* Edited by Vincent E. McHale.   Westport, Connecticut: Greenwood Press, 1983.

This entry in one of the useful guides in the *Greenwood Historical Encyclopaedia of the World's Political Parties* series describes a dozen parties and gives details of seats held in the islands' House of Representatives (1921-81). There is a brief introductory statement.

479   **Malta in the making 1962-1987: an eyewitness account.**
      Edgar Mizzi.   Malta: Printed at Beck Graphics Ltd., 1995. 481p.
The author is currently chairman of the Law Revision Commission. Before retirement
he served in the Government of Malta as an adviser to both the Nationalist Party Prime
Minister George Borġ Olivier and the Malta Labour Party Prime Minister Dom Mintoff,
being Attorney General to the latter from 1971-81. There have been relatively few political autobiographies and there are fewer by civil servants of Malta. But recently several
have provided an apologia either for their service to, or reasons for resigning from,
Mintoff's administration. This is by far the most detailed and covers the series of measures that most aroused animosity within Malta. There is little doubt that this account,
and more particularly its evaluation of policies and practices, will be challenged by
future writers. It is an important position statement that has many specific citations
from events, meetings and contemporary documents although none are referenced.
There are illustrations of the people and events that figure in this account.

480   **Maltese political parties and political modernization.**
      Godfrey A. Pirotta.   In: *Maltese society: a sociological inquiry.*
      Edited by Ronald G. Sultana, Godfrey Baldacchino.   Msida, Malta:
      Mireva Publications, 1994, p. 95-112.
The recent spread of professionally organized and managed pressure and lobby groups
has challenged the strength and influence of political parties which are no longer the sole
political agenda setters. Lately, indeed, parties have had issues – such as those to do
with the environment – forced upon them. This paper examines the influence on Maltese
parties of new pressure groups in the context of political modernization in the islands.

481   **Reports on the working of government departments for the year
      1995.**
      Valletta: Department of Information, Office of the Prime Minister,
      1996. 519p.
This is the official (annual) record of principal activities in ministries and in the House
of Representatives and in the Electoral Office. Previous annual issues reflected the
changing structure of government. In 1995, for example, there were ten ministries
reporting while, a decade and a half before that, reports were submitted by the then
forty-two departments (rather than by ministries). The annual volumes for the earlier
1990s contained about 300 pages each; issues in the 1980s ranged in size from 123 to
207 pages. The ministries reporting in the 1995 volume are Social Development,
Education, Gozo, Finance, Transport, Environment, Justice and Arts, Food and
Agriculture, Economic Services, and Home Affairs, and there are reports covering the
Office of the Prime Minister and that of the Deputy Prime Minister.

482   **Towards a new Public Service for Malta: an assessment of
      contemporary administrative initiatives.**
      Edited by Edward Warrington.   *Economic and Social Studies*, vol. 6
      (1991-92). special issue. 167p. bibliog.
Contributions to a forum on the institutional framework and on managing human
resources by different representatives of Maltese politics, industry and the civil service, are preceded by a review of the Reports of the Public Service Reform
Commission by the editor with a bibliography of the Commission's reports, and a critique of the final report of July 1989 by Godfrey Baldacchino.

Constitution and Legal System

483 **Paulo de Bono, 1848-1906: the intelligent judge.**
Joe Calleja.   Valletta: Progress Press Ltd., 1996. 184p. bibliog.
A self-made man, De Bono became a law student and educator and in due course a
judge, when he played a part in the constitutional eruptions at the end of the 19th
century and wrote a history of legislation in Malta in 1897. The appendix consists of
many documents about De Bono as well as copies of surviving correspondence from
1874-1907, when the Governor awarded his widow and children a grant from public
funds in recognition of her husband's valuable services to the Government. A few
photographs of family members are reproduced.

484 **Constitution of the Republic of Malta.**
Valletta: Department of Information, 1975. 102p.
This is the constitution under which Malta became a republic within the Common-
wealth on 13 December 1974.

485 **The law on commercial partnerships in Malta.**
F. Cremona.   Msida, Malta: University of Malta Press, 1984. 158p.
This is a detailed analysis, which first appeared in 1968, identifying types and principal characteristics of partnerships and their juridical character. There is a special
reference to limited liability, debentures, accounts, audit, and the winding-up of partnerships.

486 **Selected papers 1946-1989.**
J. J. Cremona.   Marsa, Malta: Publishers Enterprises Group (PEG)
Ltd., 1990. 289p. bibliog.
Thirty-one papers on various aspects of the law, its practice and enforcement in Malta
and the field of human rights by Malta's previous Chief Justice and the Vice-President
of the European Court of Human Rights and of the European Tribunal in matters of
State Immunity. There is a foreword by Rolv Ryssdal.

487   **The Maltese Constitution and constitutional history since 1813.**
      J. J. Cremona.   San Ġwann, Malta: Publishers Enterprises Group
      (PEG) Ltd., 1994. 172p. bibliog.

A basic review by the former Chief Justice and Professor of Malta's eleven constitutions since British rule was formalized, with the texts of each constitution. Two of the ten chapters are devoted to the Independence Constitution of 1964 and its subsequent amendments. The two appendices comprise a list of the formal publications of each constitution and a selection of documents of relevance to Maltese constitutional history.

488   **Aspects of Maltese law for bankers.**
      Philip Farrugia Randon.   Valletta: Institute of Bankers (Malta Centre),
      1983. 256p.

A reference book containing a useful index (p. 241-56), a list of cases quoted (p. 235-40) and chapters on obligations, suretyship, privileges, estates, pledge, partnerships, bankruptcy, plus details of the Acts of 1967 and 1970.

489   **The European company. A comparative study with English and
      Maltese company law.**
      J. Micallef.   Rotterdam, the Netherlands: Rotterdam University Press,
      1974. 783p.

This work compares the draft Statute for a European Company presented by the Commission of the European Communities (30 June 1970) with UK company law and with Maltese law insofar as it differs. The main comparison is between the draft for the Societas Europaea (SE) and the UK Companies Act 1948, as amended in 1967.

490   **Report of the Malta Constitutional Commission, 1960.**
      London: HMSO (Cmnd. 1261) for the Colonial Office, 1961. 75p.

A report presented by the Malta Constitutional Commission chaired by Sir Hillary Blood. Published three years before political independence, this review looks at most aspects of government and constitution and includes a range of submissions from groups involved.

Foreign Relations

491 Malta: boundaries, threats and risks.
Ewan Anderson. *Boundary Bulletin*, no. 4 (1992), p. 21-24.
The author argues that Malta's Armed Forces could effectively respond only to locally based threats to national security. In the case of regional or global threat they could act until international support arrived, he concludes. *Boundary Bulletin* is a journal of the International Boundaries Research Unit, University of Durham, England.

492 Malta in its international setting.
Salvino Busuttil. In: *The future of the Mediterranean.* Valletta: Foundation for International Studies, 1995, p. 3-54.
This is one of a collection of papers, all by Salvino Busuttil, Director General of the Foundation for International Studies, who has considerable experience of work on human settlements and sociocultural environments with UNESCO, UN, and other organizations. The author sees Malta as being placed between the wealthy north and the poor south and argues for a Mediterranean bridge between the two.

493 Malta's post-Cold War perspective on Mediterranean security.
Stephen C. Calleja. In: *Mediterranean politics*, vol. 1. Edited by Richard Gillespie. London: Pinter Publishers, 1994, p. 138-49.
Discusses Malta's role in the Conference on Security and Cooperation in Europe since 1975 and reviews the changing policies towards Libya, the European Union and other political blocks.

494 Case concerning the continental shelf (Libyan Arab Jamahiriya/Malta). Judgement of 3 June, 1985.
The Hague: International Court of Justice, 1985. 187p.
This document, consisting of 'Reports of Judgements, Advisory, Opinions and Orders', is presented bilingually (English-French). It follows a number of preliminary judgements in the matter of the delimitation of the sea between Malta and Libya,

based on the principle of equidistance. The proceedings were required by a joint 1976 agreement between Libya and Malta to submit the matter to the International Court.

495 **Malta.**
James Craig. In: *Politics, security and development in small states.* Edited by Colin Clarke, Tony Payne. London: Allen & Unwin, 1987, p. 170-83.

Identifies a phase of 'dependent sovereignty' from independence in 1964 up to 1971, followed by one of 'positive neutrality' from 1971 to 1984. Craig shows that Malta's fortunes continue to be dependent on external realities.

496 **Co-operation and security in the Mediterranean – prospects after Barcelona. Contributions to the International Colloquium, Malta, March 22-23, 1996.**
Edited by Alberto Din. Msida, Malta: University of Malta, Mediterranean Academy of Diplomatic Studies, 1996. 258p.

Eight of the twenty-eight participants are Maltese, including the islands' deputy prime minister and minister for foreign affairs who delivered the opening address in which he calls for economic and security co-operation. The initiative for – and structure of – the conference reflects current concerns in Malta about the need for new links and directions for the country within the Mediterranean. The editor holds the Italian Chair at the University of Malta.

497 **The EC: Malta at the crossroads: evaluating the effects of the islands' future relations with the European Community.**
Floriana, Malta: Market Intelligence Services Company Limited (MISCO) for Malta Federation of Industries, September 1988. 101p. bibliog.

This report, sponsored by the Lombard Bank (Malta) Limited, is mainly concerned with the likely effects on Malta's industry of future relations with the European Community. Three possible patterns are assessed: a status quo/special relationship, a customs union, and full membership (this latter involving the negotiation of transition conditions, pre-adhesion measures and long-term safeguards).

498 **The Pope considers seeking asylum in Malta, 1881-1889.**
Dominic Fenech. *Journal of Maltese Studies*, no. 15 (1983), p. 87-94.

During the troubled period following the union of Italy, the Pope seriously considered seeking asylum if the new state became a republic or sold off the property of church congregations. But his bluff was called when Crispi, the Prime Minister, made clear that he would be allowed to leave but not to return.

499 **Malta: national experiences with neutrality and non-alignment.**
Dominic Fenech. *Report of the Colloquium on neutrality and non-alignment in the post-cold war era.* Msida, Malta: The Mediterranean Academy of Diplomatic Studies, University of Malta, 1992, p. 47-57.

Recounts the different policies of the Maltese parties in power and Mintoff's support for the Arab cause contrasted with the Nationalist Party's pursuit of EC membership.

500 **Malta in the European Community: some economic and commercial perspectives.**
Michael Frendo, Josef Bonnici.   Valletta: Malta Chamber of Commerce, 1989. 172p.

This study, sponsored by the Bank of Valletta, has chapters on the European Community market, manufacturing competition and opportunities for Maltese enterprises, and the financial system and support measures. It argues that the EC (now EU) market is crucial to Malta's tourism and manufacturing – and to maintaining employment and growth levels in the islands.

501 **Europe – the case for membership.**
Michael Frendo.   Mrieħel, Malta: Offset Press Ltd., 1996. 140p.

Subtitled 'Or why Labour got it wrong', this is a political discourse focusing on why the course chosen by the Nationalist Party (PN) in 1979 is consistent with historical development and why the stand of the Malta Labour Party against European Union membership is wrong.

502 **The CSCE Mediterranean Seminar – a further attempt?**
John Paul Grech.   *Malta Review of Foreign Affairs*, vol. 3 (1993), p. 45-57.

Reviews the repeated endeavours of Malta to get the security of the Mediterranean incorporated in clauses of the various meetings of the Conference on Security and Cooperation in Europe.

503 **Malta's relations with the Holy See in postcolonial times (since 1964).**
Adrianus (Adriannes) Koster.   *Melita Historica,* vol. 11, no. 3 (1994), p. 311-23. bibliog.

After independence in 1964 the *aggiornamento* of Vatican II led towards peace between the Malta Labour Party and the local episcopate. After 1971, under Paul VI, the Vatican refused to intervene in Church-State relations. However, under John Paul II the new Archbishop of Malta was supported in conflict with Mintoff's Labour government over the financing of church schools and a new settlement was negotiated over state finance for these in return for the surrender of some Church land.

504 **Malta and the European Community – the pros and cons of membership: a study by the General Workers' Union.**
Karmenu Micallef.   Valletta: Union Press, 1990. 56p. 2 maps.

An outline of the primary industrial workers' union's view of the EC, as something to benefit from by even closer association but to avoid joining owing to the negative balance of trade, the small scale of agricultural subsidies to be expected, and the threat to dockyard work and to general living standards.

505 **Malta's foreign policy after Mintoff.**
Godfrey Pirotta. *Political Quarterly*, vol. 56, no. 2 (1985), p. 182-86.

Compares the policies of the Mintoff government in the earlier 1980s with those of the Mifsud Bonnici administration after 1984. The author sees a 'new look' in Malta's relations with Britain, Europe and NATO.

506 **Malta – EEC relations.**
Christopher Pollacco. Msida, Malta: Mireva Publications, 1992. 140p. bibliog.

This traces Malta's relations with Europe from the 1960s and concludes that, in the spirit of Malta's 'coming home', 'it is in the interest of the Maltese people to join the Community' (p. 103). The volume includes statistical tables (p. 105-27) and a bibliography (p. 129-33).

507 **The next Mediterranean enlargement of the European Community: Turkey, Cyprus and Malta?**
John Redmond. Aldershot, England: Dartmouth Publishing Company, 1993. 157p.

Malta is considered (p. 98-133) in terms of alternative views and options, the background to EC-Malta relations, the islands' politics, neutrality and size, and economic issues. The author concludes that 'The economic case for Malta joining the EC (from the Maltese perspective) seems increasingly unassailable' (p. 124). However, 'From the EC's point of view it is not easy to see how Maltese accession would be of much benefit to the existing Community' (p. 127). (The change of government in 1996 led to a review of Malta's application to join the EC.)

508 **Report by the EC Directorate to the Prime Minister and Minister of Foreign Affairs regarding Malta's membership of the European Community.**
Valletta: Ministry of Foreign Affairs, EC Directorate (distributed by Department of Information), 1990. 383p.

Represents the basis of the position of Malta's government on the islands' future links with the Community in the period prior to the 1992 election.

509 **Malta and the E.E.C.: economic and social aspects: reports and documents.**
Translated by Alfred Sant. Senglea, Malta: Malta Labour Party, Information Department, 1990. 268p. bibliog.

This sets out the Malta Labour Party view of the islands' future, summed up as 'the option of full Maltese membership of the Common Market cannot be considered as economically viable' (p. 77). There is a bibliography (p. 249-52). (The translator became prime minister of Malta in 1996.)

510 **Malta's European challenge.**
Alfred Sant. Hamrun, Malta: S. K. S. Information Department, Malta
Labour Party, 1995. 177p.

Consists of interviews, articles, and addresses by Sant, leader of the Malta Labour
Party from 1992 (and prime minister from 1996). Sant presents the economic and
other arguments for the MLP's policy of co-operation with the European Union without membership of it. This is, however, very much a personal presentation by an MLP
leader who sees Malta as a Mediterranean Switzerland.

511 **Status of petroleum exploration in Malta.**
Roger Scotto. In: *The Mediterranean in the new law of the sea.*
Edited by Victor Fenech. Valletta: Foundation for International
Studies (Malta), 1987, p. 81-86.

This paper is one of a collection presented at a conference organized by the
Mediterranean Institute (Foundation for International Studies) in collaboration with
the International Ocean Institute and the Malta Oceanographic Commission on 23 and
24 February 1987. The author describes Malta's attitude as 'wait and see' until higher
oil prices would bring funds for exploration – given the strong supply situation worldwide. The search for oil started in the mid-1950s and was renewed in the early 1970s
until halted – to the south of the islands – by the impasse with Libya. Since then Malta
has monitored technical developments. More surveys came in the 1980s. (The other
papers in this collection have some indirect relevance to Malta.)

512 **The state of the European Union, 1994.**
Edited by Peter G. Xuereb, Roderick Pace. Msida, Malta: European
Documentation and Research Centre, University of Malta, 1994. 241p.
bibliog.

This is the first of a proposed series of volumes, based on a series of public lectures,
and is to be updated in future volumes. It consists of eleven articles by seven authors,
introduced by an outline of the institutions of the European Union by Professor John
Usher and of its 'Legal Order' by Professor Peter Xuereb. Subsequent contributions
consider European integration and Malta's economic, political and commercial relations with Europe, especially with respect to law, banking and monetary union. Most
of the many references are to case judgements and documents of the European Union.

513 **Economic and legal reform in Malta: State of the European Union
Conference 1995.**
Edited by Peter G. Xuereb, Roderick Pace. Msida, Malta: European
Documentation and Research Centre, University of Malta, 1995. 419p.

The text of twenty public lectures delivered at the 'State of the European Union Conference 1995', many of which consider the impact of European Union membership on
Malta, Maltese financial services and the Maltese Competition Act, financial and
insurance service liberalization, consumer protection, and community agreements.

514 **The European Union, the IGC and the Mediterranean. State of the European Union Conference 1996.**
Edited by Peter G. Xuereb, Roderick Pace.   Msida, Malta: University of Malta, European Documentation and Research Centre, 1996. 318p.

A collection of conference presentations, most of them of relevance to Malta's regional context and situation. Three papers are specifically about the implications of European Monetary Union (EMU) for the islands – by G. Cordina, A. Demarco, and S. Gauci and J. Consiglio.

Economy

General

515 **Aspects of an island economy.**
In: *Issues.* Edited by Ernest Azzopardi, Louis J. Scerri. Malta: The New Economic Society, 1984. 51p.

Includes articles on economic development (Michael Sant), post-1945 emigration (E. P. Delia), Malta Drydocks and the Mondrogon co-operatives (E. L. Żammit, A. Gauchi), and on banking in Malta (René G. Saliba).

516 **Maltese patterns of dependence: an historical perspective.**
B. W. Beeley, W. A. Charlton. *Scottish Geographical Magazine*, vol. 110, no. 2 (1994), p. 112-20. bibliog.

Prior to 1964 Malta was controlled by outsiders and came to depend on external finance. Now there is a new dependence on tourism. The island's small land area and limited resource options arguably make one or other form of dependence inevitable, with consequent impact on land-use, landscape and on the spatial structure of the islands. Such impact varies with the changing nature of dependence.

517 **A causeway with a gate: the progress of development in Malta.**
Jeremy Boissevain. In: *Perspectives on development.* Edited by Sandra Wallman. Cambridge, England: Cambridge University Press, 1977, p. 87-97. bibliog.

Examines changing perceptions of development within Malta in terms of differing social position and political affiliation and in terms of relative levels of development among countries. The changes in perception occur within the context of progress towards a new national self-confidence and greater prosperity. The view of development as economic is now broadened to include social and political goals.

518   **The Maltese economy, and other papers.**
Lino Briguglio.   Valletta: CMTU, 1984. 57p. bibliog.
Brings together separate papers, each with references, on 'The Maltese economy, 1955-1979', 'Some findings pertaining to the Maltese aggregate labour market' and 'The Maltese official external reserves'.

519   **Factors affecting labour demand in a small open economy – the case of Malta.**
Lino Briguglio.   In: *The economic development of small countries: problems, strategies and policies.*   Edited by J. Kaminarides, L. Briguglio, H. N. Hoogendonk.   Delft, the Netherlands: Eburon Publishers with the Foundation for International Studies, Valletta, and the Faculty of Economics, University of Amsterdam, 1985, p. 143-50.
Proposes a simple macro-model to explain and quantify Malta's dependence on exports for generating employment. The model, which is assumed to be determined by domestic demand and by exports, allows for the action of price effects (arising from exchange rate changes) on the import content of exports. (See also the author's PhD thesis on 'The specification and estimation of a model for the Maltese aggregate labour market' at the University of Malta, 1982.) The publication in which this chapter is contained comprises papers presented at the International Conference on the Economic Development of Small Countries, Malta, 22-24 May 1985.

520   **The Maltese economy: a macroeconomic analysis.**
Lino Briguglio.   Msida, Malta: David Moore Publications, 1988. 210p. bibliog.
Briguglio provides a general overview of the Maltese economy and describes the magnitude of change of some of its most important macro-economic variables. The reader does not need advanced knowledge of economic theory since the contents are essentially descriptive in nature. The book has five parts. Parts one and two deal with major economic aggregates relating to output, expenditures and human resources; part three covers money and banking; part four deals with international economic aspects; and part five describes the Maltese income multiplier process (which shows how a change in any expenditure creates a change in aggregate income which may be greater than the original change in expenditure).

521   **The Maltese economy since 1960.**
Lino Briguglio.   *Hyphen*, vol. v, no. 5 (1988), p. 205-23. bibliog.
An outline of employment, sectoral scale, expenditure and the balance of payments, with a discussion of economic problems from 1960-84.

522   **The Maltese economy: a brief overview.**
Lino Briguglio.   Floriana, Malta: Malta Federation of Industry (Development House), 1989. 52p. (Publication no. 29).
A macro-economic approach, this deals with the labour market, income and expenditure, money, banking, inflation, balance of payments, the islands' international economic standing and changes over the two decades reviewed here.

523 **Island economies: plans, strategies and performance, Malta.**
Lino Briguglio.   Canberra: Australian National University, Research
School of Pacific Studies/National Centre for Development Studies,
1992. 27p. bibliog. (Economics Division Working Papers at the
Research School of Pacific Studies, ANU).
This paper identifies patterns and constraints in the Maltese economy over thirty
years.

524 **A contribution to income distribution analysis in Malta.**
E. P. Delia.   *Economics and Social Studies*, vol. 3 (1986), p. 33-48.
bibliog.
Based on data drawn from the Household Budget Survey, an evaluation of social
policy in Malta, and a survey of those aged over sixty years, the author estimates that,
as the minimum wage corresponds to the poverty income level for a family with one
child, those with large families will experience poverty as will the least educated
people over the age of sixty – probably about five per cent of Maltese households.

525 **The task ahead – dimensions, ideologies and policies: a study of the
state of the economy commissioned by the Confederation of Private
Enterprise.**
E. P. Delia.   Valletta: Cope Publications, 1987. 81p. bibliog.
There are three parts to this report. The first considers the economic system and recent
policies and relevant statistical indexes. The second analyses the market, different
political ideologies and the issue of privatization. The third part is devoted to fiscal
policies, pricing and planning, and incomes policy.

526 **Economic survey, January-September, 1995.**
Valletta: Ministry of Finance (Economic Planning Division), Nov.
1995. 335p.
This survey of the first nine months of the year covers the state of the economy,
labour, productive and service activities, income and prices, trade and finance.
Previous publications in this annual series covered similar topics, albeit more suc-
cinctly.

527 **Threads of dependence.**
John C. Grech.   Msida, Malta: University Press, 1978. 200p. bibliog.
Still the only extensive, penetrating and empirical study of the economic performance
of a section of the manufacturing sector of the Maltese economy since Independence
in 1964. Before this the Government, the British defence establishments and the brewery had been the main employers of Maltese labour. Textile manufacturing
represented one of the few significant sectors of development. The author analyses the
problem of economic development and the transfer of technology, characteristics of
the clothing industry and the results of a survey of thirty clothing firms in Malta in
1976 in the light of their effective integration in an internationalized industry. The
chapters are extensively illuminated and exemplified by tabulated data from this
survey in addition to comparative international and local sectoral economic statistics.

528 **The economic transformation of Malta in the 1960s, with particular reference to manufacturing.**
Huw R. Jones. *Scottish Geographical Magazine*, vol. 87, no. 2 (1971), p. 128-41.
The author finds that, six years after political independence in 1964, Malta seemed well on the way to the achievement of self-sustaining growth though outside capital, both official and private, was still seen to be essential for the programme of economic transformation away from dependence on British military base status.

529 **Recent developments in the political and economic geography of Malta.**
Russell King. *Tijdschrift voor Economische en Sociale Geografie*, vol. 70, no. 5 (1979), p. 258-71.
This brief but very comprehensive assessment of the economic challenges facing Malta in 1979 when the last British forces left their bases on the island puts options and trends for the economic sectors into the – unique – context of resources, population, and politics of the country.

530 **Malta – recent economic developments.**
Washington, DC: International Monetary Fund, June 1995. 113p. (IMF Staff Country Report no. 95/52).
This report prepared by R. Corker et al. reviews the implications for the Maltese economy of deregulation, private sector initiatives, and the opening up of the economy to external competition. Areas covered include the domestic economy, public finance, money and credit, payments, exchange and the trade system. Statistical data are provided by official Maltese sources.

531 **Socio-economic development and the environment in Malta.**
Leonard Mizzi. Bristol, England: University of Bristol, Centre for Mediterranean Studies, 1994. 32p. (Occasional Paper no. 9).
Since the late 1980s the Maltese government has increased the range of initiatives to limit further environmental degradation, partly in the context of the gradual harmonization of Maltese environmental legislation with that of the European Union. The writer outlines the problems for Malta as a small island economy.

532 **The restructuring of the Maltese economy.**
Edward Scicluna. Floriana, Malta: Malta Federation of Industries (publication no. 41), 1993. 74p.
This is one of a series of studies by the author for this association devoted to Malta's export competitiveness, exchange rate policy, wage/price determination, and the effect of EC membership on industry in Malta, published between 1984 and 1991. The author argues for a restructuring in the form of privatization, price and trade liberalization, and the various economic roles for government to fill.

533 **Economic adaptation and development in Malta.**
W. F. Stolper, R. E. R. Hellberg, S. O. Callander. New York: United
Nations Commission for Technical Assistance, Department of
Economic and Social Affairs, 1964. 262p.

This report, prepared for the Government of Malta, discusses constraints on development
planning in Malta and suggests a range of possible approaches and changes to policy
in respect of administration, population, education, finance and capital, and to the
economy. Assumptions behind economic projections are explained (p. 201-06). There
is an outline economic survey of Malta during the decade up to 1964 (p. 207-59).

534 **Sustainable development in Gozo: through the 90s and beyond.**
Valletta: Bank of Valletta, 1992. 62p.

Brief overviews of issues raised at a conference held at Hotel Ta'Ċenċ, Gozo, on 20
November 1992, are accompanied by texts of the papers delivered. The Bank of
Valletta organized the conference in collaboration with the Ministry for Gozo.

535 **Report of the Royal Commission on the finances, economic
condition and judicial procedure of Malta. Minutes of evidence.**
United Kingdom Government. London: HMSO, 1912. Documents
printed as Cd. 6281 (the Report is Cd. 6090).

This record of meetings held in Valletta from 13 November 1911 to 2 January 1912
constitutes one of the landmark sources on political, economic, and social change in
the islands. Submissions and reactions to questions were taken from over sixty
Maltese and locally based UK personnel. Because the main body of the document consists of sequential evidence, the index (p. 487-586) is essential as the key to the
evidence. It is classified by topic, subdivided by contributions relevant to each topic –
these are referenced by paragraph numbers. Inevitably, the balance between topics
reflects the concerns of 1912, with such subjects as administration, education, finance,
land and language having greater prominence.

Economic planning

536 **Development plan for the Maltese Islands, 1959-1964.**
Valletta: Department of Information, 1959. 96p.

Identifies Malta's main resources as its harbours, location, skilled workforce, and
equable climate – in that order (p. 2). 'The mainspring of the programme as a whole is
the aim of making Malta a variable economic unit' (p. 5). This, Malta's first comprehensive plan, assesses each main economic and social area. It was revised in 1961.
Appendix I outlines anticipated annual expenditures.

537 **Development plan for the Maltese Islands, 1964-69.**
Valletta: Department of Information, 1964. 113p.

An overview of the aims and context of the plan (p. 1-16) is followed by a series of
sector/sub-sector appendices covering specific schemes and expenditure estimates.
This, the second five-year development plan, covers the first years after independence
in 1964. It sees Malta's long-term salvation in a competitive industrial structure
largely oriented towards the export market.

538 **Development plan for Malta, 1973-1980.**
Valletta: Office of the Prime Minister, 1974. 206p.

With proportionately more text and fewer statistical tables than its predecessor, this
has chapters on the 'challenges', objectives and their economic, social, and environmental implications, a macro-framework, growth sectors (manufacturing, ship-repair
and ship-building, tourism, agriculture and fisheries, and oil), development institutions, and topics related to the commercial and economic infrastructure. The final
chapter depicts the plan as a 'rallying point' on the way to more jobs in manufacturing, a balanced foreign payments account and regulated public spending in the capital
sector. A *Supplement* appeared in 1977 (Valletta: Office of the Prime Minister. 107p.)
to 'assess progress achieved' (p. 3), identify tasks ahead and to review new opportunities. The *Supplement* includes a fold-out map of the industrial estate planned for
Marsaxlokk.

539 **Development plan for Malta, 1986-88.**
Valletta: Ministry of Trade and Economic Planning, Economic
Division, 1986. 95p.

This, the sixth development plan, covers only three years because of unpredictable
external forces expected to continue to weigh heavily upon the development of Malta.
It follows the fifth plan (see item no. 541) which aimed primarily to achieve economic
consolidation. The sixth plan aimed to strengthen the local infrastructure and to create
new jobs. The document reviews sector and sub-sector progress and objectives but
more briefly than previously and with almost no statistical figures.

540 **Joint mission for Malta. Report, 18 July, 1967.**
Valletta: Department of Information, 1967. 70p.

This joint British-Maltese mission – the Robens Report – studied the prospects for
strengthening the islands' industrial base and employment structure. It reports widely
on tourism, agriculture, the docks, manufacturing, construction, training, etc.

541 **Malta guidelines for progress. Development plan 1981-85.**
Valletta: Office of the Prime Minister, 1981. 240p.

Parts I and II review Malta's past development record. Part III outlines political, economic and social objectives, while part IV puts these into a framework distinguishing
manpower, output, resources, and payments. Monetary and fiscal policies are covered
in part V. Economic resources and human development are, respectively, the topics
for parts VI and VII while part VIII sets out sectoral development programmes. 'The
twin aims of the Fifth Development Plan are consolidation and flexibility' (p. 238).

542 **The Maltese development plan 1973-1980: an economic appraisal.**
K. I. Sams and R. Davies. *Annals of Public and Cooperative Economy*, vol. 46, part 3 (1975), p. 289-302.
This paper assesses the main provision of the plan, the fourth in the current series, in terms of whether problems were correctly identified and suggested measures appropriate and whether the quantitative forecasts made for 1979 were relevant.

543 **Third development plan for the Maltese Islands. 1969-1974.**
Valletta: Office of the Prime Minister, 1970. 134p.
After a two-page introduction, part II reviews and assesses the outcomes of the second plan (1964-69) under objectives, performance, and main features of key sectors. Part III covers the 'demographic problem' including labour supply, while part IV sets out plan policies, their implications for the overall economy and considers financing and public sector investment which is then the subject of detailed tables by annual estimates of expenditure by sector/sub-sector.

Finance and banking

544 **Bank of Valletta – Annual Report.**
Valletta: Bank of Valletta, 1978- . annual.
The 1993 edition, subtitled 'Annual Report and Financial Statements, 1993', contained thirty-three pages (in English). (See also *Rapport*, the in-house journal of the Bank.) Some issues have included articles on Maltese cultural and economic history.

545 **Bank of Valletta Review.**
Valletta: Bank of Valletta, 1990- . twice yearly.
No. 13 (Spring 1996) contained sixty-eight English-language pages of short articles etc. on business and commerce in Malta.

546 **Central Bank of Malta: Annual Report.**
Valletta: Central Bank, 1968- . annual.
Subtitled the 'Twenty-Seventh Annual Report and Statement of Accounts', the 1994 publication has ninety 'glossy' pages (in English). It covers financial developments, commercial banks and other institutions – especially Central Bank operations – plus a balance sheet and profit and loss account.

547 **Central Bank of Malta Quarterly Review.**
Valletta: Central Bank, 1968- . quarterly.
The March 1996 issue contained 116 pages, including statistical tables (p. 69-116). The text (in English) consisted of reviews of economic and financial trends in Malta.

548 **Taxation: an evaluation.**
E. P. Delia.   Msida, Malta: University of Malta, 1981. 83p.
This independent study was commissioned by the Chamber of Commerce, Employers'
Association, Hotels and Restaurants' Association, Institute of Accountants, Institute of
Bankers, Institute of Management, and the Real Estate Federation. The study covers
taxation on expenditure and savings and looks at economic growth and Value Added
Tax (VAT).

549 **Estimates, 1996.**
Floriana, Malta: Ministry of Finance, 1995. 366p.
The data are presented by government branch, with some accompanying text. Annual
volumes in this series appear in the year preceding that in question.

550 **Lombard Bank Annual Report.**
Valletta: The Lombard Bank, 1985- . annual.
This publication reflects the expanding range of interests and business of this bank. It is
also useful indirectly as a commentary on wider developments in the Maltese economy.

551 **Malta financial report 1994.**
Floriana, Malta: The Treasury, 1995. 255p.
This volume includes a comprehensive range of statistical tables with a brief text
supplement. Annual issues in this series, which appear in the year following that to
which they relate, have ranged from 176 to 255 pages in length since the early 1980s.

552 **Malta Stock Exchange Annual Report.**
Valletta: Malta Stock Exchange, 1992- . annual.
The Stock Exchange came into being on 24 January 1991 and trading commenced on
8 January 1992. The report for 1995 consisted of thirty-one glossy pages (in English) of
financial data and comment.

553 **Mid-Med Bank Report and Accounts.**
Valletta: Mid-Med Bank, 1983- . annual.
The 1995 volume, with forty-eight pages, contained a report, financial statement and
glossy illustrations. Previous reports have often included illustrated articles on
Maltese cultural and economic history.

554 **National accounts of the Maltese Islands, 1994.**
Valletta: Central Office of Statistics, 1996. 50p.
Distributed by the Information Directorate, this brief statement offers data by pri-
vate/public sectors, capital, input-output analysis, and payments, with summary tables
and appendices. There is text (p. v-xiii), statistical material (p. xiv-xv, 1-41) and notes
to tables (p. 42-50). See previous annual issues in this series (since 1954).

555 **Report of the Director of Audit for the financial year ended 31st December, 1993.**
Floriana, Malta: Audit Office, 1995. 139p.
See also previous annual issues, variously titled *Audit Report . . .*, *Auditor's Report . . .*, etc.

556 **Malta: international tax planning: a specially commissioned report.**
Patrick Spiteri and Henri Mizzi.   London: Longman Group Ltd. (UK) (Longman Law, Tax and Finance), 1989. 95p. (Longman Intelligence Reports).
Covers Malta's attractions, from a taxation point of view, for the manufacturer seeking a safe and cost-effective location and for banks and insurance companies, in an environment substantially free of governmental bureaucracy. There are sections on taxation, double tax treaties, shipping, and several on offshore trading and finance. The law stated is as at 1 July 1989. The cost of this report is shown as £125.

557 **Notes on income tax in Malta.**
Edwin A. Vella.   Valletta: Progress Press Ltd., c.1968. 272p.
This is a handbook, rather than a textbook, dealing with the operation of the law based on only some sixty court decisions on the subject – though the Board of Special Commissions has delivered about four rulings. An 'Addenda' covering the Act VIII of 1969 was published after the main volume.

Tourism and Leisure

Tourism

558 Peculiar human resources: a case study of a micro-state hotel.
Godfrey Baldacchino. *Tourism Management: Resources, Policies, Practice*, vol. 15, no. 1 (1994), p. 46-52. bibliog.

Based on research in a four-star Maltese hotel, the implications for human resource management are considered with reference to the particular relationships built up in small organizations in small countries.

559 Negotiating the tourist gaze: the example of Malta.
Annabel Black. In: *Coping with tourists. European reactions to mass tourism.* Edited by Jeremy Boissevain. Providence, Rhode Island; Oxford: Berghahn Books, 1996, p. 112-42. bibliog.

This aims to show how, in the case of Malta and in Mellieħa, one of the island's villages, the local experience of mass tourism cannot be understood unless we look at how the linkages between culture, meaning and value are maintained and transformed through a range of often flexible behaviour patterns and attitudes. This process, the topic of this case-study, gives local people a frame of reference within which to respond to the ever-encroaching pressure from visitors. The study is based on the writer's doctoral research in Mellieħa. There is a bibliography (p. 140-42).

560 The impact of tourism on a dependent island: Gozo, Malta.
Jeremy Boissevain. *Annals of Tourism Research*, vol. 6, no. 1 (1979), p. 76-90. bibliog.

Tourism has provided substantial earnings for a few hundred catering and transport entrepreneurs and farmers and a modest income for some 1,600 women and girls producing handicrafts and souvenirs at home. There is some foreign settlement in addition to large numbers of day visitors. However, tourism in Gozo is dominated by Maltese who are sometimes resented as exploiters by Gozitans.

561   **'But we live here!': perspectives on cultural tourism in Malta.**
Jeremy Boissevain.   In: *Sustainable tourism in islands and small states: case studies.*   Edited by L. Briguglio, Richard Butler, David Harrison, Walter Leal Filho.   London: Cassell, 1996, p. 220-40. bibliog.

Following research in Mdina, Malta, in 1993 and 1994, the writer is no longer optimistic about the social and cultural sustainability of tourism in Malta. Not sun, sand and sea, he notes, but culture and action have become the objects of attention of the post-modern tourist. Clearly, as the stream of visitors to Mdina's unique and venerable charm and elegance grows, the 300 residents of the 'monument' become increasingly perturbed at the sight of the hundreds of thousands of strollers through the streets each year. There is a bibliography (p. 238-40).

562   **Ritual, tourism and cultural commoditization in Malta: culture by the pound?**
Jeremy Boissevain.   In: *The tourism image: myths and myth making in tourism.*   Edited by T. Selwyn.   New York: John Wiley and Sons Ltd., 1996, p. 105-20. bibliog.

Boissevain explores the extent to which the commercialization of culture to attract tourists to Malta affects parish celebrations. He argues that the chief factor behind the growth of celebrations is a desire to combat the increase in social distance between neighbours since the 1960s. People in Naxxar and other parts of Malta are expanding their celebrations for themselves, not for tourists.

563   **Tourism multipliers in the Maltese economy.**
Lino Briguglio.   In: *Perspectives on tourism policy.*   Edited by Peter Johnson, Barry Thomas.   London: Mansell, 1992, p. 69-86 (240p.). bibliog.

This chapter estimates tourism multiplier effects using a Keynesian expenditure macro-model and an input-output model. Unlike the former, the latter contains disaggregated information about inter-sectoral relations though, at an aggregate level, they should produce similar results. Despite data limitations, this study organizes Maltese input-output tables so that they can be used in estimates of tourist expenditure, with a view to aiding policy-making.

564   **Tourism in Gozo: policies, prospects and problems.**
Edited by Lino Briguglio.   Blata l-Bajda, Malta: Formatek Ltd. for the University of Malta Gozo Centre and the Foundation for International Studies (Malta), March 1994. 102p. bibliog.

The eleven main papers are the proceedings of a seminar held in Gozo in January 1994 and include several presenting the results of research into tourists and their impact, which include statistical tables. These include: a profile of foreign visitors and their assessment of a stay in Gozo; their impact on the local economy, the environment, the island's archaeological heritage, and the local residents; planning sustainable tourism; and the views of hoteliers.

565 **The competitiveness of the Maltese Islands in Mediterranean**
international tourism.
Lino Briguglio and Leslie Vella.   In: *Island tourism: management*
principles and practice.   Edited by Michael V. Conlin, Tom Baum.
Chichester, England: Wiley & Sons Ltd., 1995, p. 133-47.

This discusses Malta's position in terms of both price, and non-price, related competitiveness compared with other Mediterranean resorts. It uses a tour-operator brochure
analysis, comparing package holidays from the United Kingdom, Germany and the
Netherlands to Malta and other destinations. The conclusion that Malta tends to be
cheaper for the two-week holiday may be explained by the competitive pricing of
daily accommodation rates. However, the writers list factors which may make Malta
an attractive destination despite being uncompetitive on price.

566 **Sustainable tourism in the Maltese Islands.**
Lino Briguglio and Marie Briguglio.   In: *Sustainable tourism in*
islands and small states: case studies.   Edited by Lino Briguglio,
Richard Butler, David Harrison, Walter Leal Filho.   London; New
York: Pinter, 1996, p. 167-79.

Argues that the negative impact of tourism on the environment in small islands, such
as Malta, tends to be relatively large, mostly on account of low carrying capacities and
high densities. It is necessary to minimize environmental damage without threatening
the short-run economic well-being of the host country. Inevitably, tourism will never
be environmentally neutral but, at least, this study heightens awareness of the problem.

567 **Tourism in Gozo: what future?: proceedings of a seminar,**
organized by the Centre for Social Research (Social Action
Movement) on the 9th June, 1989.
Edited by J. Felice Pace.   Valletta: Studia Editions, 1989. 60p.

This is a presentation by government officials on the prospects for the island in the
light of environmental concerns, the need for infrastructural changes, and the pattern
of external demand, accompanied by illustrations. (See a similar report on a 23 April
1988 conference, edited by Kenneth Wain, also published by Studia Editions,
Valletta.)

568 **Recent trends in Maltese tourism.**
D. G. Lockhart and S. E. Ashton.   *Geography*, no. 316, vol. 72, part 3
(1987), p. 255-58.

Notes improvements in the prospects for tourism in Malta including agreement
between the Maltese and UK governments, leading to a substantial revival, and the
reorganization of the National Tourism Organisation in Malta (in December 1984).
Relaxation of the law restricting foreign ownership has also promised to boost numbers of arrivals.

569   **Tourism in Malta.**
Douglas G. Lockhart, Susan E. Ashton.   *Scottish Geographical Magazine,* vol. 107, no. 1 (1991), p. 22-32. maps.
This traces the evolution of tourism in Malta since 1955 with data from a questionnaire survey of holiday visitors. The authors focus on the uneven impact of tourism, the dependence on UK visitors, and infrastructural and environmental implications. Future prospects for the industry are briefly assessed along with marketing strategies.

570   **Tourism in Malta and Cyprus.**
D. G. Lockhart.   In: *Island tourism: trends and prospects.*   Edited by D. G. Lockhart, D. Drakakis-Smith.   London: Pinter, 1997, p. 152-78 (352p.).
Tourism has developed rapidly in both islands since the early 1960s. This chapter examines the distribution of accommodation and the pattern of tourist arrivals by nationality and by season and looks at the economic and environmental impact of tourism development. The limited role of planning in both islands is discussed.

571   **A plan for Gozo. A case study of problems of tourism and conservation.**
Ian Masser.   *Town Planning Review,* vol. 40, no. 2 (1969), p. 230-50.
A report to the Director of Public Works in Malta by a group of postgraduate planning students from the University of Liverpool, England. It recognizes that Gozo's most outstanding resource is its landscape, that the island is still largely dependent on a traditional farming economy, that industrialization promises little – and would involve locational and landscape difficulties – and that tourism represents the most practicable remedy for the problems of Gozo, given its accelerator effect.

572   **Island travel yearbook. 1996.**
Terence Mirabelli (editor-in-chief).   Valletta: Island Publications Limited, 1996. 296p.
This is a glossy, comprehensive reference book for the travel trade. It offers current information on tourism in Malta, covering touristic attractions, travel, food and accommodation, special interest activities, and short biographical sketches of entrepreneurs and personalities in the tourism business in Malta and Gozo. Extensive advertising lists of addresses, etc. are also included. This volume replaces previous issues from the same source.

573   **Presenting the past: cultural tour-guides and the sustaining of European identity in Malta.**
Jon P. Mitchell.   In: *Sustainable tourism in islands and small states: case studies.*   Edited by L. Briguglio, Richard Butler, David Harrison, and Walter Leal Filho.   London: Cassell, 1996, p. 199-219. bibliog.
Examines the role of Maltese tour-guides in creating and perpetuating images of Malta which have helped to sustain tourist development. Guides present an image of continuity in a European Malta – even 5,000-year-old temple sites show the length of Malta's religious experience and, of course, such ancient sites were European . . . By promoting a European image guides may themselves contribute to the stability of

tourism. The author undertook doctoral research in Malta, particularly in Valletta, from 1992-94.

574   **National Tourism Organization: Annual Report and Accounts.**
      Valletta: National Tourism Organization, 1989- . annual.
The most recent edition, for 1995, has thirty-eight pages. It is aimed at a general readership.

575   **Maltese crossroad.**
      Terry Stevens et al.   *Leisure Management*, vol. 9, no. 2 (1989),
      p. 56-60.
This examines how a small island economy, heavily dependent on tourism, is reassessing its position in the market.

Sport and pastimes

576   **Treasures of the Maltese waters: part one: shore dives.**
      Simon Aquilina.   St. Paul's Bay, Malta: Aquilina Enterprises Ltd.,
      1995. 64p.
Introduces fifteen diving sites from the coast of Malta and includes sketch maps and coloured illustrations of aquatic flora and fauna.

577   **Goals, cups, and tears: a history of Maltese football. Volume one**
      1886-1919, the golden age of Maltese football.
      Carmel Baldacchino.   Valletta: Buġelli Publications, 1989. 427p.
This is identified as the first of a six-volume set. Volume two, on '1919-1934, the great amateur era' (1990. 591p.) was followed by volume three on '1933-1944, glory and upheaval' (1991. 456p.). Volume four was not available for examination at the time of writing. It was followed, in 1994, by volume five covering '1957-1968, the coming-of-age of Maltese football' (511p.). Volume six was said to be in press. These very substantial works of record on soccer in Malta and Gozo provide very full details of clubs, games, results, players, etc. The texts outline major events and trends during the different periods.

578   **Malta new climbs – Malta: 1986 supplement.**
      Roger Brookes, Simon Alden.   [s.l.]: Fylde Mountaineering Club,
      1987. 77p.
Supplements the first definitive guidebook for climbing in Malta, published by the Royal Navy Mountaineering Club in 1971, and reflects the resurgence of interest during the 1980s from local and visiting climbers alike. Over 156 new routes were identified in 1985-86 alone. Sketch-maps, drawings and photographs support the data on the climbs identified.

579 **The yachtsman's handbook and cruising guide to Malta.**
Roland Darmanin Kissaun.   Balzan, Malta: Commercial Advertising
Services, 1990. 79p.
A concise illustrated and data-packed guide offering basic information for yachtsmen,
with local details, coastal charts, photographs, and relevant advertising.

580 **Bird shooting and trapping in Malta: a traditional sports (sic).**
Natalino Fenech.   *Hyphen*, vol. 7, no. 2 (1992), p. 58-66. bibliog.
A review of this controversial sport in Malta, and the high percentage of the popula-
tion with a shooting licence contrasted with the small size of the island.

581 **Fatal flight: the Maltese obsession with killing birds.**
Natalino Fenech.   London: Quiller Press Ltd., 1992. 174p. bibliog.
With a comprehensive bibliography (p. 141-54), illustrations and a brief foreword by
David Bellamy, the conservationist, this is the substantive text on its subject. It covers
the practices and social context of bird shooting and looks at the development of bird
protection legislation up to the 1980s. The central argument about bird shooting is that
'the practice has got to be stopped'.

582 **Rock climbing in Malta.**
J. D. Graham.   Valletta: Royal Navy Mountaineering Club, 1971.
103p.
This survey identifies the climbing sites of Malta. There is an index of climbs and
information on equipment required in Malta.

583 **A football saga: fifty years of football in Malta.**
Joe H. Griffiths.   Hamrun, Malta: Publishers Enterprise Group, 1985.
265p.
The text, written in a racy style, traces the development of football in the 20th century.
It includes league results for 1909-84 (p. 241-65).

584 **History of water polo in Malta, 1910-1988.**
Arthur J. Leaver.   Valletta: Progress Press, 1990. 177p.
This comprehensive volume gives a detailed account of the organization and development of the sport, with information on games, teams, players and results. It is
extensively illustrated with black-and-white photographs. A supplement, *History of
water polo in Malta, 1989-1990* (21p.), was followed by further – longer – supplements in 1994 and 1995.

585 **Malta Football Association. Official handbook, 1987.**
Valletta: Malta Football Association, 1987. 242p.
The principal source for rules and regulations governing organized soccer in Malta.
An amendment published in 1990 covered alterations and additions up to 8 September
1989.

586 Scouting in Malta: an illustrated history.
J. A. Mizzi. Malta: The Author, 1989. 505p.

The text is packed with nearly 500 black-and-white photographs and other illustrations, which bring to life the progress of scouting in the islands (p. 8-428). Appendices are included on p. 429-85 and indexes on p. 487-505. This is the definitive source on the development of scouting for boys in Malta and Gozo since 1908.

587 Participation in sport. Survey results.
Floriana, Malta: Ministry for Youth and the Arts (Malta), 1992. 205p.

Provides tables of information based on a survey of 400 respondents from 20 localities in the islands. Statistical data are included on p. 25ff.

588 The football yearbook, 1996-97.
Edited by Lewis Portelli. Valletta: Mid-Med Bank, 1996. 140p.

First published in 1986, this annual coverage of results, teams, statistics, advertising, etc. is now in its tenth edition which includes new sections to offer a comprehensive survey of the whole competitive structure of the Malta Football Association.

589 The bird black hole.
Kenny Taylor. *B.B.C. Wildlife*, (May 1991), p. 324-29.

With photographs by Natalino Fenech, this article highlights the competition between Malta's government and conservationists, on the one hand, and the islands' many hunters and trappers of birds, on the other. The writer concludes that this sport – long established in Malta as in other Mediterranean areas – is at last facing serious challenge.

Trade and Industry

590 Enemalta Corporation. Annual report, 1992.
Marsa, Malta: Enemalta Corporation, 1992. 32p.
Reports on energy consumption in Malta for the year, 1 October 1991 to 30 September 1992, with a summary and financial review (p. 17-20). See also previous issues in this annual series.

591 Industrial statistics, 1992.
Valletta: Central Office of Statistics, 1995. 2 vols. 89p. + 304p.
Volume 1 offers 'summary tables' plus a 'commentary' (p. i-iii). Volume 2 presents detailed data tables. Annual volumes similar to these have appeared since 1987. From 1979 to 1986 there were annual issues of a *Census of Industrial Production* with the same format of summary and main data volumes. Prior to 1979 they carried the title, *Census of Production*. The statistics in the series derive from a postal questionnaire sent to all establishments in manufacturing, construction and quarrying in Malta. The data presented range from output, materials, fuel, value added, wages and salaries, to stocks, personnel/employment, and investment.

592 Made in Malta, 1992: manufacturers and exporters.
San Ġwann, Malta: Malta Export Trade Corporation Ltd. published in association with Crest Publicity Limited, 1992. 260p.
This glossy handbook, produced by Malta Export Trade Corporation Ltd. (METCO), replaces previous issues. It contains a wide range of information, addresses, product and service sections and substantial amounts of advertising.

593 Malta Development Corporation. Annual report and accounts, 1991.
Valletta: Malta Development Corporation, 1992. 19p.
Outlines the continuing initiatives in industrial development in the islands. Similar reports have been appearing for some years, although issues in the 1980s were longer – up to 64p.

594 **Malta Export Trade Corporation. Annual report 1994.**
San Ġwann, Malta: Malta Export Trade Corporation Ltd., 1994. 28p.
Established on Malta Government initiative in 1989 to promote trade, METCO here presents a report (18p.) and (separate) 'Financial statements' (10p.).

595 **Malta Federation of Industry. Annual report, 1995.**
Floriana, Malta: Malta Federation of Industry, 1995. 38p.
This is a colourfully illustrated glossy survey of internal developments, Federation of Industry events and contacts with the Maltese government and with local and foreign organizations. Key people are identified. This volume is one in an established annual series which began in 1977.

596 **Malta trade directory 1996.**
Valletta: The Malta Chamber of Commerce in association with Crest Publicity Ltd., 1996. 640p.
This annual directory contains a mass of data on industry, finance, docks and shipping, trade, setting up companies, tourism and public institutions. It includes classified indexes, lists of addresses, brands, etc. and a range of advertising. It has been vastly expanded since the first issue of the directory appeared in 1966.

597 **The saga of Simonds Farsons Cisk.**
Edward Sammut. Mrieħel, Malta: Simonds Farsons Cisk Ltd., 1988. 80p.
In the days when the Maltese economy was the dockyard, the defence establishments and the NAAFI, the only other single substantial employer was the brewery. Formed from the merger of several separate companies it remains a significant employer. The author, well known as a local art historian, was the company secretary from 1958 and subsequently a director. He traces the connection of Simonds brewery to Malta from 1875, followed by its merger with Farrugia & Sons, originally a milling company, in 1929 which effectively founded the brewing industry in the island. A large new art deco brewery was built in 1946-47 and the following year the company merged with the Marquis Scicluna's Cisk Brewery. The book concludes with the launch of Kinnie as a popular effervescent soft drink and the appointment of Anthony Miceli Farrugia as Managing Director. Owing to the author's death in 1984 the remaining chapters were unwritten. There are photographic illustrations of leading directors and of the various company plants.

598 **Ark, business directory, 1989.**
Edited by Ray Soler. Valletta: Ark Publishing, 1989. 578p.
This is a comprehensive source of reference on Malta's importers, manufacturers and exporters and their products, together with details of other companies and their services – plus advertising. An index of commodities and functions (p. ix-xxiv) and a detailed list of contents (p. xxv-xviii) are included. This directory indicates that further editions will follow.

599   **Malta: an emerging container port.**
Ray Towse.   *Geographical Magazine*, vol. 67, no. 3 (1995), p. 53-55.
A brief consideration of Malta's free-port development. Its investment to 1996 totals
$500 million. Some ninety per cent of Malta's container traffic is trans-shipment busi-
ness. The future looks promising.

600   **Trade statistics 1995.**
Valletta: Central Office of Statistics, 1996. 1,143p.
This compendium of data consists of three parts. The 'Preliminary report' (163p.)
includes a very brief text introduction (p. 1-2). 'Part 1' covers the months January to
March. It has an introductory text (p. i-ix) to the tables (p. x-xvi and 3-574). 'Part 2'
completes the coverage of information for the year with data tables (p. 575-1,134) and
an index (p. 1,138-43). Previous annual issues in this series appeared in varying for-
mats.

601   **The Federation of Industries: four decades of service to industry of
Malta.**
Mario Vassallo.   Floriana, Malta: Federation of Industries, 1986.
119p. bibliog.
The Federation was founded in 1946 and the four chapters trace the issues with which
it has since been involved, one of which is its relations with the socialist administration from 1971-85. The appendices include lists of founder members and office
holders and seven photographs.

Agriculture and Fisheries

602 **Cultivation and diseases of fruit trees in the Maltese Islands.**
J. Borġ. Valletta: Government Printing Office, 1922. 622p.

Though neither illustrated nor indexed, this continues to be a valuable reference work on its subject, though not all the extensive text is specifically about Malta. It also constitutes a valuable bench-mark for the time when it was compiled in view of the more recent transformation and decline of agriculture in the islands.

603 **A report on the fishing industry of Malta.**
T. W. Burdon. Valletta: Government Printing Office, 1956. 79p.

This, the first major study since that by J. Hornell in 1931, looks at the context of fishing and, in particular, at the market for fish, at boats, and at methods, and offers twenty-five recommendations. There are data on catches, boats, etc. This key study is illustrated with maps, diagrams and photographs. Its main concerns – decline in numbers of personnel, fish imports, and lack of secondary industries such as canning – remain relevant today.

604 **Malta: food, agriculture, fisheries and the environment.**
Edited by Salvino Busuttil, with François Lerin, Leonard Mizzi.
Montpellier, France: Institut Agronomique Méditerranéen de Montpellier, 1993. 192p. bibliog.

As volume 2 in a series on Mediterranean agriculture, this important publication contains brief reviews of the historical, environmental and economic contexts of Maltese farming, followed by a sectoral analysis made up of twelve articles by contributors on changing eating habits, agricultural land use, the structure plan, irrigation supply, agro-industry, wine growing and making, fishing, aquaculture, the 1988 FAO report, Malta's entry to the EC (2) and population and urban density. There is an extensive bibliography – unannotated – of over 200 titles of which all but a few are in English (p. 155-66).

605 **Census of agriculture and fisheries, 1979-80.**
Valletta: Central Office of Statistics, 1982. 75p.
Presents data collected from farm holders and livestock breeders. In 1979-80 these numbered 13,112 and there was a 95 per cent response rate. The data given are for personnel, holdings, cultivation, sales, prices, inputs/outputs, livestock, milk, machinery and implements, greenhouses, fishing population, fishing craft and implements, quantity and value of catches.

606 **Land use change in Malta.**
W. A. Charlton, B. W. Beeley. *Land Use Policy*, (April 1987), p. 96-101.
Looks at Maltese agricultural land use in general – and in particular at an area near Mellieħa – and considers changes since the 1950s against the background of political and economic transformation during those decades.

607 **Agriculture, land use and resource transformation in Malta.**
William A. Charlton, Brian W. Beeley. *Tijdschrift voor Economische en Sociale Geografie*, vol. 84, no. 5 (1993), p. 325-31. bibliog.
Uses field survey data to assess the scale and implications of changes in agricultural land use since the 1950s. The survey was conducted at eleven locations between 1984 and 1989 to identify changes evident since the Durham University survey published in 1961. The disappearance of Malta's remaining rural-agricultural landscape must be urgently reviewed for economic as well as aesthetic reasons.

608 **Report on the social aspects of Maltese agriculture.**
Renato Cirillo. Valletta: University of Malta, 1959. 120p.
This reports on pioneering intensive fieldwork carried out jointly by the Department of Geography at the University of Durham and the Royal University of Malta. A range of subjects were investigated, from farmer's perceptions and consumption patterns to practices of farming and production.

609 **The fishing industry in Malta. Past – present – future.**
Stanley Farrugia Randon. Pietà, Malta: Independence Print, 1995. 195p. bibliog.
A descriptive account of the fishing trade and its history based on research at the National Archives in Valletta as well as in fishing villages in Malta and Gozo. The author reviews the history of the Fisheries Department, the marketing system, fishing methods, fishing craft, and current aquacultural problems in the Mediterranean. Appendices contain: an outline history of fishery regulation in Malta; a statistical appendix of fish landed; black-and-white drawings of thirty-three common edible sea fish by Rio Sammut; and a brief biography of Guiseppe Despott, the first Superintendent of Fisheries.

610 **Mediterranean agriculture: subtropical fruit and grain cultivation.**
Paul A. R. Newbury. In: *A geography of agriculture.* Plymouth,
England: Macdonald & Evans, 1980, p. 170-85 (chapter xi).
Newbury takes the case of Maltese agriculture as representative of conditions in the
Mediterranean area more generally. He looks briefly at the operations of two Maltese
farmers. The author demonstrates the problems of Maltese farming in a very limited
and difficult environment.

611 **Report on the working of the Department of Agriculture during
October 1938 to September 1946 and the agricultural year 1946-47.**
Valletta: Directorate of Agriculture, 1949. 154p.
Covers the critical years of war and siege and presents a range of statistical data on
crops, cultivation, livestock, and the farming community, along with an account of
measures undertaken. It was published as *Malta Government Gazette* Supplement
no. CXVI, 8 November 1949.

612 **Agriculture in the Maltese Islands. A bibliography.**
Compiled by Nora Sammut. Msida, Malta: University of Malta
Library, 1979. n.p.
This lists 565 titles, mostly annotated, and includes an author index. Most of the titles
listed are in English as are all the annotations.

613 **Technical change and the survival of family farming in Malta:
public and private goals in resource management.**
David Short, Alan Tricker. *Journal of Rural Studies*, vol. 10, no. 2
(1994), p. 211-21.
Based on a pilot study in Malta, this paper describes the response of a group of small-
scale family farmers to superimposed technological change in the form of an
'environmentally sound' treated effluent irrigation scheme at Sant'Antnin in southeast
Malta.

614 **Traditional-style farming and values for sustainable development
in Malta.**
David Short. *Tijdschrift voor Economische en Sociale Geografie*,
vol. 88, no. 1 (1997), p. 41-52.
In rural Malta, which seems to have 'lagged behind' in an uneven modernization
process, surviving traditional styles of farming offer the prospect of more 'ecological',
less environmentally threatening, forms of production. This article presents the
findings of a survey of Maltese farm-based opinion on prospects for development in
such a context. There is a special case-study focus on the Sant'Antnin recycled
effluent irrigation scheme as an exceptional example of environmentally sensitive
government investment in the Maltese context (p. 43-50). The area covered by the
scheme was chosen for the survey because it shows the choice between 'productivist'
and 'environmentalist' development.

615   **Report on the present condition of agriculture in the Maltese Islands.**
F. A. Stockdale.   Valletta: Government Printing Office, 1934. 51p.

A report to the Secretary of State for the Colonies on a visit in March and April 1934, covering all aspects of farming and the management of agriculture in the islands. It recommends the reorganization of marketing, the early completion of a Government Farm, the immunization of goats against undulant fever, etc.

616   **Marsaxlokk: an ethnography of a Maltese fishing village.**
Finn Wilhelmsen.   Ann Arbor, Michigan: PhD thesis in Cultural Anthropology at Wayne State University, Detroit, Michigan, 1976. 665p. bibliog. Available from Ann Arbor, Michigan: University Microfilms International, 1977.

The author spent six months living in Malta's largest fishing village from 1969-70 followed by very short visits in 1971 and 1973 and a month in September 1974 during the *Lampuki* fishing season. He discusses: the significant types of people in a fisherman's network – his kin, patrons, salesmen and consumers; the regular pattern of the fishing day and year; attitudes to foreigners, other Maltese, themselves and fishing; formal rituals of the local Christian calendar; folk beliefs and cultural patterns; factors of change; networks, friendship, the crew and co-residence; and the structure of conflict and its resolution, process of socialization, and social rules. The appendices include a wealth of information on fishing practices and terminology, fish marketing, gear and boats, and local methods of classifying their fish, as well as maps of Malta and Marsaxlokk. Photographs and diagrams illustrate the text and there is a bibliography on p. 656-65.

Transport and Communications

617 **Air Malta. Annual report and accounts, 1993.**
Luqa, Malta: Air Malta, 1993. 44p.
A glossy review of the year in question precedes the financial statements (p. 28-44). In annual issues up to 1991 the financial statement section was entitled 'Accounts'.

618 **The Gozo-Malta ferry service from prehistory to present days.**
Joseph Bezzina. Valletta: Buġelli, 1991. 48p.
Despite its subsidiary title, *Il-vapur ta'Għawdex* (The Gozo ferry), this well illustrated text is in English only. It is written for a general readership.

619 **The Malta buses.**
Joseph Bonnici, Michael Cassar. Malta: The Authors, 1989. 208p.
This traces the development of the bus system in Malta from 1905 with the aid of many photographs of buses (some in colour) and of scenes involving bus transport, supported by text, tabulated data, and copies of relevant documents.

620 **The Malta railway.**
Joseph Bonnici, Michael Cassar. Malta: The Authors, 1988. 154p.; 1992. rev. ed. 192p.
This account of the narrow-gauge line between Valletta and Rabat, which was opened in 1883 and extended to Mtarfa in 1900 only to close completely in 1931, is substantially illustrated with photographs and documents.

621 **The Malta Tramway and the Barraca Lift.**
Joseph Bonnici, Michael Cassar. Malta: The Authors, 1991. 184p.
Profusely illustrated with black-and-white photographs, etc., this volume deals with the short period of electric traction in Malta and completes the trilogy on transport in the islands by the two authors.

146

622 **Broadcasting Authority. Annual report and accounts, 1995.**
Blata l-Bajda, Malta: Broadcasting Authority, 1996.
Designed for a public readership.

623 **Maritime votive paintings in Maltese churches.**
Andrew Cuschieri, Joseph Muscat. *Melita Historica,* vol. 10, no. 2
(1989), p. 121-44. bibliog.
The article outlines the function, forms and maritime details of this genre of painting
with illustrations of three of those to be found in the Żabbar Sanctuary.

624 **The *Dgħajsa – in memoriam.***
Joseph Muscat. *The Mariner's Mirror,* vol. 77, no. 4 (Nov. 1991),
p. 389-405. bibliog.
The author has established that this Maltese harbour passenger boat was adapted to
Admiralty specifications for the use of the Royal Navy in the Mediterranean. All
British warships on the station carried one as a harbour ferryboat. With the exception
of those designed for the annual regatta on the weekend of 7 September, the *Dgħajsa*
is now extinct. The author provides information on types of racing boat, their current
construction and district racing colours, and delineates the evolution of these passenger ferries from 1664 to the present in plans and profiles. The journal is published by
the Society for Nautical Research.

625 **Maltese ship and boat building, eighteenth and nineteenth
centuries.**
Joseph Muscat. In: *The evolution of wooden shipbuilding in the
Eastern Mediterranean during the 18th and 19th centuries.* Athens:
Ministry of Culture and UNESCO, 1993, p. 69-89.
A curator of the Maritime Museum in Birgu, Malta, outlines the means by which boats
were built under the Order of St. John and the types of boat constructed, followed by
the major Royal Naval dockyard and two private shipyards operating during the first
half century of British rule, and subsequent developments in order to build steam-
powered vessels as well as local arrangements for harbour ferry and fishing boat
building. This is a significant attempt to trace the growth of the Maltese mercantile
fleet during these periods. The Galley, or Dockyard, Creek was reserved for warships
but French Creek was where merchant shipbuilding expanded and provided work for
many people in the Cottonera area.

626 **In peril on the sea: marine votive paintings in the Maltese Islands.**
A. H. J. Prins. Malta: SAID International Ltd., 1989. 206p.
This significant monograph by a Dutch anthropologist consists of three parts. The first
provides both the analysis and a gazetteer of shrines and votive paintings. The second
consists of forty-five colour plates which formed an exhibition at the Cathedral
Museum in Mdina. And the third part consists of three tables, a map and forty-one
line-drawings of Mediterranean and local ships and craft by Joseph Muscat, one of the
founding curators of the Maritime Museum in Birgu.

627   **A sustainable transport policy for tourism on small islands: a case**
       study of Malta.
       Derek Robins.   In: *Sustainable tourism in islands and small states:*
       case studies.   Edited by L. Briguglio, Richard Butler, David Harrison,
       Walter Leal Filho.   London: Cassell, 1996, p. 180-98.

The author identifies ways of increasing bus use for both tourists and local people at
the expense of the private car. He also outlines other measures to control the take-over
by the automobile in Malta.

628   **Shipping and aviation statistics, 1995.**
       Valletta: Central Office of Statistics, distributed by the Department of
       Information, 1996. 186p.

Apart from a brief text summary (p. i-viii), this volume – and its annual predecessors
– consists of a range of statistical data. Topics covered are shipping (p. 3-62), aviation
(p. 65-83), passengers (p. 87-164), and tourists (p. 167-86).

629   **Telemalta Corporation. Annual report 1995-96.**
       St. Julian's, Malta: Telemalta Corporation, 1996. 33p.

This annual provides some information on the operation of the nationalized system of
telecommunications.

630   **Transport: a pillar of sustainable development in Gozo.**
       Valletta: Bank of Valletta, 1993. 65p.

This collection of presentations at a conference organized by the Bank in Mġarr, Gozo
on 26 November 1993, includes papers on the role of pricing, physical planning,
policy towards Europe, and transport itself – including its role in social and economic
cohesion.

631   **Malta aviation yearbook, 1994.**
       Edited by John Visanach.   Luqa, Malta: Malta Aviation Society,
       1994. 38p.

The preceding edition appears to have been that of 1989 (44p.) when the Society was
known as the Association of Aircraft Enthusiasts. The 1989 issue was edited by
Carmel Attard in Żabbar, Malta. These volumes collect together a range of information on aircraft and flying.

Labour and Labour Relations

632 **Industrial relations in Malta (1984): a study.**
Joseph Attard. Ħamrun, Malta: PEG Publication, 1984. 194p.
Part one provides a history of industrial relations in Malta, including the effects of legislation and the origins and functions of trades unions. Part two is devoted to the Industrial Relations Act, 1976. Part three considers the operation of worker participation in industry. This book provides a useful review of the aims and implementation of the Malta Labour Government's legislation.

633 **Wages policy at Malta Drydocks: analysis of an ambivalence.**
Godfrey Baldacchino. *Economic and Social Studies*, vol. 4 (1987-88), p. 29-50. bibliog.
Relatively high, fixed wage rates pertain in this self-managed firm operating with a substantial government subsidy, which the author attributes to a colonial work ethic. But the alternative economic and political implications for Malta of putting this labour aristocracy on the dole are not discussed.

634 **A review of Maltese trade unionism: analysis based on the annual reports of the register of trade unions.**
Godfrey Baldacchino. *Economic and Social Studies*, vol. 5 (1989-90), p. 64-82. bibliog.
An outline of trade union development as well as that of the labour market from 1976-89, and the numbers of workers banned from joining unions. Of the thirty-one unions registered in 1977, twenty-three had dissolved by 1985 and five new ones had been formed. It was a period in which the Labour Government strongly fostered its own General Workers' Union but those elected to the new compulsory works councils often represented quite different unions and political interests.

635 **Worker cooperatives with particular reference to Malta: an educationist's theory and practice.**
Godfrey Baldacchino. The Hague: Institute for Social Studies, 1990. 157p. bibliog.

The first part of the book argues the case for worker co-operatives, outlines a successful strategy and focuses on education in the ideological battle. Part two applies these to Malta and considers the local environment, the local co-operative sector, and the role of colonial experience, the Maltese labour movement, the Nationalist Party, the Roman Catholic Church, and the actual practice of co-operation in various local enterprises. The appendices comprise two maps and five tables.

636 **Cooperative ways of working: towards a Mediterranean research project.**
Edited by Godfrey Baldacchino, Saviour Rizzo, Edward L. Żammit. Msida, Malta: Workers' Participation Development Centre, University of Malta with Friedrich Ebert Stiftung, 1994. 205p. bibliog.

Two of the papers in this symposium relate to Malta. One provides an historical outline of the co-operative movement in Malta. The other is a case-study of aspects of the Spotless Cleaning and Maintenance Cooperative originally set up in 1992 to care for the grounds of the University which has subsequently extended its range of contracted operations.

637 **Graduates on the labour market: a tracer project: final report for the Foundation of Human Resources Development, the Employment and Training Corporation and the University of Malta.**
Godfrey Baldacchino. Msida, Malta: Workers' Participation Development Centre, University of Malta, 1995. 110p. bibliog.

Following the rapid expansion of higher education in Malta, both government and employers became concerned about matching supply and demand. The seventy-nine tables in this report detail the responses of graduates and employers to the questionnaires that are reproduced in the appendices. Broadly speaking both considered graduates to be flexible workers but employers considered that, excepting law, nongraduates would be just as competent. Graduates set a high priority on postgraduate education with university employment as a potential goal but employers wanted postgraduate studies to be more vocational and management orientated.

638 **Global tourism and informal labour relations: the small scale syndrome at work.**
Godfrey Baldacchino. London: Mansell, 1997. 187p. bibliog.

This book is based on fieldwork undertaken in hotels in Malta and Barbados, for which the management and employee questionnaires are provided in appendices. It offers a rare comparative analysis of the experience of work within the worldwide expansion of tourism and the encounter of global agents with local forces. In transnational hotel chains top-down corporate philosophy meets the street wisdom of local employees. This collision of values, embodied in employee relations, is described and its implications analysed with reference to professional management and organized labour. A film and discography are provided as well as tables and maps and an appendix of basic data on the world's small developing states. The author also published a summary of his research, 'Labour recruitment in the hospitality industry: a different lesson in the sustainability of small and island states', in *Sustainable tourism in islands and small states*, edited by Lino Briguglio, Brian Archer, Jafar Jafari, Geoffrey Wall (London: Pinter, 1996, p. 161-69. bibliog.).

639 **The challenges ahead: Confederation of Malta Trade Unions XIX Congress, Foundation for International Studies, University of Malta, Valletta, Malta, 24-26 February, 1993.**
Valletta: Confederation of Malta Trade Unions, 1993. 66p. bibliog.
During the years of the Nationalist Government in the decade after 1985, the Maltese trade unions witnessed a significant change in the policies of the Malta Labour Party as well as the potential challenge to be faced if Malta joined the European Union. This report outlines these problems and prospects as considered by the Congress.

640 **The labour market of schooling: Maltese girls in education and economic planning.**
Mary Darmanin. *Gender and Education*, vol. 4, no. 1/2 (1992), p. 105-26. bibliog.
An analysis of the relationship between the planners' perception of the market, school curricula, the available jobs, and the general maintenance of feminized choices for girls. This pattern could change with the redirection of the economy away from low-skilled industrial work for women.

641 **Landmarks in medical unionism in Malta 1937-1987.**
Lino J. German. Attard, Malta: Media Centre Publications, 1991. 236p.
Part of Malta's post-war politics is epitomized by Prime Minister Mintoff's conflict with the local medical profession, a well-trained and numerous body providing private but cheap general practice and a largely free government hospital service. The first clash with a Labour Government in 1956 was won by the Maltese branch of the British Medical Association but the second in 1977 lasted a decade and led directly to the closure of the university and the dismissal of local doctors who refused to sign the government's directive. The author was Hon. Sec. of the Medical Association of Malta from 1973-88 and here provides his account of the conflict, supported by thirteen documentary appendices and details of significant people and events. The conflict concerned the status and clinical direction of the medical profession, and their freedom to conduct private practice outside the public hospital. It also concerned the direction of junior doctors and those about to graduate from the medical school.

642 **The industrialization of Malta: a historical analysis of the formation, control and response of Labour.**
In: *Issues*. Malta: The New Economic Society, 1988, p. 60-87. bibliog.
A useful review of phases and types of industrialization and the response of organized labour, with six tables showing the size and strike action of trade unions under different government policies.

151

643   **Factors affecting the size of the Maltese labour force.**
Carmel Inguanez, Lino Briguglio.   *Economics and Social Studies*,
vol. 3 (1986), p. 7-22. bibliog.
The labour force has increased in line with the population of working age. As wage
rates increase, more women enter the labour force. Future trends are discussed.

644   **Transition to workers' self-management: its dynamics in the
decolonising economy of Malta.**
Gerard Kester.   The Hague: Institute of Social Studies, 1980. 255p.
bibliog. (Research Report Series no. 7).
During Mintoff's second Labour Government from 1971, the Malta Drydocks was
reorganized on the basis of workers' participation in management through the General
Workers' Union. This study charts this process and its extension to other parastatal
industries by a government whose role is characterized as being 'manipulatory
reformist'.

645   **The General Workers' Union, Malta: information dossier.**
Edited by Karmenu Micallef.   Valletta: Union Press, 1990. 112p.
2 maps.
A handbook of information on the primary industrial workers' union in Malta, outlining its history, organization, functions, relations with the Malta Labour Party and trade
union laws, rights and freedoms in Malta. From representing the dockyard workers,
the union attained a much more general membership during the rise and periods in
office of the Malta Labour Party, to which it was formally attached.

646   **Child workers in Malta: critical perspectives on a new underclass.**
Ronald G. Sultana.   *Economic and Social Studies: Journal of Malta*,
vol. 7 (1993-94), p. 44-66. bibliog.
After outlining the legislative restrictions on child labour, the paper explains the susceptibility of the Maltese economy to such practice, including the high percentage of
children attending private tuition after school hours. The bulk of the text discusses relevant aspects of a survey carried out in trade schools and in Gozitan secondary
schools.

647   **The University of Malta. Workers' Participation Development
Centre. First annual report (March-December, 1981).**
Msida, Malta: University of Malta, 1981. 7p.
This is a brief statement and accounts of the WPDC established in March 1981, to
promote and co-ordinate workers' participation in the Maltese economy. Most of the
activities of the WPDC involve training courses and seminars. (Subsequent annual
reports were longer: e.g. the report for 1989 was 26p.)

648   **Women workers in industrial estates: a survey of their needs and facilities: a report prepared for the Commission for the Advancement of Women.**
Msida, Malta: Workers' Participation Development Centre, University of Malta, 1992. 29p.

A report of the results of a survey in seven areas of Malta and Gozo. In nine tables a wide range of basic social data is presented, as well as that on working conditions, wages, and the facilities for child care available to working mothers. The publication concludes with a set of recommendations.

649   **Transition to workers' self management.**
Edward L. Żammit, Edward J. Scicluna, Adrian Gauci, Pauline Mireli. Msida, Malta: University of Malta Press for the Institute of Social Studies, The Hague, and the Workers' Participation Development Centre, University of Malta, 1981. 75p. (Workers' Education Series, no. 1).

This reports on the Maltese experience of the development of workers' participation since 1971 but traces its origins back to 1920, when the Malta Labour Party was founded. The compilers focus on the context of worker participation through the run-down of the dockyard and defence bases and the transition to workers' self-management in Malta and the establishment of a Workers' Participation Development Centre at the University of Malta.

650   **A colonial inheritance: Maltese perceptions of work, power and class structure with reference to the labour movement.**
Edward L. Żammit.   Msida, Malta: Malta University Press, 1984. 195p. bibliog.

This abridged version of the author's DPhil thesis consists of seven chapters incorporating fieldwork data and the results of surveys of the attitudes to work etc. of workers at Malta Drydocks and a quota sample from the general population administered in the years just before the closure of the British base in 1979. Separate chapters are devoted to their perceptions of work, power, and the local class structure after discussion of more general historical and socio-economic background setting the political and industrial scene. The author was particularly interested in Malta's introduction of workers' participation which had been developed at the Drydocks. The appendices outline aspects of the main and supplementary surveys and the text of the main questionnaire.

651   **Malta: Malta Drydocks.**
Edward L. Żammit.   In: *Workers' self-management and participation in practice, vol. 1 case studies.*   Edited by Alés Vahcic and Vesna Smole-Grobovsek.   Ljubljana, Yugoslavia: International Centre for Public Enterprises in Developing Countries, 1986, p. 105-23. bibliog.

A useful outline of the situation at the Drydocks followed by an economic analysis and the report of a survey of workers' attitudes to their participatory system, the role of the union, and issues of power and control. The appendices include Maltese labour and economic data.

652   **Workers' participation in Malta: options for a future policy.**
Edward L. Żammit.   Msida, Malta: Workers' Participation
Development Centre, University of Malta with the Ministry for Social
Policy, 1988. 104p.

The thirteen papers and addresses included were given at a national seminar. They
include contributions from the employers' association, trade unions, the co-operative
movement, political parties, and government departments, as well as the International
Labor Organization.

653   **Workers on the Board – a sociological comment on recent
developments in workers' participation in Malta.**
Edward L. Żammit, Godfrey Baldacchino.   *Economic Analysis and
Workers' Management*, vol. 23, no. 1 (1989), p. 79-94. bibliog.

The challenge of workers' participation to established managerial prerogatives is discussed in relation to traditional patterns for the local management of powerlessness.
The election of worker directors became the focus of political and trade union competition but it is argued that they are not legally differentiated from other directors. The
paper sets out seven proposals for action. The appendices chronicle: the introduction
of worker directors, mainly in public corporations and parastatal companies; the way
this issue became a matter of confrontation between the GWU and the new Nationalist
Government in 1987; and the statute establishing a Federation of Worker Directors.

Environment and
Water Resources

654 **The Maltese Islands: a threatened coastline.**
Ewan A. Anderson, John A. Schembri. In: *Environmental and
economic issues in small island development.* Edited by Douglas
Lockhart and David Drakakis-Smith. London: The Commonwealth
Foundation, 1991, p. 5-21. maps. (Monograph no. 6, Developing Areas
Research Group).
This is a brief resumé of a full report, produced by the writers in 1989, on a survey of
the coastal zones of both Malta and Gozo. The report included an executive summons,
100 land-use maps at a scale of 1:2,500, and some maps at 1:25,000 and other scales
depicting ecological patterns. This resumé outlines the categorization of coasts by
accessibility, tourism, industry, maritime activity, agriculture, vegetation, waste dis-
posal, development and building. It stresses the urgent need to safeguard the few
remaining stretches of accessible lowland coast.

655 **Big holes in a small place. The stone quarrying dilemma in the
Maltese Islands.**
Roger Balm. *Geography*, no. 350, vol. 81, part 1 (1996), p. 82-86.
map.
Examines the environmental impact of a major extractive industry in the context of a
small island where concerns for economic viability lead to land-use conflict.

656 **The public gardens and groves of Malta and Gozo.**
Joseph Borġ   Attard, Malta: The Author, 1990. 3rd ed. 149p. bibliog.
This illustrated descriptive guide is classified by palace, fortification, town and village, commemorative, and newer, gardens. There is some discussion of policy
regarding the zoning of land for national park status, nurseries, afforestation, etc.

657   **Malta. Background for development.**
H. Bowen-Jones, J. C. Dewdney, W. B. Fisher.   Durham, England:
Durham University, Department of Geography, 1961. 356p. bibliog.

This important volume reports on a major survey of land use, environment and development potential by more than twenty contributors from Durham University between
1955 and 1958. As the most comprehensive stock-taking of the economic and social
geography of Malta and Gozo in the last years of the colonial period, it is still con-
sulted by planners and others. Section I deals with the physical setting – geology,
geomorphology, water and soils (p. 25-99). Section II, on the people, considers the
main social, economic and demographic trends, particularly since 1800 (p. 102-85).
These two sections set the scene for Section III, on agriculture, which summarizes and
analyses the findings of the survey of land use in which every field in the islands was
visited (sometimes more than once to get an indication of seasonal contrasts). This
remarkable enterprise resulted in the compilation of maps showing the distribution of
individual crops in the islands and to the preparation of detailed field-plot plans and
sketches. These appear in this section along with a comprehensive text description and
analysis (p. 188-348): the result is a unique inventory of the reality of rural Malta
before it was hit by accelerating modernization, especially building. This very detailed
and critically analysed work concludes with an assessment of the cultural landscape in
Section IV (p. 349-53). In addition to the maps and plans, the book includes many
graphs, diagrams and photographs.

658   **Malta – an essay in historical ecology.**
Howard Bowen-Jones.   In: *Human ecology in the Commonwealth.*
Edited by Howard Bowen-Jones.   London: Charles Knight & Co.
Ltd., 1972, p. 59-74.

This essay (in a volume containing the proceedings of the First Commonwealth
Conference on Development and Human Ecology, Malta, 18-24 October 1970) takes
an informed and broad-brush look at the relationship, since earliest times, between the
Maltese environment and the human impact upon it. The notion of ecosystem is
applied to the evidence of Malta where the facts of small sizes and long history and
prehistory combine to generate unique local outcomes. The writer sees any event or
decision, over time, external or internal, inexorably affecting movements already in
train to produce a changing balance in its ecosystem.

659   **Structure plan for the Maltese Islands.**
Colin Buchanan & Partners, Generale Progetti SpA, in association with
Planning Services Division, Government of Malta.   Beltissebh
(Floriana), Malta: Ministry for Development of Infrastructure, 1990.

This is the first comprehensive attempt at co-ordinated planning in the islands' history.
The first to appear was *Malta. Structure plan brief* (1988. 108p.). In the following year
came *Malta structure plan: inception report* (147p.). In 1990 the main plan appeared
in three parts: *Draft final written statement and key diagram* (125p. map); *Explanatory
memorandum* (154p. maps); and *Summary of public consultation* (283p.). A number of
technical reports appeared with the plan. One of these was *Planning legislation and
related matters: appraisal and outline proposals* (no. 9.1. 58p.). The collection of data
during the preparation of the plan makes this a bench-mark source while the attempts
to identify priorities and targets summarize Malta's (official) view of itself in the late
20th century. Apart from being a substantial inventory of the resources and spatial and

built realities of the islands, the proposals contained here constitute the first set of co-ordinated plans for Malta and Gozo.

660   **The rainfall of Malta.**
B. F. Bulmer and K. Stormonth.   London: Her Majesty's Stationery
Office for the Air Ministry, Meteorological Office, 1960. 20p. maps.
(Scientific Paper no. 3).
Attempts to produce a homogeneous record of rainfall over a century and to assess
spatial and temporal variations.

661   **Socio-economic aspects of man and his environment in Malta.**
Salvino Busuttil.   In: *Human ecology in the Commonwealth.*   Edited
by Howard Bowen-Jones.   London: Charles Knight & Co. Ltd., 1972,
p. 105-33.
This outlines progress on a multi-disciplinary pilot ecological study, first proposed in
the late 1960s and later involving specialists from a range of disciplines. It is argued
that Malta is at a crossroads between decline, on the one hand, and the achievement of
perfect ecological balance, on the other.

662   **The climate of the Maltese Islands: a review.**
Deborah Chetcuti, Anton Buħaġiar, Patrick J. Schembri, Frank
Ventura.   Msida, Malta: University of Malta Press, 1992. 108p.
bibliog.
This very useful and well illustrated concise assessment of Malta's climate and
weather includes a comprehensive annotated bibliography of more than seventy titles
(p. 98-104).

663   **A review of research work on natural products carried out during
1964-1978 at the University of Malta.**
V. Ferrito.   In: *Natural products: proceedings of the Symposium on
Natural Products held in Malta in June, 1992.*   Edited by Anthony
Serracino Inglott, Maurice Żarb Adami.   Msida, Malta: University of
Malta Press, 1993, p. 31-47 (148p.).
Describes the personalities and research activities in the University of Malta's Faculty
of Science (constituted in 1958) from 1963 when the first science graduates appeared.

664   **Malta: past, present, and future.**
Edited by J. Quentin Hughes.   *The Architectural Review,* vol. cxlvi,
no. 869 (1969), p. 1-82.
This special issue includes contributions from J. Quentin Hughes (the associate editor
for this special issue), James Morris, Richard Demarco, Richard England, Ian Masser,
Peter Richardson, Joseph Tonna, Salvino Busuttil, and J. G. Huntingford. It provides a
well-illustrated survey of the origins and prospects of the urban and rural built envi-
ronment in Malta – 'a veritable museum of architectural history'. See especially: the
'Foreword' on p. 3-6; 'The perils of non-planning' by Ian Masser, p. 57-60 (including
'Mellieħa' p. 58-59); 'Malta future' by J. Quentin Hughes and Peter Richardson, p. 67-68;

and 'Town planning law', by J. G. Huntingford, p. 79-81. One of the messages coming through clearly in this publication is that 'if Malta accepts laisser-faire development, the whole island will be obliterated by buildings' (p. 68).

665 A new deal for planning in Malta?
Huw R. Jones. *Town and Country Planning*, vol. 39, no. 9 (1971), p. 402-05.

This notes that the building boom from the mid-1960s damaged the harmonious relationship between the cultural and natural environment. Yet Malta possesses much of the infrastructure for effective physical planning – and protection of the unique traditional landscape – though the lack of a development plan hindered both economic and physical planning.

666 Soils of Malta and Gozo.
D. M. Lang. London: Her Majesty's Stationery Office for Colonial Research Studies, no. 29, 1960. 112p.

This survey of soils, their geological basis and role in agriculture, is supplemented by a map, plates, and plans.

667 Sustainable development and environmental management: the case of the small Mediterranean island of Gozo.
Anthony Macelli. In: *Sustainable development and environmental management of small islands.* Edited by W. Beller, P. d'Ayala, P. Hein. Paris: UNESCO; Carnforth, England: The Parthenon Publishing Group, 1990, p. 169-81. (Man and the Biosphere Series, vol. 5).

The idea of sustainable development is questioned and, after an overview of links between humankind and its environment and of structural change processes on Gozo – which point to the inadequacy of environmental management – the case is made for new institutional arrangements including full citizen participation. The series editor is J. N. R. Jeffers.

668 Gozo: the human ecosystem on an island.
Tony Macelli, Peter Serracino Inglott, Nora Sammut. Msida, Malta: University of Malta, 1979. 92 + 107 + 39p. bibliog.

This report to UNESCO's Division of Human Settlements and Socio-Cultural Environment has three parts. Part one, by Serracino Inglott, is a synthesis of the studies of human-environment interactions in Gozo – on the basis of a dossier assembled by Macelli who prepared part two, on the analysis of water use. Part three consists of charts, tables, and a bibliography compiled by Nora Sammut. Tony Macelli's contribution paralleled his PhD work at the University of Malta ('The interaction of multiple processes of human settlement in a Mediterranean island ecosystem: Gozo', 1980).

669   **Malta's national report to the United Nations' Conference on Environment and Development, 1992.**
Floriana, Malta: Office of the Parliamentary Secretary for the Environment, 1992. 72p.

Reviews background information and looks at sectoral trends, with a main focus on environmental issues and prospects in the context of the national Structure Plan.

670   **Marine pollution in Malta. Proceedings of a Conference on the Management of Marine Contamination Hazards organized by the Malta Council for Science and Technology 15-16 December, 1994.**
Msida, Malta: Malta University Press, for the Council, 1996. 212p.

This volume includes summaries of some thirty presentations by Maltese specialists at the above conference in the Freeport Centre at Kalafrana, Malta. The principal finding was that the need for effective quality monitoring of marine conditions is an urgent prerequisite for co-ordinated, comprehensive resource and environment management.

671   **The water supply resources of Malta.**
T. O. Morris.   Valletta: Government Printing Office, 1952. 125p.

A study describing the position from the 17th century up to 1945 and surveying storage, distribution, irrigation, and boring at the time of writing. It includes graphs and a valuable map.

672   **The effects on water production in islands with high population and tourist densities: the case of Malta.**
George Peplow.   In: *Les resources en eau et le tourisme dans les îles de la Méditerranée.* (Water resources and tourism on Mediterranean islands.)   Edited by Salvino Busuttil and Christiane Villain-Gandossi et al.   Valletta: Foundation for International Studies (Malta), 1989, p. 171-80.

A brief overview of an important aspect of the water constraint in Malta, published in association with the European Co-ordination Centre for Research and Documentation in Social Sciences (Vienna).

673   **Localities with conservation value in the Maltese Islands.**
Patrick J. Schembri et al.   Floriana, Malta: Ministry of Education, Environmental Division, 1987. 27p.

Lists, and gives very brief descriptions of, sixty-six sites, of which thirty-nine are in Malta, sixteen in Gozo, and eleven on minor islands. There are photographs but no bibliography.

674 **Development and the natural environment in the Maltese Islands.**
Patrick J. Schembri, Edwin Lanfranco. In: *The development process in small island states.* Edited by D. G. Lockhart, D. Drakakis-Smith, J. Schembri. London: Routledge, 1993, p. 247-66. bibliog.

The pressure of population on a very limited space over many centuries has had a profound impact on the islands' environment. Natural landscapes have been replaced by anthropic ones and there has been a general degradation of the natural environment coupled with increased habitat disturbance characterized by adventive species, often in competition with the indigenous biota. Only recently has there been substantial awareness of the need to protect the natural environment and to control development.

675 **Recurrent problems of water supply in Malta.**
A. S. Tricker. *Geography*, vol. 62, part 2 (1977), p. 118-21.

In 1967 the first sea water distillation plant promised an end to the problem of maintaining adequate supplies. By 1970 four plants were in operation. The writer assesses the likely impact of distillation on Malta's ability to meet growing demands for water.

Education

General

676 **Secondary education in Malta.**
Paul A. Attard, with Andrew J. Buħaġiar.   Strasbourg, France: Council of Europe Press, 1996. 82p.
This is one in a series of guides to secondary education in Europe, edited by Denis Kallen. The series aims to give a systematic and coherent exposition for each signatory state to the European Cultural Convention and to identify problems in each case. The Malta volume contains a factual introduction to the islands and a section giving an overview of the education system there. A section on the issues is followed by a brief assessment of efficiency and performance while a final section looks at eight problems and prospects ranging from teacher shortages and resource allocation to information technology and the use of schools as community centres. References are indicated (p. 81-82).

677 **The evolution of education in Malta. A philosophy in the making.**
James Calleja.   *Revue du Monde Musulman et de la Meditérranée,* no. 71 (1994), p. 185-97.
A paper comprising a brief overview of the major past developments, followed by an examination of reforms and counter-reforms since 1945, the systematization of education in Malta, and teacher training. It appears in a special theme issue of the *Revue,* entitled *Le Carrefour Maltais* (The Maltese crossroads).

678 **Education's role in the socio-economic development of Malta.**
Carmen M. Caruana.   Westport, Connecticut; London: Praeger, 1992. 132p. bibliog.
An outline of the policy aims and structure of Malta's system of education since earliest times, with substantial emphasis on the period since 1945 and during the Labour

161

Government from 1970-85. The author adopts the 'human resource' approach to education as an investment in national development, and outlines the islands' economic goals and strategies. The appendices chart the scale and components of the educational system and its administrative structure at c.1985.

679 Education Statistics.
Valletta: Central Office of Statistics, 1951/52- . annual.

Recently, this series of tabulated data has been published, with short introductory commentaries, as follows: 1984-85 (1987). 168p.; 1985-86 (1987). 122p.; 1986-87 (1988). 129p.; 1987-88 (1989). 123p.; 1989-90 (1991). 174p.; 1992-93 (1994). 237p.; 1993-94 (1996). 239p; and 1995 (1996). 233p. The contents of the most recent issue are as follows: introduction, p. i-xv; primary schools, p. 1-47; government secondary and post-secondary schools, p. 50-77; technical institutes and trade schools, p. 80-114; private schools, p. 115-63; special education, p. 166-74; academy of dramatic arts, p. 176-81; school of music, p. 184-85; evening classes, p. 188-95; and the university, p. 198-233.

680 Collegium Melitense quartercentenary celebrations (1592-1992): collected papers.
Edited by Roger Ellul-Micallef, Stanley Fiorini. Msida, Malta: The University of Malta, 1992. bibliog.

This publication was designed to celebrate the academic achievements of one of the oldest universities in the (British) Commonwealth and to demonstrate the revival of an institution officially shut down by the government and superseded by another from 1980-87. The first editor, since 1996 the rector of the university, provides the foreword to twenty-one essays by different members of staff. Those devoted to the physical sciences, chemistry, medicine and mathematics have a universal point of reference. But the book also provides a useful source of reviews of current research and studies of a wide range of Maltese subjects, for example: sexuality in Maltese megalithic art; sources on 'The Maltese Paleaochristian hypogea'; 'The Latin-Arabic alphabet of the Maltese language'; 'A survey of congenital anomalies in Malta'; 'Baroque architecture in Malta'; 'Language and nationhood in the Maltese experience'; 'The fauna of the Maltese Islands'; and 'Architectural and Urbanistic traditions in Malta'. The absence of demographic and sociological entries is surprising.

681 Education in Malta: a look to the future: proceedings of a national workshop for further training of educational advisors and school principals in Malta.
Edited by Charles J. Farrugia. Valletta: UNESCO for the Foundation for International Studies, 1988. 184p. bibliog.

Consists of the texts of papers and workshop reports on the following: the Maltese educational system; the impact of examinations; the curriculum; teacher education; educational support services; and administration and management. Also included are appendices on the participants and a programme of the conference. This national workshop was organized with assistance from UNESCO, the Foundation for International Studies and the Faculty of Education at the University of Malta on 12 October 1987.

682 **Malta: educational development in a small island state.**
Charles J. Farrugia. *Prospects*, vol. XXI, no. 4 (1991), p. 584-94.
bibliog.
An account of the effects of small-scale, economic, and cultural dependency, and
other factors affecting the role and practice of education in Malta.

683 **Foundation for International Studies at the University of Malta.**
Annual report and statement of accounts.
Valletta: Foundation for International Studies, 1995. 42p.
Founded in 1985, the Foundation is active in research, publication, teaching and con-
ferences on a variety of international issues. This colourfully illustrated report details
the initiatives and personalities involved.

684 **De la Salle College. Vol. 1. 1903-1938. A study in growth.**
Victor Mallia-Milanes. Malta: De la Salle College, 1979. 94p.
A short history of one of the influential schools run by the Christian Brothers, in
Cospicua in the heart of Malta's docklands, together with a biographical list of staff
who served there.

685 **De la Salle College. Vol. 2. Life at Cottonera 1939-1971.**
Alfred Spiteri. Malta: De La Salle College, 1988. 206p.
This volume provides an account of this influential church school from its role as a
preparatory school for HM Dockyard apprenticeships to its success as a grammar
school pioneering several aspects of secondary education. Illustrated with many photographs of staff, pupils and buildings, it also contains appendices on brothers who
have served at the college, and college statistics.

686 **Themes in education: a Maltese reader.**
Edited by Ronald G. Sultana. Msida, Malta: Mireva Publications
Ltd., 1991. 321p. bibliog.
The eleven papers of which this reader is composed are all by Maltese authors on
aspects of the situation of education in the islands, after drawing on other unpublished
material submitted for courses in education. It is therefore also a useful bibliographical source. It is introduced by a paper by Professor Paul Hirst. The subjects of the
papers include: motivation and education; discipline; classroom decision making; language in the classroom; schools and their curriculum; the values, uses and problems of
assessment and its form; gender differentials and subject choice in Maltese secondary
schools and their particular relevance to science; and the relationship between social
class, educational attainment and types of schooling.

687 **Education and national development: historical and critical**
perspectives on vocational schooling in Malta.
Ronald G. Sultana. Msida, Malta: Mireva Publications Ltd., 1992.
494p. bibliog.
Due no doubt to the small scale of its economy and the high density of its population,
Malta has had a long history of 'practical educational' policies. The first part of this

impressive monograph outlines this history in 19th- and 20th-century Malta and the rise of vocational schools until the re-introduction of more general education since 1987. Part two raises questions about the economic assumptions on which such schools are based and the opportunities offered to their students, and the educational goals of such schools, as well as the wider social and ideological aims put forward for them. Part three considers four possible lines of development for vocational development and concludes that the problem lies in Maltese society and education as much as in this sector of schooling. Several photographs illustrate part one.

688 **Adult education and the politics of knowledge: the relevance of Malta's Dun Ġorġ Preca.**
Ronald G. Sultana. *International Journal of Lifelong Education,*
vol. 15, no. 4 (July-August 1996), p. 276-85. bibliog.
This paper is about the contribution of Fr. Preca (1880-1962) to the development of adult education in the islands. Preca was committed to the democratization of knowledge and to teaching, if appropriate, at the grass roots rather than the formal institutional level. He was responsible for launching the M.U.S.E.U.M., a movement of lay religious instructors which has the structure and fundamentalist enthusiasm of a national confraternity.

689 **University of Malta Annual Report.**
Msida, Malta: University of Malta, 1905- . annual.
Between 1905 and 1912 the Report of the Department of Public Instruction included reports on the University. The first report from the University itself was that for 1913-14. The most recent annual report is that for 1994-95 (62p.). Reports cover teaching sectors, student numbers, plans and finances.

690 **Education in Malta: a handbook.**
Joe Żammit Ciantar. Malta: Ministry of Education and Human
Resources, 1993. 92p.
A useful outline of the legal framework, management, structure, curricula, and the location of all departmental offices, government and private schools in the islands.

691 **Education in Malta.**
J. Żammit Mangion. Valletta: Social Action Movement (Studia
Editions), 1992. 596p. bibliog.
Section one of this comprehensive survey deals with the growth and development of education in six chapters. Section two covers state, private, and higher education at the time of writing, and also looks at aspects of examinations, teacher training and teaching unions. Part X of section two provides a particularly interesting 'critique' of Maltese education. Section three consists of nine appendices, including: lists of senior officials; the national curricula; various codes, regulations and arguments relating to innovations and disputes over the last twenty years; salary scales; a valuable glossary (p. 490-587) and an extensive bibliography (p. 588-96).

Curriculum

692 **Malta's national curriculum: a critical analysis.**
Carmel Borġ, Jennifer Camilleri, Peter Mayo, Toni Xerri.
International Review of Education, vol. 41, no. 5 (1995), p. 337-56.
bibliog.

The writers argue that the recently introduced National Minimum Curriculum for primary, secondary and post-secondary levels is, like similar national curricula elsewhere, underpinned by conservative ideology. It discriminates against women, undervalues non-European cultures, and promotes hierarchical rather than democratic education.

693 **A national minimum curriculum for Malta: proceedings of the Maltese Workshop on the National Minimum Curriculum for the Primary Level: January 1991.**
Edited by Charles Farrugia. Malta: Foundation for International Studies and Ministry of Education, Malta, 1991. 146p. bibliog.

The 1988 Education Act repealed that of 1974 and introduced a national curriculum. These papers review the form, evaluation and experience of the new curriculum and its implementation. There are summaries of eight contributions on the curriculum in part two followed by thirteen more in part three on experiences in teaching mathematics, history, religion, languages, reading, art, sport and leisure, environment, and science. The six recommendations from the workshop are on p. 16.

694 **Language and the science curriculum.**
Frank Ventura. *Education*, vol. 4, no. 2 (1991), p. 15-18. bibliog.

Compares a sample of boys and girls taking the Form I Science Test, using its Maltese or English versions, and looks at the expectations of their teachers.

695 **The Maltese national curriculum: a critical evaluation.**
Kenneth Wain. Msida, Malta: Mireva Publications Ltd., 1991.
122p. bibliog.

The three chapters review the politics underlying the introduction of these curricula for primary and secondary schools, the form and content of the curricula, and the alternatives that could be adopted in the context of lifelong education. The appendices reproduce the relevant sections of the legislation introducing the primary curriculum in 1988 and the secondary curriculum due to start in 1990.

Teachers and pupils

696 **Beyond schooling: adult education in Malta.**
Edited by Godfrey Baldacchino and Peter Mayo. Msida, Malta:
Mireva Publications, 1997. 506p. bibliog.

This large book draws on the experience and views of many Maltese educators and practitioners in this field which has growing significance in local educational policy. The twenty-nine articles are grouped in four sections entitled: the historical context; adult education practice: alternatives to chalk and talk; worker education: developing worker resourcefulness; and adult education as a change agent, each of which has its own editorial introduction. The editors previously wrote on this topic in: 'Multi-functionalism, volunteers and the "school culture": adult education in the Maltese context', in *International yearbook of adult education 13 and 23*, edited by Joachim H. Kroll (Cologne, Germany: Böhlau Verlag (1995), p. 228-44. bibliog.). They outlined the traditional difference between government literacy programmes stressing the medium of English and religious associations encouraging non-socialist trade unions and rural co-operatives, and the different lines of approach being taken by more recent voluntary and political groups.

697 **Stress and job satisfaction among primary school teachers in Malta.**
Mark G. Borġ, Joseph M. Falzon. *Educational Review*, vol. 41, no. 3
(1989), p. 271-79. bibliog.

This analysis cites evidence indicating that thirty per cent of teachers felt their job was very stressful, a response negatively correlated with both job satisfaction and the desire to return to teaching a second time. In collaboration with various colleagues, Mark Borġ has published a series of papers on various aspects of these problems, some of them re-analysing his data using different statistical and computer-assisted theoretical methods, a selection from which is included here.

698 **Coping actions used by Maltese primary teachers.**
Mark G. Borġ, Joseph M. Falzon. *Educational Research*, vol. 32,
no. 1, Spring (1990), p. 50-58. bibliog.

Another part of research into teachers' stress in Malta, which found that teachers most frequently coped by trying to relax after work, to avoid confrontation, and to nip potential sources of stress in the bud. The gender, teaching experience, age and ability-stream of pupils were all relevant factors in these responses.

699 **Teachers' perception of primary school children's undesirable behaviours: the effects of teaching experience, pupil's age, sex and ability stream.**
Mark G. Borġ, Joseph M. Falzon. *British Journal of Educational Psychology*, vol. 60 (1990), p. 220-26. bibliog.

The results of a survey of 844 Maltese teachers, which presents the statistical analysis of their responses in relation to 16 different types of behaviour. These were regarded as most problematic in the case of the older children, and by the less experienced teachers. The ability of the children was not significantly related to teachers' attitudes.

700 **Occupational stress and satisfaction in teaching.**
Mark G. Borġ, Richard J. Riding. *British Educational Research Journal*, vol. 17, no. 3 (1991), p. 263-81. bibliog.

The paper, derived from the Maltese primary teachers' stress survey, demonstrates the finding that teachers reporting greater stress were not only less satisfied with their job and less likely to take it up again, but more likely to be absent from work (and for longer periods) as well as to leave the teaching profession altogether.

701 **Predictors of overall performance in a B.Ed. course and in educational psychology.**
Mark G. Borġ, Joseph M. Falzon. *Assessment and Evaluation in Higher Education*, vol. 16, no. 2, Summer (1991), p. 149-56. bibliog.

Reports a study of the association between entry qualifications, performance in educational psychology, and the final results of BEd students. Maths/science students tended to perform better in educational psychology and those doing well in the latter tended to have better final results. Female students out-performed their male colleagues.

702 **Streaming in Maltese primary schools.**
Mark G. Borġ, Joseph M. Falzon. *Research in Education*, vol. 45 (1991), p. 1-12. bibliog.

A report of research into the age and gender differences of children in each of the three ability streams, the transfer rate between streams, and any age or gender differences in the latter. Girls were more highly placed and kept to their stream. Boys were more commonly demoted and transfer rates were considerably higher than in Britain.

703 **Stress in teaching: a study of occupational stress and its determinants, job satisfaction and career commitment among primary schoolteachers.**
Mark G. Borġ, Richard J. Riding, Joseph M. Falzon. *Educational Psychology*, vol. 11, no. 1 (1991), p. 59-75. bibliog.

A principal components analysis of the responses to the teachers' stress survey revealed four heavily loaded factors: pupil misbehaviour, time/resource difficulties, the need for professional recognition, and poor relationships. The teachers' gender and the ability group of children they taught interacted significantly with stress. Those feeling most stressed were less satisfied with, and less committed to, teaching if they had another choice of career.

704 **Occupational stress and job satisfaction among school administrators.**
Mark G. Borġ, Richard J. Riding. *Journal of Educational Administration*, vol. 31, no. 1 (1993), p. 4-21. bibliog.

An extension of the previous assessment of the stresses experienced by school teachers to heads and their deputies, with the finding of a similar level of problem and likelihood of the pressures being intensified. Greater stress was reported by more experienced heads who were also usually older.

705 **Teacher stress and cognitive style.**
Mark G. Borġ, Richard J. Riding. *British Journal of Educational Psychology*, vol. 63 (1993), p. 271-86. bibliog.

A cognitive styles analysis of responses of Maltese secondary-school teachers to a sample survey of overall stress and the severity of four main areas of job stress which are listed in the appendix: pupil misbehaviour, poor working conditions, poor staff relations, and time pressures. The two types of style analysis are described and the patterns of association with stress levels discussed.

706 **Age and sex differences in performance in an 11-plus selective examination.**
Mark G. Borġ, Joseph M. Falzon, Arthur Sammut. *Educational Psychology*, vol. 15, no. 4 (1995), p. 433-43. bibliog.

During the 1970s the Malta Government abolished and then re-introduced selective secondary education. This is an analysis of pupils born in 1981 who had just sat the examination for the first time and is based on the raw scores in five subjects. Girls out-performed boys in Maltese, English and religious knowledge, especially the languages, but performance in mathematics and social studies was similar. Older pupils tended to be more successful than younger pupils and girls more likely to pass the whole examination than boys.

707 **Birth date and sex effects on the scholastic attainment of primary schoolchildren: a cross-sectional study.**
Mark G. Borġ, Joseph M. Falzon. *British Educational Research Journal*, vol. 21, no. 1 (1995), p. 61-74. bibliog.

The results of an analysis of the year-end examinations in Grades 3, 4 and 5 of twelve Maltese primary schools. It found that there was a strong and consistent age effect on scores in Maltese, English and mathematics, and that girls consistently performed better than boys in each of these.

708 **Malta's teachers and social change.**
Mary Darmanin. In: *The politics of teacher unionism: international perspectives*. Edited by Marti Lawn. London: Croom Helm, 1985, p. 158-90. bibliog.

An extensively documented account and analysis of the role and major activities of the Malta Union of Teachers (now the Movement of United Teachers) in response to political and systemic changes in the form of, and policies for, education.

709 **Maltese primary school teachers' experience of centralized policies.**
Mary Darmanin. *British Journal of Sociology of Education*, vol. 11, no. 3 (1990), p. 275-308. bibliog.

The classroom strategies adopted by teachers faced with great changes in their work as a result of the dictates of educational policy may negate the aims of the policy makers who might have been more effective if they had involved the teachers in the process.

710 **Career-choice and sources of occupational satisfaction and frustration among teachers in Malta.**
Charles Farrugia. *Comparative Education*, vol. 22, no. 3 (1986), p. 221-31. bibliog.

This report of a representative sample survey of teachers evidences the occupational commitment sustained by the rewards of pedagogical interaction as well as their material frustrations and disappointments, which are more publicly voiced.

711 **Education and social transition: vocationalism, ideology and the problems of development.**
Ronald G. Sultana. *International Review of Education*, vol. 41, nos. 3-4 (1995), p. 199-221.

An assessment of the Malta Labour Party's aims and limited achievements in the practice of trade schools, which were a place to occupy children unsuccessful in the main stream of education rather than a positive social mixing ground and avenue to occupational opportunity.

712 **Gender, science choice and achievement: a Maltese perspective.**
Frank Ventura. *International Journal of Science Education*, vol. 14 (1992), p. 445-61. bibliog.

Presents the results of a study of boys and girls in their choice and ultimate goals of achievement in national scientific courses at school.

Literature

Prose

713 No strangers in the silent city.
Anne Agius Ferrante.   Valletta: Andrew Rupert Publishing, 1992.
128p.
Contains twenty-six reminiscences and stories about people the author has known during her life in Mdina, illustrated with lively line-drawings by Mario Muscat.

714 Pynchon, V., and the Malta connection.
Arnold Cassola.   *Journal of Modern Literature*, vol. 12, no. 2 (1985),
p. 311-31. 2 maps. bibliog.
The American author Thomas Pynchon's obviously close knowledge of aspects of Maltese history and Valletta leads to an investigation of his likely sources for the novel, and the buildings and Strait Street premises to which he refers in 1956. A glossary provides further information on the historic figures and the places which are referred to in the novel, as well as other Maltese names, events etc. Pynchon's apparent reclusiveness has made his visit, presumably on an American warship, an intriguing mystery.

715 In the eye of the sun: a novel set in Malta.
Francis Ebejer.   London: Macdonald, 1969. 158p.
A powerful story, set in Malta, of a student who faces a psychotic return to his peasant origins and traumatic past.

716 A wreath of Malta innocents: a novel.
Francis Ebejer.   Valletta: Buġelli, 1981. 261p.
This novel, revised by the author, originally appeared as *A wreath for the innocents* (London: MacGibbon & Kee, 1958). It is about class conflict against a background of

170

different brands of Catholicism. Although the author denied it, the book does present a message about the condition of Maltese society in the 1950s.

717 **For Rozina . . . a husband, and other Malta stories.**
Francis Ebejer. Valletta: Progress Press, 1990. 157p.

Some of these sixteen short stories were previously published during the 1980s. 'Most', says Ebejer, 'were written during those intervals between the completion of more demanding works . . .'. All, certainly, carry the flavour of Malta and its people and show the skill of this versatile, bilingual Maltese writer who is known for his more than fifty plays and several novels. He has received the Malta Literary Award four times.

718 **The collected short stories of Sir Temi Żammit.**
Translated by Godwin Ellul. Qormi, Malta: Polidano Press Ltd., 1995. 144p.

Sir Themistocles Żammit (1864-1935) was one of the most remarkable figures of modern Malta. Discoverer of the brucellosis vector, Professor of Chemistry, Curator of the Museum and archaeologist, and Rector of the University, he collected and wrote these thirty stories in idiomatic Maltese. They were first published in 1987. In a short introduction Professor Aquilina commends this translation of short stories which 'are really extended anecdotes, with humour playing a conspicuous part in the unfolding of the "plot" leading to a surprise conclusion but which are often used to apply a moralistic comment in the gentlest of ways imaginable'.

719 **In search of a national identity: a survey of Maltese literature.**
Oliver Friggieri. *Durham University Journal*, Dec. 1985, p. 121-36.

The writer looks at history – especially history in prose – as the basis of national mythology. What he calls 'the aesthetic myth of the people as the truest poet' is 'the primary motive of the revival of Maltese as a means of literary and especially versified expression' (p. 128). Gian Anton Vassallo (1817-68) was the first leader in this direction for poetry. The outstanding Maltese poet, Dun Karm Psaila (1871-1961), wrote in Italian from 1889 to 1912 and only then started to use the local language. This article identifies most of the key figures in the field. A version of this paper served as an introduction to *Cross winds. An anthology of post-war Maltese poetry* (see item no. 734).

720 **A turn of the wheel: a novel.**
Oliver Friggieri, translated from the Maltese by Grazio Falzon, with an introduction by Grazio Falzon and Konrad Hopkins. Paisley, Scotland: Wilfion Books, 1987. 77p.

This volume is one of a 'UNESCO collection of representative works, European series'. It opens with some comment on the growth of Maltese literature (p. 1-7) and a brief note about Friggieri, the university teacher, writer, and editor whose literary (and academic) work appears in several languages (p. 7-9). In this novel, Friggieri produces a vibrant picture of life in a small, self-enclosed island society where one young man, Baruch, is a misfit – which is roughly the translation of *L-Istramb*, the title of this work in its earlier Maltese version (Valletta: Gulf, 1980).

721 **Koranta and other short stories from Malta.**
Oliver Friggieri, translated from the Maltese by Spencer Levy.
Msida, Malta: Mireva Publications, 1994. 214p.

This collection of twenty-five stories by a prolific Maltese writer who also produces novels, poetry, and literary criticism in English, Italian, and Maltese, constitutes a microcosm of social behaviour culled from this versatile writer's youthful experiences in his Mediterranean island. Critical to this collection is the fact that Friggieri's protagonists are all strongly conditioned by the insularity of an island-state.

722 **A short history of Maltese literature.**
Oliver Friggieri. In: *Riding out. New writing from around the world.*
Edited by M. Jurgensen. Queensland, Australia: Phoenix-Outride
Co-Production, 1994, p. 68-83.

After a brief discussion of language in Maltese writing (Maltese, English and Italian), the writer proposes that the two genres which characterize the fullest development of Maltese literature are the narrative and the lyrical. Consequently he devotes the rest of this paper to prose and poetry. He sees the 'contribution of the dramatists dovetailing into this mainstream' while theatre 'in the modern sense is only a recent achievement'.

723 **The Stolen Faldetta: an intriguing story in Malta and Gozo during the plague epidemic of 1813 and 1814.**
Mary Grech. Malta: Publishers Enterprises Group Ltd., 1991. 199p.
map.

A novel based on accounts of this terrible epidemic and of some of the people involved.

724 **Individual and community in Commonwealth literature.**
Edited by Daniel Massa. Msida, Malta: The University Press, 1978.

The papers of the 1978 Conference of the Association for Commonwealth Literature and Language Studies include three papers on the situation in Malta: 'The bicultural situation in Malta' by Francis Ebejer, 'Disillusionment after Independence in Maltese literature' by Joe Friggieri, and 'The Faustus of Malta: an interface of fact and fiction in Pynchon's *V*' by Peter Serracino-Inglott.

725 **The Kappillan of Malta.**
Nicholas Monsarrat. London: Cassell, 1973. 576p.

This novel is a powerful evocation of the 1939-45 war in Malta. It is based on the life and work of the Kappillan Father Salvatore, and written in the form of reminiscent retrospections during the course of his funeral.

726 **In the trickster tradition: the novels of Andrew Salkey, Francis Ebejar [sic] and Ishmael Reed.**
Peter Nazareth. London: Bogle-L'Ouverture, 1994. 262p. bibliog.

The second chapter (p. 95-166) situates the work of Francis Ebejer in its local and national context and compares it with that of other writers whose work reflects social change. Ebejer's first two novels were written before Malta became independent in

1964; his later works deal with post-independence problems. There is a valuable bibliography (p. 242-57).

727 **Lost letters: an ostensibly historical divertimento.**
Nicholas de Piro.   London: Pedigree Books, 1986. 96p. bibliog.
This collection of letters, purporting to emanate from well-known and imaginary characters in Maltese history, is amusingly illustrated by Kenneth Żammit Tabone in a style reminiscent of S. R. Behrman. Some parody the writing of their assumed authors and others present comments on their times.

728 **V.**
Thomas Pynchon.   London: Jonathan Cape Ltd., 1963. Reprinted, London: Pan Books, 1975. 492p.
This novel, written by an American author who is reticent about his autobiography recounts a search for the mysterious V from New York to Egypt and Malta. The Vaudeville of characters includes sailors, spies, priests, philosophers and bums, not a few of whom seem to have been based on the author's own experiences of the harbour bars and Strait Street during his draft in the US Navy. The novel and its author have attracted considerable interest amongst Maltese *literati*.

Verse

729 **Dun Karm: poet of Malta.**
A. J. Arberry and P. Grech.   London: Cambridge University Press, 1961. 217p. bibliog. (Oriental Publications, no. 6).
An important selection of poems translated by the first author with a substantial introduction (52p.), notes and glossary by the second. This is the most accessible and comprehensive English-language publication on Malta's national poet Dun Karm Psaila. His poetic idiom and use of Maltese impressed the late Professor of Arabic at Oxford, Frederick Beeston, as bearing comparison with the classical Arabic poetry of early Mediaeval Baghdad.

730 **Malta. The new poetry.**
Edited by Mario Azzopardi, with an introduction by Francis Ebejer.
Valletta: Klabb Kotba Maltin, printed at the Lux Press, 1971. 187p.
Eight Maltese poets (Mario Azzopardi, Victor Fenech, Oliver Friggieri, Joe Friggieri, Daniel Massa, Achille Mizzi, Lillian Sciberras and Kenneth Wain) are introduced by the playwright and novelist Francis Ebejer (p. 9-13). All the poems are presented in both Maltese and English. 'The [Maltese] poets of the sixties have thrown overboard traditional diction, imagery and versification, and have rejected the traditional word-picture which formed the essential background of their predecessors' work' (Paul Xuereb, writing in *The Times*, London).

731 **Primitive infancy, nature, death, religion and life beyond death in the works of two romantic poets from Gozo.**
Arnold Cassola. *Journal of Maltese Studies*, vol. 4, no. 1 (1994), p. 97-111. bibliog.
Examines the poetic production of Ġorġ Pisani (1909-) and Roger Scicluna (1898-1942) who wrote in Maltese and English respectively and argues that their prevailing mythology is typically Mediterranean.

732 **Malta: poems.**
John Cremona. Valletta: Klabb Kotba Maltin with the Foundation for International Studies, University of Malta, 1992. 67p.
This collection of poems by the retired Chief Justice and Vice-President of the European Court of Human Rights has an introduction by Peter Serracino Inglott reviewing the author's moods and evocation of place which tie his writing in English to his Maltese national identification.

733 **Rebel in the mind: the poetry of Mario Azzopardi.**
Grazio Falzon. *Hyphen*, vol. V, no. 1 (1986), p. 19-38.
An analysis of the innovative literary forms of a contemporary poet who satirized popular beliefs and customs and broke loose from the archaic influences of the Italian *Risorgimento*, looking instead to current American forms but expressing his ideas in Maltese.

734 **Cross winds. An anthology of post-war Maltese poetry.**
Compiled by Oliver Friggieri, edited by Konrad Hopkins, Ronald van Roebel. Paisley, Scotland: Wilfion Books, 1979. 125p.
A representative collection of contemporary Maltese poetry compiled by an ardent advocate and exponent of this means of expression in Maltese.

735 **Mario Azzopardi: Malta's new experience through poetry.**
Oliver Friggieri. *The Journal of Commonwealth Literature*, vol. 16, no. 1 (1981), p. 40-44.
This is about the poetry of perhaps the main exponent of the Maltese avant-garde. Born in 1944, a poet, teacher and freelancer to numerous local newspapers and magazines, Azzopardi was co-founder, in 1966, of the Movement for the Promotion of Literature.

736 **Malta and the poetics of national awareness: a brief account of modern poetry.**
Oliver Friggieri. *Scripta Mediterranea*, vol. 5 (1984), p. 39-54.
The unifying motive of the significant Maltese poets and novelists from the mid-19th to the mid-20th centuries is the presentation of their home islands as an autonomous entity. Foremost representative of the national awareness was Dun Karm Psaila (1871-1961). This article takes the discussion past independence in 1964 and looks at modern Maltese poets concerned with the challenge of being self-aware.

737 **The evolution of poetry in Malta.**
Oliver Friggieri. *The Journal of Commonwealth Literature*, vol. 19, no. 1 (1985), p. 22-26.
A very brief survey – indicating major names such as Gian Anton Vassallo, Dun Karm, and Manwel Dimech – of poetry in Maltese since the later 19th century.

738 **Malta siege verse: 1941-1942-1943.**
John Snook. Bridport, England: Koons, 1990. 76p.
Some forty poems with supporting prose annotations by one who endured siege conditions in Malta during the Second World War.

739 **The Duque De Rivas, John Hookham Frere and the tribute to Malta in *El Moro Exposito*.**
Peter Vassallo. *Melita Historica*, vol. 9, no. 4 (1987), p. 315-28.
bibliog.
This Spaniard, a liberal in exile, was befriended by Frere who had been a British diplomat in Spain, and wrote poetry drawing on romantic Maltese themes. *The Lighthouse of Malta* is translated in an appendix and illustrated from a much earlier engraving as well as portraits of the two men.

The Arts

General

740 The Cathedral Museum, Mdina, Malta.
John Azzopardi.   Malta: Lombard Bank, 1990. 29p.

A comprehensive review of the components of the museum and its collections with good, if small, coloured illustrations of specific coins, pictures, ecclesiastical treasures and prints as well as an account of the types of archive housed at the museum relating to the diocese, its courts and those of the Roman Inquisition in Malta, and rare musical scores from 1568-1798. This museum director's account was originally published in the *Annual Report of the Lombard Bank* (q.v.) of 1990.

741 The Cathedral Museum, Notabile, Malta: catalogue.
R. Bonnici Cali.   Mdina, Malta: Malta Metropolitan Cathedral, 1954. 39p.

A useful list of the contents of the museum before it was resited at its current location in the ex-seminary. This includes items that have remained *in situ* in the treasury and other rooms of the Cathedral Chapter as well as its meeting hall and library, and many that are not now on permanent display and therefore unlisted in the other available short publications of what is to be seen by visitors.

742 Malta: history and works of art of St. John's Church, Valletta.
Dominic Cutajar.   Malta: M. J. Publications Ltd., 1989. 112p.

Although not as exhaustive as Sir Hannibal Scicluna's great work, this superbly colour-illustrated guide provides a mine of specifically documented information on every aspect of the fabric, decoration, furnishing and monuments of the Order's conventual church and a brief summary of the tapestries and liturgical vestments, antiphonals and plate in the adjacent museum.

743 **Museum of Fine Arts, Valletta, Malta: a commentary on its history and selected works.**
Dominic Cutajar. Valletta: Museums Department, 1991. 64p.
A well-illustrated cross-section of the paintings on view in the two primary floors of the splendid 18th-century palace that previously housed Portuguese Knights and the C.-in-C. of the Royal Navy's Mediterranean fleet. Not all the attributions are secure but short accounts of the artists are provided. Of the exhibits demonstrating the history of the Order, in the basement, only the Sicilian Majolica vessels are discussed, but this section has been under rearrangement since the opening of the Maritime Museum in Birgu to which several items have been transferred.

744 **Maltese baroque: proceedings of a seminar on 'The Baroque Route in Malta' held at the Ministry of Education, Beltissebħ, Malta, on 3rd June, 1989.**
Edited by Giovanni Mangion. Malta: Ministry of Education; Strasbourg, France: Council for Cultural Cooperation of the Council of Europe, 1989. 176p. bibliog.
Twenty-three short essays comprise this extensive review of many aspects of Maltese art and architecture, illustrated by numerous excellent black-and-white photographs and thirty-two in colour as a final section, many of them showing details of buildings or pictures. Although many of these brief accounts do not offer much new information, they do include a useful summary of Leonard Mahoney's findings on 18th-century palace design, the work of the painter Nicolo Nasoni (1691-1773), and the Maltese architect Carlo Gimach (1651-1730) in Portugal, and articles on Maltese music, maps and literature.

745 **Liber Amicorum: essays on art, history, cartography and bibliography in honour of Dr. Albert Ganado.**
Edited by Joseph Schirò, Sven Sorensen, Paul Xuereb. Msida, Malta: Malta University Library, 1994. 138p. bibliog.
This is a Festschrift for the leading collector of Melitensia, scholar of prints and maps, and research encourager of Malta since its independence. It comprises twelve articles by Maltese and foreign scholars on topics divided equally between art, history, books and maps. These include a 13th-century codex of Mdina Cathedral, a letter by Mattia Preti, the ultimately sad story of the water-colourist Vicenzo D'Esposito (1886-1946), relations between Malta and Djerba (1241-1798), the case of a Maltese Huguenot, and printing during the British Protectorate (1804-05). The collection concludes with a bibliography of seventy publications by Ganado and his other contributions to scholarship.

746 **The Church of St. John in Valletta: its history, architecture and monuments, with a brief history of the Order of St. John from its inception to the present day.**
Sir Hannibal Scicluna. Rome: Casa M. Danesi, 1955. 344p. bibliog.
This massive, well-researched and extensively illustrated volume was published privately by the author, a past librarian of what is now the National Library of Malta and repository of the Order's voluminous archives. Although many more discoveries and

attributions have been made with reference to specific items in this large and intricately decorated building, this book remains the fullest compendium of information and sometimes the only available description due to wartime damage. Except for this and one major destructive programme in the Chapel of the French Langue in the early 19th century, St. John's remains generally as the British found it in 1800. Its monuments of the grand masters, tapestries, frescoes and oil paintings make it one of the most complete baroque ensembles in Europe. All these are well illustrated in black-and-white photographs, although the colour plates are disappointing. The floor of the church consists of particoloured marble ledgers memorializing past members of the Order, all of which are both illustrated in the plates and transcribed in an appendix.

Fine arts

General

747 The Rhodes Missal: a commentary.
Eustace A. Alliott.   London: The Order of St. John, 1980. 47p. bibliog.

In his foreword Professor Lionel Butler describes the arrival of the Order's cargo ship with the French Prior Charles Aleman de Rochenard's gifts to the conventual church at Rhodes in 1511 and a contemporary record of this knight's other donations, including land, cannon and this illuminated missal. The author describes its safe passage to Malta in 1530 and its disappearance after 1798 until it was acquired in 1929 by the Venerable Order in England from a Florentine bookseller. He considers the French artists in whose circle it was produced followed by a general description of the manuscript and details of its illuminations, many of which are illustrated in colour or monochrome. In an appendix he outlines the forms and functions of a shepherd's *houlette* (crook). The missal was one of the finest adornments of St. John's high altar and is now on view at the Order's museum in Clerkenwell, London.

748 Some late Medieval and early modern panel paintings in Malta.
Mario Buḥaġiar.   *Melita Historica*, vol. 8, no. 3 (1982), p. 177-89. bibliog.

Eight religious paintings on panels are discussed which survive from the large altar panel paintings that were replaced by oil paintings on canvas later in the 17th century. Technically, as well as artistically, primitive, these pictures would have been the usual products of local craftsmen until the impact of Mattia Preti's productive and long-active studio in Malta in the last half of the 17th century.

749 **The iconography of the Maltese Islands 1400-1900: painting.**
Mario Buḣaġiar. Valletta: Progress Press for World Federation of
Salesian Past Pupils of Don Bosco – Lions Club (Malta), 1987. 202p.
bibliog.
By far the most important, informative and superbly colour-illustrated book so far
published on painting in Malta. The author reviews the artists with examples of their
work through nine chapters devoted to: late Mediaeval and early 16th-century works;
the late Mannerist painting of d'Aleccio and others; Caravaggio and Mattia Preti with
their respective schools; later baroque works especially by the Erardi family, G. N.
Buhagiar and F. V. Zahra and their French Knight contemporary Antoine de Favray;
and the Maltese artists strongly influenced by the succession of 19th-century artistic
practices and styles in Rome. This ordering of data and evaluation of significant artists
will provide the basis for any subsequent discussion of local painting for many years.
It is biased towards religious art and other painting to be found in public collections
with the result that still lifes, genre groups, and some portraiture and landscape is
under-represented in both the text and illustrations. Given the inaccessibility of local
private collections to most Maltese citizens this is not surprising. But it does mean
that iconographic portraiture, for example, is not discussed. With such a wealth of
great artists invited to Malta in each generation by the Order, Maltese artists were
exposed to marvellous models, although their own formative years were usually spent
in Rome, often at the Accademia di San Luca.

750 **The international dictionary of artists who painted Malta.**
Nicholas de Piro. Valletta: Said International Ltd. for Mid-Med
Bank Ltd., 1988. 208p.
In addition to its obvious value as a unique compendium of information on the many
foreign and local artists who have included the depiction of Maltese subjects in their
oil painting, water-colours, prints and drawings, this book provides invaluable evidence of their type of work in its many coloured illustrations. It is a remarkable
achievement even if the additional data on the lives, dates and viewable collections of
each artist's work is inevitably not always certain or complete. Artists to whom the
larger illustrated sections are devoted include: Charles F. von Brocktorff (1775-1850),
Salvatore Busuttil (1798-1854), Edward Caruuna Dingli (1876-1950), Leslie Cole
(1910-76), Vincenzo Fenech (late 18th-early 19th century), Joseph Galea (1904-85),
Alfred Gerada (1895-1968), Girolamo Gianni (1837-c.1895), Nicholas Krasnoff
(fl.1920s), Edward Lear (1812-88), Albert W. C. McFall (1862-1923), Alberto
Pullicino (1719-59), Giorgio Pullicino (1780-1852), five members of the Schranz
family and General Sir George Whitmore K. C. H. (1775-1862). In many cases these
are the only easily available reproductions of the artist's work and all have been taken
from excellent photographs.

751 **The provenance of the paintings on permanent display at the**
National Museum of Fine Arts.
Antonio Espinosa Rodriguez. *Proceedings of History Week, 1983*
(1984), p. 97-124. bibliog.
This digest of available sources on the paintings displayed in the museum lists their
current attributions to artists as well as their provenance. Nine are of unknown origin,
7 presented under the terms of the Antiquities Act 1925, 7 from various chapels of the
Order of St. John, 9 by donations from abroad, 57 by donation or bequest within

Malta, 9 from Government sources including the National Library, the University, the Orphans' Asylum and the Central Hospital, 44 from the Grand Master's Palace collection, 10 purchased abroad and 112 purchased for the museum locally. The medium, support, and exhibition of each work are also given, with published references. No records were found of collections once held in the auberges of the Order although such registers are referred to in the *spoglie* (inventories of effects acquired by the Order from its deceased members) of some grand masters.

752 **Paintings at the National Museum of Fine Arts in Malta.**
Antonio Espinosa Rodriguez.   Valletta: Said International Ltd., 1990. 275p. bibliog.

This is a grand catalogue of 270 paintings in the collection, fully illustrated in colour, with details of their medium, support, dimensions, provenance, museum no., and published references, and descriptive and critical notes on each entry. These entries, which are listed by school and date of execution, are preceded by a brief account of the collection and the museum's history. A few attributions are unstable and this excellent publication will assist in their deliberation.

753 **European paintings in the Cauchi Collection at the Cathedral Museum, Mdina, Malta: Dr. Victor Captur Memorial Lecture No. 1.**
John T. Spike.   Mdina, Malta: The Cathedral Museum, 1994. 48p.

Joe Cauchi (1913-92), curator of the National Museum of Fine Arts in Valletta and an art historian who had studied at the Courtauld Institute in London, formed a collection of nearly 200 paintings, drawings, water-colours and engravings that he bequeathed to the Cathedral Museum. This publication is an illustrated catalogue of the sixty-one paintings selected for long-term exhibition in their own gallery at the museum, with a commentary on most of them by Spike and a list of Cauchi's published work by John Azzopardi. Primarily examples of Italian baroque religious art, they also include mythological paintings and work by Flemish, French, German, Swiss and English artists. Cauchi's is the most significant private collection formed in Malta since 1945 and one of the few great donations to a public institution in the islands in recent years.

16th-18th centuries

754 **Francesco Zahra 1710-1773.**
J. Azzopardi, M. Buħaġiar, J. A. Cauchi, A. Espinosa Rodriguez, E. Montanaro.   Mdina, Malta: Friends of the Cathedral Museum, 1986. 147p. bibliog.

The primary source on this accomplished Maltese painter, this includes eighteen illustrations from the exhibition for which it was the catalogue. The book includes biographical data as well as a list of the artist's works in Mdina Cathedral and its museum (with forty-four documents relating to Zahra's work in their original Italian), and in Żurrieq Parish Church and in Gozo.

755   **Our Lady of Damascus: the story of an icon.**
      Papàs Vito Borgia.   Kettering, England: Catholic Truth Society, 1992.
      11p.
A summary of what is known about this probably 12th-century icon in the Greek-
Catholic church in Valletta, transported from Rhodes in 1523, and judiciously cleaned
and restored in Rome in 1963-66.

756   **Alberto Pullicino: his artistic commissions, life and times in
      eighteenth-century Malta.**
      David M. Boswell.   *Melita Historica*, vol. 9, no. 4 (1987), p. 347-67.
      bibliog.
The discovery of four views of the harbour cities with an inscription giving the artist's
name, date of 1749 and style of execution, and the patron, a French knight who subsequently led a French expedition to Guyana, led to further research into this artist's
family and works. In total a set of eight distinct views were recorded in different com-
binations in several collections in Malta and elsewhere. They transformed the way in
which Malta was depicted over the next half-century. Other documented commissions
included the decoration of St. John's vestry and treasury and the depictions of the
Order's reliquaries and other treasures that constitute the illustrations bound in their
inventory of 1756, which is now in the Cathedral Museum at Mdina. A well-illustrated
extension of this research, with an appendix of Pullicino's views in different media
and in different collections is '"Malta's Canaletto", Alberto Pullicino: a "painter after
nature" and his circle' in *Apollo*, vol. cxxxii, no. 346 (new series) (Dec. 1990), p. 302-98.
bibliog.

757   **Eighteenth century Malta represented: the significance of Alberto
      Pullicino's urban harbour views.**
      David M. Boswell.   *Treasures of Malta*, vol. 1, no. 3 (1995), p. 9-16.
      bibliog.
This article updates the author's previous research on this artist and his various commissions and indicates the form of view painting that became established in Malta for
some fifty years. The twelve well-reproduced colour plates include details of
identifiable historical events depicted in some of Pullicino's sets of views as well as
pictures by his nephew, Giorgio, which appear to be derived from some of Alberto's
paintings.

758   **Marian art during the seventeenth and eighteenth centuries.**
      Edited by Mario Buħaġiar.   Mdina, Malta: Friends of the Cathedral
      Museum, 1983. 83p. bibliog.
A set of essays by the author and two Maltese art historians sets the scene for the catalogue of the twenty-eight paintings included in an exhibition at the Cathedral Museum
in Mdina. A further essay on votive paintings introduces the catalogue of fifty-three
ex-votos exhibited. Nineteen inferior illustrations complete this informative little
book.

759   **Images of the Grand Tour: Louis Ducros 1748-1810.**
Edited by Paul Chessex.   Geneva: Editions du Tricorne, 1985. 111p.
bibliog.

In addition to the catalogue of an exhibition of this Swiss artist's work held at
Kenwood, London, The Whitworth Art Gallery, Manchester, and the Musée Central
des Beaux-Arts at Lausanne, Switzerland, the book includes six articles. The four by
art historians include a biographical history, essays on Ducros's relations with some of
his British patrons and artists (unfortunately not including General Graham or other
patrons during their take-over of Malta from the French in 1800), Swiss artists in
Rome 1775-93, and Ducros's views of the Museo Pio-Clementino in Rome. The other
two essays are devoted to Ducros's methods of painting and the methods adopted to
conserve his water-colours. Ducros used a variety of media in producing the gorgeous
and luscious effects in his highly finished paintings. Five of these in the Bayfordbury
Collection were of Maltese subjects. They were bought in 1945 by the National Art
Collections Fund and given to Malta where they may be seen in the Fine Arts
Museum. Some of them have since then been so destructively 'cleaned' that their sublime original impact can only be inferred from two excellent coloured reproductions in
this book of virtually identical versions in Lausanne. Eight paintings of Malta are
reproduced in black-and-white on p. 70-73. They mark the first major change in representing Malta since Pullicino's views of 1749 (see item nos. 756 and 757).

760   **Mattia Preti – monografie di artisti.** (Mattia Preti – monographs on
artists.)
Edited by Erminia Corace.   Rome: Fratelli Palombi for Mid-Med
Bank Ltd., 1989. 188p. bibliog.

This is the only comprehensive monograph devoted to one of the most influential, as
well as one of the most prolific, of the Italian painters invited to work for the Order of
St. John in Malta. A native of Taverna, *Il Calabrese* (The Calabrian) as Preti (1613-
99) was nicknamed, had a thorough formation in the artistry of Rome, Venice and
Emilia and executed significant religious frescoes in Rome, Modena and Naples
before going to Malta in 1659 where he accomplished an extensive range of murals
and oil paintings for the churches and chapels of the Order as well as some parish
churches and small chapels. The book consists of four parts. The first part includes a
short essay on Preti's origins in Taverna, and a substantial review by John T. Spike of
the artist's long career with an appendix of thirty documents transcribed with their original Italian from Maltese sources. F. Piccirillo provides a biography supported by
facsimiles from the Vatican archives on Preti's admission to the Order as a Knight of
Obedience. Part 2 comprises 116 coloured reproductions of Preti's paintings and
drawings, not always photographed in ideal conditions, and part 3 includes essays on
the development of the artist's style of painting and his followers and on the diverging
artistic style of Preti's brother Gregorio. The final part includes indexes of all the
works mentioned in the book and details of where they may now be found as well as a
comprehensive bibliography of publications in Italian and English.

761   **An inventory of Alessio Erardi's paintings and books.**
John Debono.   Malta: The Author, 1989. 30p.

The son of Stefano, a successful painter of religious subjects whose practice he continued, Erardi (d.1727) left a will of 1726 and inventory of his effects. The latter
included 629 works of art, half of which were of religious subjects, and another third
still lifes, land and seascapes. The full text describing each in Italian is printed.

762 **Malta views: a catalogue of topographical prints and drawings in the Museum of the Order of St. John.**
Stella Dyer. London: The Order of St. John, 1984. 68p.
A well-illustrated and chronologically arranged demonstration of the ways in which Malta has been viewed since the 17th century, with introductory chapters on the island and the development of its depicted image. The collection is especially rich in works by French artists and those producing art in the period of British rule.

763 **Three artistic links between Malta and Seville.**
Antonio Espinosa Rodriguez. Mdina, Malta: Friends of the Cathedral Museum, 1985. 16p. bibliog.
A fully documented account of the Spanish patronage of two artists who worked in Malta, Mattia Perez d'Aleccio (1547-c.1616), and Mattia Preti (1613-99), and a Spanish Knight of St. John who became an artist in Malta and returned to Seville as a friend of Murillo, Don Pedro Nuñez de Villavicencio (1640-c.1700).

764 **Caravaggio in Malta.**
Edited by Philip Farrugia Randon. Malta: Mid-Med Bank Ltd., 1989. 143p. bibliog.
This useful collection of nine articles and essays is well documented but uneven in the quality of its contribution to this popular subject. After Cutajar's review of the artist's work and followers in Malta, John Azzopardi traces the sources for Caravaggio's eventful year in Malta in 1607-08 and his subsequent trial, and also for his admission to the Order. Seven of these documents are reproduced in facsimile and transcribed in their original Latin and English translation with four extracts from 17th-century biographies of the artist. Edward Sammut's short article (1978) on the artist's trial is also reprinted as well as a translation of Cesare Brandi's report (1952) on the state of *The beheading of St. John the Baptist*, with J. A. Cauchi's account of the restoration of that painting and *St. Jerome* in Rome in 1955/56. Vincenzo Pacelli provides an article in Italian on the last works produced by Caravaggio and Peter Serracino Inglott one on the symbolism underlying the artist's 'realism'. The book concludes with a long and rather rambling commentary on the huge painting in the Oratory of St. John's church already discussed in the articles by Brandi and Cauchi mentioned above.

765 **Matteo Perez d'Aleccio's engravings of the Siege of Malta of 1565.**
Albert Ganado. *Proceedings of History Week, 1983* (1984), p. 125-61. bibliog.
An extremely well documented analysis of the contents of, intention behind, and reception of, the engravings the artist based on his frescoes in the Grand Master's Palace, Valletta, which were published in Rome in 1582. In 1631 they were re-engraved by A. F. Lucini in Rome, with an additional plate delineating the grand masters, and these were subsequently reprinted twice in Bologna. Three appendices include descriptions of the fifteen plates as well as their Italian inscriptions and identification keys and texts. The map sources available to d'Aleccio are described as well as the influence of his own maps on the subsequent cartography of Malta. A group of eight plates reproduce a portrait drawing of d'Aleccio and several of his maps and other documents. Another appendix provides a concordance of places included in d'Alleccio's engraved and fresco maps, Lafreri's map of 1551 and that of the United Kingdom War Office in 1854, which indicates changes in settlement

pattern. The article is a major documentary source on this key representation and phase of Malta's history and population distribution.

766 **The identity of Caravaggio's 'Knight of Malta'.**
John Gash. *The Burlington Magazine,* vol. CXXXIX, no. 1128 (March 1997), p. 156-60. bibliog.

The subject of a striking portrait in the Pitti Palace at Florence has at last been convincingly identified as Antonio Martelli, a Knight of St. John from c.1558 who was resident in office in Malta during Caravaggio's short sojourn on the island in 1607-08 and promoted to prior of Messina where he repaired in 1608 before his final return to Tuscany in 1609. The author also provides useful information on the artist's other Italian patron in the Order, the Marchese Ippolito Malaspina, who owned the *St. Jerome* now restored to the chapel of the Italian Langue in the co-cathedral of St. John in Valletta after its theft from the adjacent museum.

767 **The maritime siege of Malta 1565.**
George Nash. London: HMSO for National Maritime Museum, 1970. 33p.

A fully illustrated account of the eight paintings of the Turkish siege by Perez d'Alecchio, which have been in the royal collection since the 16th century. Nash compares them with engravings based on the larger series in Malta's Grand Master's Palace. Other sections discuss the galleys and Battle of Lepanto in 1571. This short work was published in connection with an exhibition at the National Maritime Museum.

768 **The context of Caravaggio's 'Beheading of St. John' in Malta.**
David M. Stone. *The Burlington Magazine,* vol. CXXXIX, no. 1128 (March 1997), p. 161-70. bibliog.

The recent dismantling of this large canvas behind the altar of the Oratory of St. John's Co-Cathedral in Valletta provided the opportunity for the author to compare what was revealed with a view of the chapel engraved in 1650 and other documentary evidence. Used for novices in training as well as the criminal tribunal, the context of Caravaggio's work, which associated the heroism of the Order with that of its patron saint, is discussed. This was substantially modified by Mattia Preti when he remodelled the chapel's decorative scheme to incorporate his series of paintings of Christ's Passion.

769 **Image of a knight: portrait prints and drawings of the Knights of St. John in the Museum of the Order of St. John.**
Julia Toffolo. London: The Order of St. John, 1988. 101p. bibliog.

Published in association with an exhibition at the Museum of St. John's Gate, Clerkenwell, London, this catalogue is prefaced by an essay on the commissioning of portraits by the Order and the form of the collection in the Museum. Although some of the portraits were fanciful and many after oil paintings, the likenesses of these noble warriors of Catholic Christendom, accompanied by their heraldic achievements, with some of the Inquisitors and artists of Malta, stare out over the centuries. Textual inscriptions are transcribed and accompanied by brief biographies of the sitters and their notable achievements and how they are portrayed. Where known, brief information is given on the artist and many of the entries are illustrated, including the period since

1798. Sets and series are listed in full and bibliographical information is provided on books which include such portraits. The dates of all the grand masters from c.1099-1798 are listed in one appendix and another provides brief biographies of grand masters whose portraits do not figure in the main catalogue.

19th-20th centuries

770 **Count Saverio Marchese (1757-1833): his picture-gallery and his bequest to the Cathedral Museum.**
John Azzopardi. *Proceedings of History Week, 1982* (1983), p. 28-43. bibliog.

A brief account of Count Saverio Marchese's life precedes that of the acquisition of his art collection from 1793-1833. There is a register of eighty-five paintings with their subjects, attributions and provenance and the inventory of family portraits and other paintings accompanying his last will under which the bulk of the collection ultimately came to the museum. Two appendices list these items with notes on the subsequent history and attribution of some of them.

771 **The Schranz artists: landscape and marine painters in the Mediterranean (active XIX century).**
Edited by John Azzopardi. Mdina, Malta: Gulf Publication for the Friends of the Cathedral Museum, 1987. 72p. bibliog.

This is an important book on one of several foreign families of artists who settled in Malta in the 19th century and produced the representations of the harbour areas and the countryside that characterized the British period. Published in association with an exhibition at the Cathedral Museum, the book comprises three parts, which are extensively illustrated in black-and-white with a few good colour reproductions of works by members of the Schranz family. The first part includes five short essays on the monastic town of Ochsenhausen where Anton Schranz was born, the artistic environment in which the family worked in Minorca, Greece and Malta and their patrons in the Royal Navy. The second part consists of biographical essays by Kurt Diemer, Egon Schneider and Albert Ganado on Anton Schranz (1769-1839) and his sons Giovanni (1794-1882), Antonio (1801-after 1864) and Joseph (1803-after 1853). The final part includes the exhibition catalogue of their paintings, water-colours and sketches by Antonio Espinosa Rodriguez, and of prints by Albert Ganado, all items borrowed from Maltese private and public collections.

772 **Anton Inglott 1915-1945.**
Edited by John Azzopardi. Mdina, Malta: Friends of the Cathedral Museum, 1988. 86p. bibliog.

Three essays precede the catalogue to the museum's exhibition of oil paintings, water-colours, pastels and drawings by one of the last Maltese art students to attend the Accademia di Belle Arti in Rome before Mussolini took Italy into the Second World War. The sources and range of his art are outlined as well as his major work of the *Death of St. Joseph* in the main apse of Msida parish church. Inglott died of diabetic complications before he could execute other murals in this church. The illustrations provide a poor reproduction of the artist's works.

773 Girolamo Gianni in Malta.
Edited by Giovanni Bonello.   Malta: Progress Press and Melitensia
Art Gallery Publications, 1994. 110p. bibliog.

This book was produced in connection with an exhibition mounted by the Fondazzjoni
Patrimonju Malti (Foundation for the Maltese Patrimony), in which 133 of this
Neapolitan artist's views of 19th-century Malta were shown, mostly from local private
collections, together with a few pictures by others painting in his manner. This colourfully illustrated catalogue is preceded by essays on Gianni's life (1837-95) by Albert
Ganado, on his Neapolitan predecessors by Dominic Cutajar, and on his varied subject
matter and their appeal by five other authors. A curious sunset glow seems to characterize most of these oil paintings, many of which provide the traditional views around
the harbour cities and street scenes of *festa* celebrations and clergy that have appealed
to British servicemen and now to Maltese collectors.

774 Giuseppe Cassar: Malta watercolours.
E. V. Borġ.   Pietà, Malta: Independence Print, 1992. 22p. + 100
full-page plates.

Giuseppe Cassar (born 1917) is a professional photographer who took up painting
during wartime detention in Italy as an anti-Fascist British citizen, but only returned to
it in retirement in the 1970s. His accomplished water-colours, illustrated here in
colour and monochrome, depict the land, sea and townscape of the island and have
been the subject of several exhibitions at the Cathedral Museum in Mdina.

775 Giuseppe Calleja, 1828-1915, the man, the teacher, the artist.
Joe Calleja.   Malta: The Author, 1992. 168p. bibliog.

A product of great-grand nepotal piety, this is a sumptuous record of a rather indiffer-
ent artist, whose ordinariness makes the book of unusual interest. It was published to
accompany an exhibition of Calleja's paintings at the Cathedral Museum in Mdina, for
which part 2 is the catalogue of 172 works, followed by lists of his 59 published lithographs and 23 works of restoration and other designs, and various writings. Part 1
consists of three essays on Calleja's life, his work as drawing master in primary
schools, and his artistic output, much of which has since been replaced by the work of
subsequent religious subject painters. Part 3 comprises a group of substantial documents, including the artist's own inventory of his collection of pictures and prints, the
text of his autobiography in Italian, copies of 235 letters written by Calleja between
1885 and 1895, and the last wills of Calleja and his art teacher Giuseppe Hysler,
whose Nazerene style was to influence his own.

776 School for sightseers: topographical artists in Malta 1800-50.
Anne Crosthwait.   *Country Life*, 4 October (1984), p. 936-37.

This article reviews the work of several of the foreign artists who worked in Malta,
sometimes establishing their families as artists, during the first fifty years of British
rule. The works of five artists are illustrated.

777 **The lure of the Orient: the Schranzes, the Brockdorffs, Preziosi and other artists.**
Dominic Cutajar. *Hyphen*, vol. 5, no. 3 (1987), p. 101-36. bibliog.
A useful if raw account of the various foreign artists who settled in Malta but, along with some Maltese artists, sought other subjects in the eastern Mediterranean when Malta ceased to be a prosperous entrepot in the mid-19th century. Evidence of the different voyages made by members of the Schranz family are listed as well as Preziosi, five members of the Brockdorff family, Michele Bellanti, and eight other artists, all drawn from the arrival and departure entries in the Port Books of the Malta Government Archives.

778 **Malta. Six modern artists.**
Dominic Cutajar, Emanuel Fiorentino, Kenneth Wain. Msida, Malta: Malta University Services Ltd., 1991. 181p.
This elegantly produced volume, with an introduction by Peter Serracino Inglott, offers profiles of the artists Josef Kalleya, Vincent Apap and Emvin Cremona (by Dominic Cutajar), Esprit Barthet and Frank Portelli (by Kenneth Wain) and Antoine Camilleri (by Emmanuel Fiorentino). Some of the many photographs are in colour.

779 **Contemporary sacred art in Malta: an exhibition organized by the Malta Society of Arts, Manufactures and Commerce on the invitation of the Metropolitan Cathedral Chapter commemorating the twenty fifth anniversary of the opening of the Cathedral Museum.**
Edited by Dominic Cutajar. Mdina, Malta: Cathedral Museum Publications, 1994. 63p.
Three short essays introduce the biographies of forty living artists. An example of each of their work is reproduced in colour, followed by the catalogue of works exhibited.

780 **The painting of the cathedral dome at Mdina: a case study in ecclesiastical artistic patronage in Malta in the nineteenth and early twentieth century.**
Antonio Espinosa Rodriguez. *Proceedings of History Week 1986* (1992), p. 39-68.
As the result of an earthquake in 1856, the dome had to be partially rebuilt and Manno's frescoed *Paradiso* replaced. This article recounts the disputes surrounding the restoration of this painting, first by Giovanni Gallucci in 1859, and then owing to further structural decay, by the Italian Mario Caffaro-Rore, after a long wartime delay, in 1955. There are few historical articles on these more recent ecclesiastical commissions in Malta.

781   **Nicola Camilleri alias Nicolas Cammillieri a Maltese ship-painter.**
Antonio Espinosa Rodriguez.   *Melita Historica*, vol. 11, no. 2 (1993),
p. 143-56. bibliog.
This artist (c.1773-1860) was a prolific painter of ships, using settings identifiable as
Malta and Marseilles, from which he had returned by 1822. Appendices include documents, a list of foreign museums holding the artist's paintings, and illustrations of the
five given to the Maritime Museum in Malta by the Mid-Med Bank in 1992.

782   **Giuseppe Calì 1846-1930.**
Emanuel Fiorentino, Louis A. Grasso.   Valletta: Said International
Ltd., 1991. 172p. bibliog.
The son of a Neapolitan musician and scenographer at the Manoel Theatre, Calì studied in Naples and returned to make his name with *The death of Dragut* in 1867. The
book, which is copiously illustrated with excellent colour plates, proceeds to discuss
his substantial oeuvre of religious paintings, his portraits, and other works including
the allegorical decoration of a cinema underneath the Casino Maltese in Valletta that
is now a fashionable café.

783   **Willie Apap 1918-1970.**
Emanuel Fiorentino, Louis A. Grasso.   Sliema, Malta: Carmelo
Zammit la Rosa, 1993. 187p. bibliog.
The artist divided his career between Malta and Rome, where he spent most of his life
after first going to study there in 1937 at the Royal Academy of Fine Arts. In 1946 he
was detained in Italy with other Maltese who had surrendered their British passports
and remained in Italy during the war, but was acquitted after a trial in Malta in 1947.
The book is primarily devoted to the different types and subject matter of his art, profusely illustrated here in colour: his artistic formation, religious works, portraits,
human figurative compositions, landscapes and still lives. Finally, there is a review
and list of his exhibitions.

784   **Malta in British and French caricature 1798-1818, with historical
notes.**
Albert Ganado, Joseph Sammut.   Valletta: Said International Ltd. for
the Central Bank of Malta, 1989. 164p. bibliog.
One hundred and fifty-five caricatures are listed of which forty-nine are illustrated in
full colour and often at full size, accompanied by a textual description and historical
commentary. They indicate the significance attached to Malta in this struggle for the
mastery of Europe and the Mediterranean.

785   **Sacred art in Malta 1890-1960.**
Edited by Gino Gauci.   Valletta: Said International Ltd., 1990. 96p.
A book associated with an exhibition mounted during the papal visit of that year. All
the pictures are illustrated in colour with notes by the curators of fine art at the
National Museum, and an introductory essay on religious art in the context of Malta's
experience of cultural bipolarization by the editor and Peter Serracino Inglott.

786 **The people and places of Constantinople: watercolours by Amadeo Count Preziosi.**
Briony Llewellyn, Charles Newton.   London: Victoria and Albert Museum, 1985. 56p. bibliog.
This catalogue of an exhibition at the Victoria and Albert Museum is prefaced by an informative account of the life, artistic work and environment of Preziosi (1816-82), a Maltese nobleman who trained as a graphic artist in Paris before proceeding to Istanbul in 1842 where he spent the rest of his life until killed in a shooting accident. The fifty-four works in the exhibition are fully described and many are illustrated in black-and-white or full-page colour plates of portraits, costume and views of Istanbul and Bucharest. An appendix details Preziosi's publications of lithographs of Eastern Life (in Istanbul), Cairo and Bucharest, but the essay indicates that he was commissioned to provide illustrations for other travellers' published accounts as well as for *The Illustrated London News*. Preziosi was one of the great popularizers of the Orient and an unusually accomplished example of one of the many Maltese who migrated along the Mediterranean littoral in the 19th century. His significance and artistic skills are strangely unsung.

787 **Homage to Willie Apap (1918-1970).**
Edited by Edward Sammut.   Mdina, Malta: Friends of the Cathedral Museum, 1984. 60p. bibliog.
This illustrated catalogue to an exhibition of thirty-four painted portraits, religious and other subjects and fourteen drawings, is prefaced by the editor's account of the artist's life in Italy as a Rome scholar and his trial for treason after the war. The work also includes an assessment of his painting by Carlo Liberto in Italian as well as extracts from published criticism of his works.

788 **Anton Agius: Maltese sculptor.**
Godwin Scerri.   Malta: PEG Ltd., 1986. 61p.
An expressively illustrated personal account and assessment of the natural forms and representational figures of one of Malta's most commissioned and prolific contemporary sculptors since Sciortino. He virtually became the official artist to Mintoff's second government and his monuments fill the squares of Valletta, Msida and Birgu *inter alia*.

789 **Contemporary Maltese artists.**
Adrian Stivala.   Valletta: North Star Publications, 1985. 128p.
A biographical dictionary of ninety-two local artists with several illustrations of their work as well as a photographic portrait of each in alphabetical order.

790 **Luciano Micallef: a study.**
Kenneth Wain.   Msida, Malta: Malta University Service (MUS) Ltd., 1993. 79p.
A monograph, extensively illustrated in colour with the abstract and figurative paintings of this contemporary artist.

Architecture

General

791 **Mdina. The cathedral city of Malta: a reassessment of its history and a critical appreciation of its architecture and works of art. Vol. I.**
Mario Buħaġiar, Stanley Fiorini, photography by the Marquis Cassar de Sain. Valletta: The Central Bank of Malta and Gutenberg Press Ltd., 1996. 350p. bibliog.
This comprehensively written and magnificently illustrated book covers the history and development of Mdina from Roman times through the Mediaeval period to the building of the new cathedral in the last years of the 17th century and the early part of the 18th century. The final chapter deals with the religious orders. This is a feast of art and architecture, as much as it is a history.

792 **Mdina: a reassessment of its history and a critical appreciation of its architecture and works of art. Vol. II.**
Mario Buħaġiar, Stanley Fiorini, photography by the Marquis Cassar de Sain. Valletta: The Central Bank of Malta and Gutenberg Press Ltd., 1996, p. 353-775. bibliog.
This second volume evokes the same superlatives as the first. It deals with the secondary churches of the city and with its fortifications. The rest of the volume traces the evolution of the city under the Knights of St. John and up to the present day when there is, however, 'the danger of speculative greed. The insensitive urge to make easy cash, to prostitute her monuments for the amusement of tourists . . .' (p. 685). Indeed the two volumes are published as concern about the very number of visitors to the (once) 'silent city' mounts. This volume concludes with a Select Corpus of Inscriptions (p. 689-97), a list of plates, a substantial bibliography (p. 717-52), and an index. As in volume I the photography is particularly noteworthy for its breadth of coverage, from the grandest building and most celebrated work of art to pictures of the humble and the everyday, and from the detail of a balcony to a simple view of an alley, or a railway train.

793 **Architecture in Malta 1. Historical aspects.**
Edited by Patrick Calleja. Msida, Malta: Society of Architecture and Engineering Students, University of Malta, 1986. 64p. bibliog.
The text is based on eight public lectures given by local students of Maltese architecture, some of which were later published in book form. Information not as fully aggregated elsewhere may be found in the essays devoted to neo-classical and neo-gothic architecture in the 19th century by Konrad Buħaġiar and Michael Ellul respectively, and mediaeval hypogea and cave churches by Mario Buħaġiar. There is also Leonard Mahoney's summary of his thesis on the design of St. John's conventual church.

794 **Mdina: a history of its urban space and architecture.**
Denis de Lucca.   Valletta: Said International Ltd., 1995. 152p.
bibliog.
This mediaeval cathedral citadel has been the subject of numerous informative guides
and articles, several by this author. This well-illustrated and produced monograph represents the results of twenty years' research. The five chapters are devoted to the city
in ancient, mediaeval, early and late baroque, and more recent, times. Many original
plans and designs are reproduced as well as photographs by Creative Design Systems
detailing matters discussed in the text. Excellent comparative plans of street patterns
and individual buildings are provided as well as a series of plans showing the development of both overbuilt and public spaces in different quarters of the city. The volume
would have benefited from being produced in the smaller format for which many of its
sketch-plans were originally drawn.

795 **Casa Rocca Piccola: an historic house, home of a Maltese noble
family, 74 Republic Street.**
Marquis de Piro.   Valletta: Said International Ltd., 1991. 27p.
The guidebook to the only private Maltese house which is open to the public. The
interiors are illustrated in colour and the personal history of significant furniture,
paintings and other memorabilia is described, as are some previous occupants of the
house. Owners have included the Langue of Italy, notable Knights of the Order and
latterly Cassar Torreggiani, the author's grandfather and a prominent businessman in
Malta.

796 **The girna: the Maltese corbelled stone hut.**
Michael Fsadni, OP, translated by L. J. Scerri.   Malta: Dominican
Publication, 1992. 120p. map. bibliog.
First published in Maltese in 1990, this publication won that year's Malta Government
Literary Award gold medal. Buildings roofed by corbelled domes have been constructed
since prehistoric times and various forms can be found around the Mediterranean as
well as Africa. Although, like caves, some of these structures have been used as
dwellings in Malta until very recently, the majority are to be found in the rocky out-
crops to the north and west of Malta where they acted as shelters for those working the
land, watching flocks far from their home-villages or rearing livestock. Motorized
transport has made them redundant and the author set out to record their uses and
types of construction before they disintegrate. This account, illustrated from ninety-
eight excellent coloured and black-and-white photographs, two plans and a map of the
areas most extensively provided with surviving *girna*, is a unique record with the
added value of a typological constructional analysis.

797 **Fortress: architecture and military history in Malta.**
Quentin Hughes.   London: Lund Humphreys, 1969. 284p. 2 maps.
In this book, profusely illustrated with outstanding black-and-white photographs, the
author covers the whole built environment of Malta from prehistoric to modern times.
It is a useful summary of much that is published in his more specific books. The
remaining copies were issued in paperback by the Progress Press in Malta.

798   **Housing in the Maltese Islands: an analysis of the influences in built form.**
M. J. King.   Unpublished MA thesis, Faculty of Architecture,
University of Malta, 1971. 93p. bibliog.

For all the attention devoted to the highlights of Maltese ecclesiastical architecture and the conventual and other buildings of the Order of St. John, little attention has been paid to the greater and lesser residential palaces and houses built for Maltese domestic use. King partially fills this gap, illustrating his text with appropriate perspective sketches and a series of plans and elevations, urban as well as rural, from all periods of Maltese vernacular architecture. Courtyard and row houses are delineated as well as some of the tourist complexes then under construction. The design principles and modes of construction are outlined and an appendix of Maltese, Italian and English building and other terms is provided.

799   **A Maltese mosaic.**
Kilin (Mikiel Spiteri).   Malta: Gutenberg Press, 1990. 74p.

Comprises rare records of the history and buildings of 100 of the many rural and urban wayside chapels on the Maltese islands which were originally published each week in the 1970s in the Maltese newspaper *Lehen is-Sewwa* (Voice of Truth) and in three little pocket-books. They are ordered according to their period of foundation, their type of founder, or the reason for their foundation. Every entry includes a full-page reproduction of the author's lively sketch of the chapel, which is often the only evidence for the actual construction of the building as it now stands. Owing to the survival of these chapels' small endowments and local devotion to their occasional but regular use, these important examples of popular religion and diminutive architecture may still be seen throughout the island. In many countries they have either long since disappeared or been replaced by vast pilgrimage churches.

800   **A history of Maltese architecture from ancient times up to 1800.**
Leonard Mahoney.   Malta: Veritas Press, 1988. 360p. bibliog.

This is the most important original book on Maltese architecture, since Tonna and de Lucca's revisions of traditional local attributions accepted by Quentin Hughes. But here the author adopts the full scope of Hughes's books. The first part is devoted to St. John's conventual church, the similarity of its facade to Michelangelo's design for S. Lorenzo in Florence and the 'harmonies' of its proportions (an example noted by Sir Howard Colvin of intricate mathematics not necessarily making for the best architecture). Part two provides a brief review of Maltese mediaeval architecture and the mainly Sicilian origins of terms for tools etc. The third and largest part contains descriptions of many of the churches, civic and conventual buildings built between 1530 and 1800, but little on the private, secular palaces of the Maltese nobility. Within several of these accounts are most of the author's original discoveries and attributions. These have established the significant designing roles of the Order's chief engineers, as different from the Maltese masters who erected these buildings (other than actual fortifications), and the Maltese architect, Andrea Belli, who introduced the imperial staircase to Rabat in the 18th century. For these latter reasons, rather than its rather muddled layout, the book will set the agenda for a generation of architectural research in Malta. A substantial section of illustrations and many plans augment the text.

801 **5000 years of architecture in Malta.**
Leonard Mahoney. Valletta: Valletta Publishing, 1996. 399p. bibliog.
This comprehensively written, beautifully illustrated, and elegantly produced, volume
contains chapters on prehistory and the Romans, the Middle Ages, town and country
houses, Renaissance and baroque, and architecture from 1800 to 1939. All are abun-
dantly illustrated with black-and-white and colour photographs, line-drawings and
plans. Each chapter has extensive notes and references and there is a bibliography
(p. 329-37). There is a valuable section of biographical notes on architects and engineers who practised in Malta (p. 371-99). The volume complements that published by
the author in 1988 (see previous entry) without being unduly repetitive. The final
preparation of this book, which 'contains the end result of the author's lifelong
research . . .' (Foreword, p. v), was completed by the four daughters of Leonard
Mahoney who also included the design proposal for the National Arts Centre which
their father had submitted a few months before his death in 1993 (p. 340-62).

802 **The Maltese vernacular expression: in search of a humane
architecture.**
Conrad Thake. Unpublished Bachelor of Engineering & Architecture
dissertation: University of Malta, 1987. unpaginated. bibliog.
The seven chapters outline the characteristics of Maltese vernacular architecture, its
humble origins, the Maltese farmhouse, control of the natural environment, and village characteristics, and contain a critique of patterns of house planning and a
consideration of current and future building expressions. Each chapter makes extensive use of plans and photographic details.

803 **Architecture in Malta 2. Evolution of a culture.**
Edited by David Xuereb. Msida, Malta: Society of Architecture and
Engineering Students, University of Malta, 1990. 76p. bibliog.
The text is based on eight public lectures given in 1989 by Maltese scholars and recent
graduates on philosophical, aesthetic and social aspects of architectural design and
planning. The most novel, in a local context, are those on the delicate relationship
between decoration and architecture by Mario Buhaġiar, a planning critique by Paolo
Gauci, and Richard England's outline of the principles of design apparent in Malta's
buildings.

16th-18th centuries

804 **Mdina and the earthquake of 1693.**
Edited by John Azzopardi. Malta: Heritage Books, 1993. 88p.
bibliog.
The four essays that make up this book formed part of a set of seminars to commemorate the major Sicilian earthquake of 1693, which also did extensive damage in Malta.
Frank Ventura and Pauline Galea review seismic activity in the region. Michael Ellul
summarizes the extent of damage recorded throughout the islands by Blondel, the
Order's senior resident engineer. Denis de Lucca provides a detailed list of the
rebuilding works in Mdina and Albert Ganado introduces a newly rediscovered project
(c.1572-73) by Gabrio Serbelloni (1509-80), the assessor of Laparelli's plans to build

Valletta. This plan is reproduced as well as another manuscript plan of late 17th-century Mdina and other relevant plans, sketches and photographs.

805 **A city by an Order.**
Roger de Giorgio. Malta: Progress Press Co. Ltd., 1985. 259p. bibliog.

The first major re-examination of the planning and building of Valletta in the 16th and 17th centuries since Quentin Hughes's *The building of Malta during the period of the Knights of St. John of Jerusalem 1530-1795* (see item no. 811). It is by the Maltese architect responsible for major public works on the Knights' fortifications during the decade since 1987 and clearly influenced his decisions on 'restoration'. The fully referenced text is augmented by many plans drawn for the book as well as reproductions of original documents. But the use of buff-coloured paper obscures the photographic details in this otherwise extremely thorough account.

806 **French military engineers in Malta during the seventeenth and eighteenth centuries.**
Denis de Lucca. *Melita Historica,* vol. 8 (1980), p. 23-33.

Provides a useful summary of these French fortification engineers, some of whom were also responsible for architectural projects, from 1645-1733. They included the Compte de Pagan (1645), Blondel des Croisettes (1645-95), Claude de Colongues (fl.1703); Réne Jacob de Tignè (1715, 1717, 1723); and Charles François de Mondion (1715-33).

807 **The genesis of Maltese baroque architecture: Francesco Buonamici (1596-1677).**
Denis de Lucca, Conrad Thake. Msida, Malta: University of Malta, 1994. 50p. bibliog.

This short book adds some biographical and practical information to the detective work already published by Leonard Mahoney. It includes data on his work in Lucca and Syracuse as well as comparative plans and photographs of his Maltese buildings and works by other architects in Rome and Milan.

808 **Carlo Gimach (1651-1730) – architect and poet.**
Michael Ellul. *Proceedings of History Week 1986* (1992), p. 15-38. bibliog.

Much is now being published on the foreign military engineers and architects who came to Malta during the era of the Order of St. John. Gimach, however, was a significant export. A Maltese merchant's son, Gimach was taken up by the future Grand Master Lascaris, educated at the Jesuit college in Rome, and undertook architectural commissions for several Portuguese knights, including what became the Auberge de Baverie, a palazzo now divided into several houses in Old Bakery Street, Valletta, and a small shipyard. One of his patrons took Gimach to Portugal where he is renowned as an architect of Oporto and a poet. He went to Rome in the retinue of a subsequent patron who had become the Portuguese ambassador to Rome, and stayed on to serve a new Portuguese cardinal for whom he restored Sant Anastasia. In the 1720s Gimach undertook extensive work at the Palazzo Malta, now the Roman headquarters of the Sovereign Military Order of Malta in Via Condotti.

809 **Malta: naval base of the baroque.**
John Fleming. *The Architectural Review*, vol. 99 (1946), p. 169-76.
A significant evaluation of Maltese architecture from an historical perspective, with excellent black-and-white illustrations, which predates most of the documentary architectural research but observes the main characteristics with precision.

810 **Malta: the Palace of the Grandmasters and the Armoury.**
Michael Galea. Malta: M. J. Publications Ltd., 1988. 64p.
An extensively illustrated guide to the Valletta Palace with one of the few lists of commemorative paintings to be found in the friezes and lunettes of the grand master's apartments and the corridors of the *piano nobile*, and a brief note on the Armoury exhibits of which there are several illustrations. It concludes with a list of grand masters, governors and presidents of Malta.

811 **The building of Malta during the period of the Knights of St. John of Jerusalem 1530-1795.**
Quentin Hughes. London: Alec Tiranti, 1967. Reprinted, Valletta: Progress Press Publications, 1986. 242p. bibliog.
This modern classic remains the most handy, comprehensive account of Maltese architectural development during these formative years, although it has been superseded in important respects by the research and publications of de Lucca and Mahoney. The 92 plans and elevations and the section of 332 architectural photographs are directly related to the text. The four substantive chapters are devoted to: military architecture and town planning; churches; palaces, public buildings and houses; and building materials and methods of construction. The second appendix provides biographical information on the architects and military inquirers mentioned in the text. A glossary is included, mainly consisting of Anglo-French constructional terminology.

812 **In search of Vittorio Cassar – a documentary approach.**
Victor Mallia-Milanes. *Melita Historica*, vol. 9, no. 3 (1986), p. 277-70. bibliog.
The great architect and engineer who executed Laparelli's plan for Valletta and designed the conventual buildings for the Order of St. John was Girolomo Cassar. The missing link between him and subsequent 17th-century architects has been assumed to be his son Vittorio but the author has only been able to find twenty-nine documents referring to him, all of which are transcribed in their original Latin in an appendix. However, these do not provide evidence for the buildings attributed to him, nor for his immediate succession to his father's post as resident engineer, but refer to modifications to the citadel in Gozo and a tower overlooking Mġarr harbour. At least three other *capomaestri* (master builders) are named as building for the Order during this period.

813 **Valletta 1566-1798: an epitome of Europe.**
Victor Mallia-Milanes. *Annual Report and Financial Statements, Bank of Valletta*, 1988, p. I-XXXVIII. bibliog.
Written in the form of a comprehensive historical overview, this account includes many specific details and a large number of excellent coloured reproductions of portraits, views and plans, as well as prints and maps from the collection of Dr. Albert Ganado.

814 **The building of a new church dedicated to Saint Julian in 1682.**
Eugene F. Montanaro. *Melita Historica*, vol. 9, no. 1 (1992),
p. 35-58. bibliog.

A discussion of the evidence from a series of contracts, attributing the design of this church to Vincenzo Casanova (born c.1645, died 1706), who came from a family of builders in Senglea and was a contemporary of Giovanni Barbara and Lorenzo Gafa. The 1693 earthquake damaged the church which was rebuilt between 1716 and 1730. But the evidence provided by these contracts launches another potential architect of baroque Malta to our attention.

815 **Baroque churches in Malta.**
Conrad Thake. Malta: Arcadia Publishers, 1995. 113p. bibliog.

Fifty-five full-page plates of monochrome photographs by Carmel Psaila are provided with an introductory history and commentaries on each church by the author who draws on the published work of previous architectural historians and indicates the possible architect(s) of each building. However, the quality of the printing is grey and the texts often too brief for useful reference compared with other available architectural publications.

19th-20th centuries

816 **Transformations, Richard England, 25 years of architecture.**
Chris Abel. Malta: Mid-Med Bank Ltd., 1987. 176p.

This is a sumptuously laid-out, and some might feel rather pretentious, book on the concepts and work of Malta's best known contemporary architect. It is lavishly illustrated from the subject's own perspectives and photographs of works projected and executed in Malta, Gozo, the Middle East and elsewhere. The author provides an evaluative introduction and the subject's aphorisms are printed to accompany drawings and finished buildings. Reference is as usual made to the motifs adopted from Maltese vernacular architecture but none is made to the appearance of many of these in the works of Sir Basil Spence long before he retired to live in Malta. Sadly the ambience of the buildings and the standard of their construction do not always live up to their intentions and photographic image.

817 **Manikata church 1962-1974, Richard England.**
Chris Abel. London: Academy Editions, 1995. 80p. bibliog.

A pictorial survey of the church in colour and monochrome, accompanied by a plan and drawings by the architect, follows two essays. The first, on the design of this church in the context of liturgical reform after the Second Vatican Council in 1963 is by Peter Serracino Inglott and the second, by the author, is focused on the architect and the concept behind his design.

818   **On Tower Road: a critical analysis.**
       Carmen Abela.   Unpublished Bachelor of Engineering & Architecture
       dissertation, University of Malta, 1988. 84p. bibliog.

The four main chapters discuss, with extensive photographic illustrations, the urban
context of Tower Road (the Sliema seafront), its visual analysis and a case-study of St.
Anne Square. The appendices map the street development of Sliema from 1865-1986
(6 maps) and tabulate the population by comparison with Valletta from 1947-87.
There is no other account of this transformation of a high status Maltese residential
area to become the centre of new commercial and tourist activity with accommodation
in hotels and apartments instead of terraced villas with gardens.

819   **Views of Malta: photographic album of Malta, its harbours and
       defences.**
       Anon.   London: Gale & Polden Ltd., c.1903. Facsimile reprinted,
       Malta: Gutenberg Press, 1994. 28p.

An extensive range of Ellis & Sons' photographs (q.v.) with the original accompanying pages of advertisements, which are even more informative on the trade and social
values of Britain's primary military and naval base in the Mediterranean.

820   **Giorgio Pullicino, 1779-1851, architect and painter.**
       John Azzopardi, Michael Ellul, Albert E. Abela, Antonio Espinosa
       Rodriguez.   Malta: Friends of the Cathedral Museum, Mdina, 1989.
       148p.

This book, which includes the catalogue of an exhibition of over sixty of this university drawing-master's works, contains the only significant discussion of his life and
career as an artist and architect. It represents the height of attributions to Pullicino,
several of whose buildings and paintings have subsequently been reassigned on documentary evidence to General Sir George Whitmore (1775-1862) and to J. T. Serres
(1794-1882). Pullicino's system for reproducing the same subject in different media at
different sizes marks him as an early practitioner of cheaper forms of the tourist views
that his uncle, Alberto, had established in a series of large oil paintings in 1749.
Although he was eventually accorded qualified status as an architect, Giorgio was
employed to teach drawing at the re-established University of Malta and had his shop .
and studio a few doors away in the same street as the new Doric entrance to the
University.

821   **A Grecian architectural revival: General Whitmore's
       achievements.**
       David M. Boswell.   In: *Treasures of Malta*, vol. 3, no. 1 (1996),
       p. 39-45. bibliog.

A review and reassessment of the buildings which can be attributed to this accomplished British military engineer by documentary evidence. These include the Main
Guard, the Royal Naval Hospital, several monuments and garden buildings and an
unbuilt church in Malta, and the Palace of St. Michael and St. George as well as the
Maitland Monument on the esplanade at Corfu. Whitmore took up and remained faith-
ful to the baseless Doric order of the Greek revival even in his suburban garden
designs of 1857, but his claim to fame is his reintroduction of the style to its
Mediterranean countries of origin as the built statement of the *Pax Britannica*.

822   **The Msida Bastion Cemetery, Malta: a brief history of the Msida
Cemetery and the research conducted by R. G. Kirkpatrick.**
Edited by James Cannon.   Hedgerley, England: Cannon Associates,
1990. 41p. bibliog.

This cemetery used the top of one of the bastions below the former Lintorn Barracks
between c.1806 and 1880. A survey in 1930 charted 269 graves in 3 zones. In the
1980s Kirkpatrick documented 528 names of those interred or memorialized on their
stones. Severely vandalized in recent years, these graves commemorate some of the
most distinguished, mainly British, protestants resident in Malta during the period,
including John Hookham Frere, Sir Henry Hotham, Sir Henry Pottinger, Walter
Rodwell Wright and the unmarked site of Mikiel Anton Vassalli's burial. A full list of
individuals, grave sites, dates of death and other information is provided in alphabetical order, as well as a similar listing by zones as amended from Zammit's plan of
1930, and the regiments and ships recorded on the graves or elsewhere. An appendix
provides some information on the nearby Quarantine Bastion Cemetery that became
the site of the Excelsior Hotel.

823   **Victorian Malta.**
H. M. (now Sir Howard) Colvin.   *The Architectural Review*, vol. 99
(1946), p. 179-81.

In this early work by the doyen of post-war British architectural historians, a full
description is provided of the disastrous first attempt to build the 'Anglo-Classical'
pro-cathedral for the Church of England in Valletta in 1841. British 'face' and the
building was saved by the competent intervention of William Scamp (1801-72), who
came to Malta for the Admiralty and designed the Steam Bakery in Vittoriosa. Brief
summaries are provided of the other Protestant churches built during the second half
of the 19th century as well as E. M. Barry's Opera House. The illustrations include the
interior of the Anglican Cathedral before it was reoriented for the third time.

824   **George Whitmore on Corfu: the Palace of St. Michael and
St. George and the Maitland Monument.**
Jordan Dimacopoulos.   Athens: Ministry of Culture, ICOM – National
Hellenic Committee, 1994. 104p. bibliog.

General Sir George Whitmore's years in Malta, 1812-28, as commanding officer of
the Royal Engineers, were highly significant for the adoption of neo-classical architecture on the island. Having been given formal responsibility for civil architecture, his
designs were adopted for public buildings in Valletta and the redecoration of their
interiors as well as the long proposed Naval Hospital at Bighi. Whitmore's greatest
work was the design of the Palace for the British Lord High Commissioner of the
Ionian Islands who was also Governor of Malta, Sir Thomas Maitland, and his memorial on the esplanade at Corfu. They were built in Maltese stone by Maltese masons and
the grand rooms of St. Michael and St. George have recently been restored. All these
are well illustrated in colour and the author traces the origins of their design to similar
models in ancient Greek, Roman and Italian, and English Palladian architecture. A
consideration of this substantial and complex building indicates both Whitmore's
competence and the likelihood that he did design those buildings in Malta to which he
laid claim in his memoirs. The illustrations include reproductions of painted views of
Whitmore's buildings c.1830 by Joseph Schranz, one of the family of artists who settled in Malta from Minorca.

825   **In search of silent spaces.**
Richard England.   Malta: MRS Editions, 1983. 116p.
An integrated presentation of thoughts and images, mostly of Malta, and of the author's designs and garden constructions.

826   **St. Paul's Anglican Pro-Cathedral.**
R. G. Kirkpatrick.   Malta: St. Paul's Cathedral, 1988. 9p.
A short and factual summary of the foundation, architecture, memorials and office-holders of the diocese and chancellorship.

827   **Manikata: the making of a church.**
Charles Knevitt.   Malta: Printex for Manikata Church, 1980. 48p.
A beautifully illustrated celebration of the new parish church designed for this small village by Richard England and the ancient local building principles upon which he based his design – principally a low profile and interlocking mural circles which are found in both the rustic *girna* (corbelled stone hut) and the neolithic temples. Unlike these and the walls of the small terraced fields of Malta, Manikata church was built of dressed rather than rough dry stones which were only used in it for decorative effect. A clear plan is provided as are several reproductions of the architect's series of ideas for this project.

828   **Architect Andrea Vassallo (1908-1928).**
Leonard Mahoney.   *Melita Historica*, vol. 10, no. 3 (1990), p. 225-36.
In 1908 Vassallo was granted the Maltese warrant of Land Surveyor and Architect without ever having sat for an examination, but he had already been admitted to the corresponding English institutions. This article attributes works to him using contemporary documents. They include the domes of Siġġiewi and Ħamrun churches, a group of gothic villas for Baron de Piro in Rabat and Mdina, the Casa Said and Villa Rosa in an art nouveau style, Sliema Government School and the Blue Sisters' hospital, and the neo-romanesque pilgrimage church of Ta'Pinu, Gozo. Seven of these are illustrated.

829   **The Malta siege bell memorial.**
Edited by Roger Mifsud.   Valletta: Progress Press Ltd., 1992. 28p.
A colourfully illustrated album of the Queen's dedication of this memorial to those who died in Malta during the Second World War. In addition to the plan and sections, there are many illustrations of Michael Sandle's design as it developed, of the bell, of the catafalque with its recumbent bronze figure, and of the ceremony itself on 29 May 1992. The bell is situated on the bastion beside the lower Baracca in Valletta and its cupola is a prominent monument in the Grand Harbour.

Fortifications

830 The Victoria Lines souvenir guide.
Edited by Ray Cachia Zammit. Valletta: Progress Press Ltd., 1996. 72p.

Profusely illustrated with photographs, maps, and plans, this detailed and comprehensive guide for visitors clearly indicates major features and access routes. The lines constitute a twelve-kilometre stretch of defensive walls and forts across north-central Malta built by the British army between 1870 and 1899, when the strategy was for the British army to hold the line if foreign troops invaded until the Royal Navy was able to take up its seaward position and cut off their supply routes. The military relevance of the lines faded soon after they were completed and by the 1939-45 war the aim was to secure *all* of Malta and Gozo and the lines were no more than a secondary defence.

831 Fort St. Elmo – Malta: a brief history.
Michael Ellul. Valletta: Progress Press, 1988. 71p.

This well-illustrated case-study concerns the most important early fortification built for the Order of St. John in 1552, which withstood the Turkish siege of 1565 for so long as to have a significant impact on its ultimate outcome. The chapels within the walls are described and illustrated in detail but little attention is devoted to repeated modification of the fortress to meet new defensive requirements during the later years of the Order or the 150 years of British use. An appendix lists the castellans and governors from 1551-1722.

832 Malta: a guide to the fortifications.
Quentin Hughes. Valletta: Said International Ltd., 1993. 283p. bibliog.

In this book the doyen of British fortification historians returns to his first subject – Malta. Nine short chapters, covering the periods from the Middle Ages to the Second World War, precede the gazetteer of fifty different types or sites of fortification in the islands. These are arranged alphabetically by name, which is appropriate for the many that have been modified several times over the centuries to meet new defensive requirements, but less helpful if one wishes to compare those built at one time and left virtually unchanged. Plans are provided of every entry, and often accompanied by reproductions from the original plans, elevations and sections drawn by the author or his students at the University of Malta between 1968 and 1972.

833 Gozo citadel, Malta: report submitted to the Division of Cultural Heritage, U.N.E.S.C.O.
Anthony Luttrell. Malta: The Author, 1981. 186p. bibliog.

The Gozo citadel forms one of the most significant relatively undisturbed areas of long-term settlement in the island, much of it abandoned above the entrance *Piazza* and the *Matrice* (now the Cathedral). This report and proposals for the conservation of the area were based on the work of a team with the author. It has ten chapters devoted to the rural context, geology and archaeological strata, history, fortifications and standing structures, modes of public presentation and specific proposals. The appendices include Mederico Blondel's report after the earthquake in 1693, early information on the citadel, the evolution of the fortifications, some exhibitions in the cathedral museum, and suggestions on flora conservation. Many plans and photographs of building details are included in the plates and figures.

834 Scipione Campi's report on the fortifications of Valletta, 1576.
Victor Mallia-Milanes. *Melita Historica*, vol. 8, no. 4 (1983),
p. 276-90. bibliog.
A discussion of one of the first reports submitted after the death of the Italian designer of Valletta, Laparelli, followed by the full Italian text by this distinguished Spanish engineer.

835 The coastal fortifications of Gozo and Comino.
A. Samut-Tagliaferro. Malta: Midsea Publications, 1993. 373p.
An extensively illustrated account of the defences projected and erected by the Order of St. John in these Maltese Islands, making use of aerial photographs taken in 1991. The three main parts are devoted to the historical background, the coastal watch-towers, and 18th-century coastal defences, with an epilogue covering the transition from the rule of the Order, via the French, to the British. The appendices include the nominal roll of those interred in the Protestant cemetery, in Fort Chambrai, which was being destroyed in preparation for a building site. This is one of several recent publications advocating an approach to the conservation of historic buildings which respects their functional modifications over time rather than official policies to 'restore' buildings to their appearance at one time or obliterate them for immediate commercial gain.

836 The Knights' fortifications: an illustrated guide of the fortifications built by the Knights of St. John in Malta.
Stephen C. Spiteri. Malta: Print Services Ltd., 1989. 212p.
A comprehensive gazetteer, which provides a short history of the Order, and of all the types and sites of its fortifications in the islands, making extensive use of maps, plans, sections and photographs, many of them made by the author.

837 The British fortifications: an illustrated guide to the British fortifications in Malta.
Stephen C. Spiteri. Malta: Print Services Ltd., 1991. 243p.
The companion volume to the author's guide to the Knights' fortifications (see previous entry), with a short history of both the structures and the development of coastal artillery, followed by an extensive gazetteer of defensive forts, lines, batteries and pillboxes. The work is informatively illustrated by maps, plans, elevations, photographs and functional diagrams, many of them made by the author.

838 Fortresses of the Cross: Hospitaller military architecture (1136-1798).
Stephen C. Spiteri. Malta: Heritage Interpretation Services, 1994.
674p. bibliog.
This is a spectacular record, analysis and technical presentation of the Order of St. John's fortifications in Asia Minor, the Greek Islands and Malta, which fully deserves its fullsome presentation by the current Grand Master of the Sovereign Military Order

of Malta and the foreword by Professor Quentin Hughes. In addition to the maps, plans, elevations, photographs and functional diagrams which are provided in his other gazetteers, the author has drawn a series of large bird's-eye perspective views of the major fortresses which convey all the necessary information without the clutter and misleading shadows of many photographs. In addition, there are descriptions of the uses of these buildings and adjacent settlements, separate sections devoted to the methods of building and garrisoning these strongholds and a glossary of military architectural terms. This book ranks as one of the most thoroughly researched, informatively presented and well-illustrated publications in a decade that has enjoyed a remarkable series of fine studies of Maltese history and architecture.

839 British military architecture in Malta.
Stephen C. Spiteri.   Valletta: The Author, 1996. 561p. bibliog.

This comprehensively detailed and illustrated volume is the definitive work on its subject. After a general introduction, it has sections on harbour fortifications (p. 139-240), forts (p. 241-360), fortified lines (p. 361-404), major batteries (p. 405-96), field defences, pillboxes, and AA batteries (p. 497-557). There is a full supporting text with diagrams, etc.

Decorative arts

840 The silver of Malta.
Alaine Apap Bologna.   Malta: MAG Publications for Fondazzjoni Patrimonju Malti, 1995. 271p. bibliog.

This technically well-illustrated book is a splendid demonstration of the silverware produced in Malta throughout the period of the Order of St. John and the subsequent years of British rule. It also forms the catalogue of 995 items, or groups of items, exhibited in the Supreme Council Chamber of the Grand Master's Palace by the Foundation in 1995. It is prefaced by the author's essay on the influence of European silver on Maltese silversmithing from 1650-1800 and has an appendix illustrating all the known maker's marks with any known dates and their items in the exhibition. It is the definitive work on Maltese silver but the illustrations in earlier books are often larger and show more examples of any one type of vessel etc. and are therefore still of considerable use.

841 Gozo lace: an introduction to lace making in the Maltese Islands.
Consiglia Azzopardi.   Gozo: The Author, 1991. 130p. Accompanying pack of prickings. 44p.

A fully illustrated account and demonstration of the craft, which was revived and introduced into Malta and Gozo as a means of providing an income for women. A separate pack includes seventy-two prickings of the patterns related to the eight chapters, including basic stitches, motifs, floral and other doilies and borders.

842 **The Sovereign Military Hospitaller Order of St. John of Jerusalem of Rhodes and of Malta: the Order's early legacy in Malta.**
Edited by John Azzopardi.   Valletta: Said International Ltd., 1989.
124p. bibliog.

This is essentially a catalogue of paintings, sculpture, relics, plate, church vestments, manuscripts, books and prints exhibited at the Cathedral Museum, Mdina. They were selected because of the tradition that they were brought to Malta in 1530 after the Order was evicted from Rhodes in 1522 and spent the rest of that decade in exile. After a general essay on the Order's time in Rhodes by Anthony Luttrell, Mario Buħaġiar and others provide detailed entries on each of the 102 items, all of which are well illustrated in colour. A documentary appendix includes an inventory of items from the conventual church treasury in Rhodes which were considered dispensable in 1475, evidence on the Byzantine icons brought from Rhodes dating from 1558-59, and excerpts from the inventory of 1756 illustrated by Alberto Pullicino (1719-59), which includes plate dating from before 1534. The entries are often well documented and bring together most useful information.

843 **The hidden gem: St. Paul's Shipwreck Collegiate Church, Valletta, Malta.**
Canon John Ciarlò.   Malta: Progress Press, 1993. 72p.

A colourfully illustrated guide to this important secular parish church *en fête*, with information on its plate, paintings, statuary and chapels.

844 **The goldsmiths of Malta and their marks.**
Victor F. Denaro.   Florence, Italy: Leo S. Olschki, 1972. 241p.

This richly illustrated study deals with the work of gold- and silversmiths from the 16th to the 20th centuries. Appendices cover measures of weights and tables of gold and silver standards.

845 **The sedan chair in Malta: Is-Suġġetta.**
Nicholas de Piro.   Malta: Fondazzjoni Patrimonju Malti for the
Parliamentary Secretariat for Tourism, 1993. 72p. bibliog.

Published to accompany the Foundation's exhibition, this book contains a commentary, and coloured photographs by Patrick Fenech, on each of the twenty sedan chairs known to survive in Malta as well as a general account of their uses. Most of these are preserved in the ecclesiastical premises from which they issued forth with the Blessed Sacrament for the *Viaticum* (last rites). Most of those surviving date from the 18th century but several were in use until the 1930s.

846 **The Grandmaster's Palace and the Gobelin Tapestries.**
Joseph Ellul.   Siġġiewi, Malta: The Author (printed at the Gutenberg
Press, Tarxien, Malta), 1996. 75p.

An accessible guide to the magnificent palace in Valletta, with twenty-seven beautiful colour illustrations of paintings, tapestries and rooms. The Gobelin Tapestries in the Council Chamber receive special attention (p. 44-57). There is a supporting text with plans and diagrams. The author published a complete set of excellent coloured reproductions of Mattia Perez D'Aleccio's frescoes of the siege in the Grand Master's Palace, with a brief text, in *1565: the Great Siege of Malta* (Siġġiewi, Malta, 1992. 67p.).

847 **Antique Maltese domestic silver.**
Jimmy Farrugia.   Valletta: Said International, 1992. 347p. bibliog.

A significant work with 130 new names and marks of Maltese gold- and silversmiths as well as assay marks discovered by the author. It also includes the names and marks of craftsmen licensed since the publication of V. F. Denaro's *The goldsmiths of Malta and their marks* (q.v.).

848 **Silver at St. John's Gate: Maltese and other silver in the collection of the Museum of the Order of St. John.**
Julia Findlater, Pamela Willis.   London: The Order of St. John, 1990.
32p. bibliog.

The catalogue of an exhibition of 129 items at the Museum of St. John's Gate, Clerkenwell, London. It is introduced by an essay on the Order's plate and on Maltese silver. Many of the items are illustrated, some in colour, others with their marks. Although much of the silver is of Maltese manufacture, a substantial proportion post-dates the Order's years on the island, and a lot of the silver associated with the Order originated with French or other non-Maltese silversmiths. There have also been dona-tions to the Venerable Order since its foundation in the 19th century and to its church of St. John, Clerkenwell, which are associated with its use by the Church of England between the Reformation and its restoration to the new, Anglican, Order of St. John in the British realm.

849 **Artists, artisans and craftsmen at Mdina Cathedral in the early sixteenth century.**
Stanley Fiorini.   *Melita Historica*, vol. 10, no. 4 (1991), p. 321-52.
bibliog.

Using the Mandati documents (records of Cathedral directives – see item no. 154), this article traces details of those who were paid for various works at the old cathedral before its destruction by the earthquake of 1693. Four documents, a contemporary plan, and several of the works produced, are illustrated.

850 **Antique Maltese furniture.**
Joseph Galea-Naudi, Denise Micallef.   Valletta: Said International
Ltd., 1989. 198p.

This is the first major publication on the subject and provides a short commentary on 210 excellently photographed items which date mainly from the 17th, 18th and 19th centuries. It is particularly useful in demonstrating the forms of antique coffer, chest of drawers, cabinet, table, bureau-bookcase, prie-dieu, chair, stool, bench, games-table, portable altar, cupboard, bed, clock, display cabinet, mirror etc. to be found in Malta today and their approximation to Sicilian, British or other models. Apart from a short reference to materials and condition for dating purposes, there is no discussion of actual cabinet-makers or their marks (if any), or the modification of furniture since its construction, which is obvious in the case of bureau-bookcases. Until the influx of British 19th-century taste and goods, there were only a few standard items of Maltese furniture and these varied most in their level of finish and decoration rather than their structural forms and uses. The mass of occasional furniture for very specific uses that was characteristic of French 18th-century, and then other European, furniture is notably absent from Malta.

851   Guide to Maltese furniture: a complete handbook on Maltese
       furniture 1700-1900.
       Joseph Galea-Naudi, Denise Micallef.   Msida, Malta: Orbit Ltd.,
       1993. 254p.
This colourfully illustrated book provides a wide range of examples of different types
of furniture to be found in, and manufactured in, Malta, with short textual descriptions
preceding each section. Although some of the examples illustrated are in public collections, most are in private homes. Sizes are given but no information on makers'
marks or other documentation seems to be available.

852   Another sculpture by Ciro Ferri in Malta.
       Hanno-Walter Kruft.   *The Burlington Magazine*, vol. cxxii, no. 934
       (1981), p. 26-29.
In addition to the bronze reliquary designed by Ferri (1634-89) and donated by Grand
Master Caraffa (1680-90), the author attributes the latter's tomb to the artist, on the
grounds of the great stylistic similarity between his bronze and marble putti in these
two works and others executed by him in Florence and Rome. If correct, this attribution significantly adds to the evidence on another of the remarkable series of
monumental sculptures in St. John's conventual church.

853   Antique Maltese clocks.
       Edited by John Manduca.   Valletta: Progress Press Ltd. for
       Fondazzjoni Patrimonju Malti, 1992. 144p. bibliog.
This splendidly illustrated volume was published in association with the first exhibition of the National Cultural Foundation at the Auberge de Provence. John Manduca
provides a review of the uses to which the auberge has been put and Giovanni Bonello
outlines aspects of the history of time-keeping in Malta. Other authors provide short
essays on the wall-clocks characteristic of Malta and their movements, the clock tower
at Vittoriosa that was destroyed in 1942, Maltese turret clocks, sundials, and the
career of the noted turret clock maker Michelangelo Sapiano (d.1912). The catalogue
entries are by Louis Busuttil.

854   Silver and banqueting in Malta: a collection of essays, papers and
       recent findings.
       Edited by Mark Micallef.   Valletta: Progress Press for Fondazzjoni
       Patrimonju Malti, 1995. 221p. bibliog.
This collection was published in connection with the Foundation's exhibition of
Maltese silver in the Grand Master's Palace at Valletta in 1995. It comprises three
very different parts. The first part begins with a discursive essay by the editor on the
depiction of banqueting tables, a few of them by artists of Malta (Mattia Preti and
Antoine de Favray) in the early modern period, and two short essays on the silver at
St. John's Gate and the hallmarking influence of the Worshipful Company of
Goldsmiths of London. Giovanni Bonello provides a wide-ranging series of notes on
aspects of eating and food in Malta which include coloured illustrations of the depictions of Maltese food in the murals of the refectory of the 18th-century Jesuit retreat
house in Floriana (now the Archbishop's Curia) and an engraving after Louis Ducrot
of the snow depot near the wharf c.1801. Shorter essays describe: the trial by the
Inquisition in 1564-75 of the Flemish silversmith Simon Prevost who was responsible

for designing the coins and medals of Grand Master de la Valette; the silversmiths Antonio Massa, Pietro Roselli, Michele Arcangelo Pianta, and Salvatore Falzon; assay marks on Maltese silver from 1530-1798; and the coats of arms and assay marks of grand masters and some local families. The final item in this part is a reprint of Sir Charles Oman's articles on 'The treasure of the Conventual Church of St. John in Malta', originally published in *The Connoisseur* (February, March and April 1970) which is well illustrated from Alberto Pullicino's water-colours in the *Inventory* completed in 1756 now held by the Cathedral Museum. Part two reprints three articles by the late Victor F. Denaro on 'Maltese silver and the Red Hand of Ulster', 'Maltese silver coffee pots', and 'The Hand of John the Baptist', originally published in different journals in 1968, 1970 and 1958 respectively. Part three comprises a short essay on the Grand Master's Palace, and a bibliography of the laws, regulations, publications and documents relating to gold and silver articles made in Malta.

855   **Maltese sundials.**
      Paul I. Micallef.   Malta: Union Print Co. Ltd., 1995. 125p.

A brief introduction and information on some designers of sundials in Malta is followed by a gazetteer of examples known to the author, in alphabetical order, with photographs of each one. Although many have been placed on historic buildings they are often of much more recent origin.

Performing arts

Drama

856   **The La Valettes: an experimental dramatic work with a meaning for the twentieth and twenty-first centuries, based on Friedrich Schiller's *Die Malteser* and its literary background of the eighteenth century as well as on the historical background of the Siege of Malta and the founding of Valletta in the sixteenth century.**
      Francis Cachia.   Valletta: Progress Press Co. Ltd., 1990. 67p.

An experimental dramatic work for television originally written for academic secondary pupils at a German school. It was based on Schiller's *Die Malteser* and has an 18th-century literary, as well as a 16th-century historical, background. Illustrations in colour and monochrome are selected from the Great Siege frieze and other Maltese sources.

857   **Collected English plays.**
      Francis Ebejer.   Valletta: A. C. Aquilina & Co., 1980. 3 vols. vol. 1, 254p.; vol. 2, 245p.; vol. 3, 317p.

These plays, by 'the finest dramatist that Malta produced hitherto' (Paul Xuereb) are preceded by brief notes and, where applicable, cast lists for their first performances.

Volume one contains 'Mark of the zebra', 'Cleopatra slept (badly) here', and 'Bloody in Bolivia'. Volume two contains 'Boulevard', 'Golden Tut', 'Hour of the sun', and 'Mcrz'. Volume three contains 'Saluting batteries', 'The cliffhangers', 'Hefen plus zero', and 'Summer holidays'. Ebejer also wrote novels in English (q.v.) and in Maltese.

858 **Il Teatro Italiano a Malta (1630-1830).** (Italian drama in Malta, 1630-1830.)
Joseph Eynaud. Malta: Lux Press, 1979. 127p.

The only comprehensive account of this type of drama presented at the Manoel Theatre, Valletta, under the Knights and early British-engaged impresarios. Several rare or unpublished texts are printed in the appendices. The text is in Italian as suits its subject and it has no counterpart in English. Italian was the primary cultural language of Europe, except for France, until the mid-18th century, but remained that of the Maltese until the Second World War.

859 **The M.A.D.C. story 1910-1985: a personal account.**
Joseph C. Mompalao de Piro. Malta: MADC, 1985. 129p.

This recounts the history of Malta's leading amateur dramatic company which has produced plays in English for the Maltese stage since 1910. The author is a long-term member and past chairman of the company. The appendices list all known public performances, performances for club members, and the company's chairmen and honorary secretaries.

860 **The Manoel Theatre: a short history.**
Paul Xuereb. Malta: Mid-Med Bank for the Friends of the Manoel Theatre, 1994. 176p. bibliog.

A comprehensive summary of the vicissitudes of one of the oldest extant theatres in Europe, originally built in 1731 but extensively remodelled internally in the first half of the 19th century. The theatre's darker years are outlined after 1866, following the opening and rebuilding of Barry's Opera House, also in Valletta, and its most recent restoration in association with the national schools of music and drama is described. The work is enhanced by twenty-nine illustrations of plans, playbills, portraits and production photographs.

Music

861 **Francesco Azzopardi's '*Il musico prattico*': an annotated translation and critical study of its French editions by Framéry (1786) and Choron (1824): vols. I and II.**
Oliver Brantley Adams. Ann Arbor, Michigan: University of Ann Arbor, University Microfilms International, 1991. 2 vols. vol. I, 213p.; vol. II, 241p. bibliog.

The two volumes comprise the text of the author's PhD thesis in three chapters in volume one, with the second volume devoted to the annotated translation of *Le musicien pratique* (The practical musician). Azzopardi (1748-1809) was a Maltese cleric, composer, organist and teacher. Educated in Naples, he returned to become *Maestro di cappella* (head of music) at the cathedrals of St. Paul and St. John. Most of his 250 unpublished works are being collected and catalogued by the Cathedral Museum in Mdina. This manual on counterpoint and composition was written from 1782-85 in Italian but published in French. The author analyses the latter and places the manual in the context of 18th-century musical theory. The appendices list the composer's sacred and secular works from 1768-96, the contents of the three editions of his manual, and additional material provided in Choron's edition.

862 Nicolò Isouard de Malte.

Edited by John Azzopardi. Mdina, Malta: The Friends of the Cathedral Museum with Alliance Française de Malte, 1991. 88p. bibliog.

This important collection of fully documented articles on Malta's primary musician of 1775 (or 1773) to 1818, was published when Professor Alain Blondy brought eight full scores of his operas to Malta, one of which was then performed at the Manoel Theatre, and these were exhibited at the Museum with scores by two of Isouard's descendants, Anne Nicolette and Sophie. In the first two articles, Canon Azzopardi and Joseph Vella Bondin attempt to establish evidence of the composer's birth and life in Malta, where he was admitted a Donat of the Order of St. John and became organist of its *cappella* in 1796. After the French occupation, Isouard was appointed Commissioner of the Theatre and he left with Vaubois's forces in 1800, taking all his musical compositions. Alain Blondy provides an essay on the intellectual and political context of the composer, whose bust was one of those later erected on the Paris Opéra. In addition to the catalogue of scores, the texts of thirty-one documents in their original languages are appended, mostly related to Isouard's work in Malta.

863 The piano music of Charles Camilleri.

Edited by Michael Bonello. Valletta: Andrew Rupert Publishing, 1990. 73p.

An analysis of the composer's music, interposing extracts from his and other writings with examples from his scores. The appendices provide a select list of Camilleri's (b. 1931) works for piano, a selected discography and four scores.

864 The Royal Opera House, Malta.

Joseph Bonnici, Michael Cassar. Malta: The Authors, 1990. 104p.

E. M. Barry's building (1862-66) must be one of the first major constructions in Malta to be covered from first to last by contemporary photographs. These, as well as many plans and elevations, illustrate this informative case-study. The Opera House was one of Malta's grandest buildings and entrusted to the son of the architect of the British Houses of Parliament. It was burnt out in 1873 and reconstructed to a modified design by Webster Paulson after which it ran a chequered but seasonally glittering career until its devastation by the German *Luftwaffe* in April 1942. Although its front terrace and column plinths still survive, the site continues to convey the message of Malta's sacrifice for being British in the Second World War. The ruins surround a car park which flanks the 'neo-Fascist' *piazza* built inside Valletta's main gate just after Independence in 1964. There have been many schemes to reconstruct both the *piazza* and the Opera House, some of which are discussed here. The book concludes with several pages of theatre bills and the text and portrait studies of those who participated in the 1934-35 opera season, which help to bring the building to life.

865   **Octaves of reflection: stone, space and silence.**
Charles Camilleri, Richard England.   London: John Arthur Studios,
1987. 96p.
Peter Serracino Inglott provides a philosophical introduction to a collection of short
maxims and reflections on today's world by the authors interposed with scores by
Camilleri and photographs and drawings by England, respectively a leading Maltese
composer and architect.

866   **Mediterranean music.**
Charles Camilleri, Peter Serracino Inglott.   Malta: Foundation for
International Studies of the University of Malta in collaboration with
the International Council of Music, UNESCO, 1988. 70p. bibliog.
The text of a long recorded interview of the composer Camilleri by the philosopher
Serracino Inglott, followed by a list of musical techniques and sounds found in
Mediterranean music, a glossary of terms, and several scores of Camilleri's music.

867   **The Maltese Cross: background to an opera on the mystery of
Schiller's** *Die Malteser.*
Edited by Toni Cortis.   Msida, Malta: Malta University Publishers,
n.d. 240p. bibliog.
The German text of the opera *The Knights of Malta* printed opposite an English trans-
lation by Albert Friggieri is followed by ten essays on various aspects of the text, de la
Valette's life and its presentation by different authors (which gave Schiller his
sources), the institutions of the court jester and chivalry, the language of honour, and
Goethe's relation to Malta. The book concludes with the libretto of the new opera in
three acts, *The Maltese Cross,* written by Peter Serracino Inglott with music by
Charles Camilleri (not printed here) and illustrations by Richard England, which was
first produced in Malta at the fifth centenary of de la Valette's birth.

868   **Carmelo Pace a Maltese composer: thematic, annotated and
illustrated catalogue of works: catalogue of the music archives of
the Malta Cathedral Museum vol. III.**
Marcel de Gabriele and Georgette Caffari with the collaboration of the
composer.   Mdina, Malta: Foundation for the Promotion of the Music
of Carmelo Pace, The Cathedral Museum, and Hill Monastic
Manuscript Library, St. John's University, Minnesota, 1991. 481p.
bibliog.
This is far more than a catalogue of the substantial archive (including all his original
scores) that the composer (born 1906) donated to the Cathedral Museum. It includes
many photographs of productions and soloists as well as theme tune scores, the outline
of librettos, and the texts of shorter works set to Pace's music. Most of his choral
works were religious but his other works were for every type of instrument. The
appendices provide a chronological catalogue of his works, the names of lyricists,
autograph manuscripts in this publication, and a list of the subjects of the many illustrations. Volumes I and II are in the course of preparation.

869 **Church music and musicians in late medieval Malta.**
     Stanley Fiorini. *Melita Historica*, vol. 10, no. 1 (1988), p. 1-11.
     bibliog.
A brief account of the staff and instruments at some of the primary churches in Malta
followed by the full text of five relevant documents. This represents the situation prior
to the major innovations and elaborations introduced by the Order of St. John after
1530.

870 **Singing and politics: Maltese folk music and musicians.**
     Marcia Herndon.   PhD thesis, Tulane University, New Orleans,
     Louisiana, 1971. bibliog.
One of the traditional forms of Maltese folk-singing is essentially contemporary in
content. Although some forms are sung privately, even in melancholy solitude, others
take the form of antiphonal performances on a public platform, loudly amplified and
encouraging a response from the audience to the personal and political innuendoes in
the chants.

871 **The music of Charles Camilleri: an introduction.**
     Christopher Palmer.   Valletta: Midsea Publications, 1975. 80p.
An important review of the leading modern Maltese composer's earlier music for
orchestra, piano, organ and other instruments, with many examples of his scores.

872 **Charles Camilleri: portrait of a composer.**
     Edwige Sapienza, Joe Attard.   Valletta: Said International Ltd., 1988.
     111p. bibliog.
Preceded by short essays on the ideas underlying Camilleri's art and music, this biographical album comprises photographs, designs and musical programmes, tracing this
modern composer's life and career.

873 *Musica Restituta*: **a revival programme of seventeenth century**
     Maltese sacred music.
     Edited by Maestro Joseph Vella.   Mdina, Malta: Cathedral Church of
     St. Peter and St. Paul, 1980. 24p.
This choral concert programme includes useful summaries of the sources and editing
of performed works by three composers, for whom biographical notes are provided.
There is a description of the cathedral before the 1693 earthquake with a contemporary plan and an elevation of the current building designed by Lorenzo Gafà that
succeeded it. The cathedral archives include many musical scores etc. that have been
edited for performance in recent years.

Numismatics and philatelics

Numismatics

874 **Malta: the history of the coinage.**
Emmanuel Azzopardi. Valletta: Said International Ltd., 1993. 336p.
maps. bibliog.
Comprises descriptions of 1,400 coins, 1,200 of which are illustrated, with some reproductions of depictions of events and personalities of the various periods, in 4 substantial chapters devoted to ancient Malta, mediaeval Malta, the Order of St. John, and French, British, and the Central Bank of Malta coinage.

875 **The coins of Muslim Malta.**
Helen W. Brown. *Melita Historica*, vol. 11, no. 1 (1992), p. 1-18.
bibliog.
A review of eleven collections in Malta, the Muslim coins in which seldom had an assured Maltese provenance. Details are provided of coins found in several local hoards and eight are illustrated.

876 **Mdina hoard of Muslim coins: 1698.**
Anthony T. Luttrell. *Melita Historica*, vol. 11, no. 1 (1992), p. 19-25.
bibliog.
A review of the documentary evidence on this discovery, which was divided between the Church and the Grand Master and mostly melted down.

877 **The coinage of the Knights of Malta.**
Felice Restelli, Joseph C. Sammut. Valletta: Emmanuel Said
Publishers, 1977. 2 vols. vol. I, 219p. bibliog.; vol. II, 199p.
Volume I gives a textual account of the coinage; see especially the introductory section (p. 1-20) and bibliography (p. 21-23). The coins described are comprehensively illustrated in volume II. This definitive study provides a precise and detailed description of every known coin of the period and illustrates them. The information provided gives insights into the history of the Order.

878 **Bank and currency notes in Malta.**
Joseph C. Sammut. *Annual Report and Financial Statements, Bank of Valletta Ltd.*, 1987, p. 24-61. bibliog.
A fully illustrated account of the various issues by private, as well as government, banks from 1809 until the date of publication, with some discussion of economic policies and the impact of major historical events.

879 **Currency in Malta: a brief history.**
Joseph C. Sammut. Valletta: Central Bank of Malta, 1988. 70p. bibliog.
Part 1 describes the coins of Malta since ancient times (p. 1-20) and part 2 deals with bank and currency notes from 1809 (p. 20-23). There are coloured illustrations of representative coins and notes (p. 43-67) and a list of references (p. 39).

880   **From Scudo to Sterling: money in Malta 1798-1887.**
Joseph C. Sammut.   Valletta: Said International Ltd. for the Central
Bank of Malta, 1992. 199p. bibliog.

After the French intervention in Malta, followed by the British in 1798-1800, all sorts
of currency circulated including that of Spain and Sicily and the Order of St. John.
British coins were declared the legal currency in 1825 including a British Grain which
was struck for use in Malta until 1913. However, South American dollars were introduced in 1833 because of the scarcity of Spanish dollars, although Sicilian currency
predominated by the time local commercial institutions were established in the 1840s
and 1850s. But after the demonetization of Bourbon and papal coins by the Kingdom
of a United Italy in 1885, Sicilian currency was undermined and the ecclesiastical
authorities and the Chamber of Commerce called on the Government to organize the
withdrawal of this currency which was totally replaced by sterling. The book is copiously illustrated with excellent clear reproductions of the various coinages and many
coloured reproductions of portraits and caricatures of the principal authorities.
Appendix 1 outlines the different Currency Laws and Regulations over the whole
period and the rest list various categories of government officials with their dates in
office.

Philatelics

881   **Cyprus, Gibraltar, and Malta.**
Ringwood, England: Stanley Gibbons Publications, 1985. 19p.

The stamps of Malta are comprehensively listed in part 3 of this 'Commonwealth two
reigns stamp catalogue'.

882   **The Officio della Posta and its functionaries.**
Albert Ganado.   *The Philatelic Society of Malta Magazine*
(Summer 1983). 12p.

An account of postal services under the Order, the French occupation and the British
institution of a postmaster. Sources are indicated (p. 22-24).

883   **The growth of the Malta Post Office 1802-1886.**
Albert Ganado.   *The Philatelic Society of Malta Magazine*, vol. 15,
no. 3 (1986), p. 10-36. bibliog.

A detailed account of the operation of the Post Office and its officials with illustrations of its headquarters. References, sources, and appendices are included, p. 29-36.

884   **The J. B. catalogue of Malta stamps, 1992.**
Sliema, Malta: Sliema Stamp Shop, 1991/92. 138p.

This is the ninth edition of this annual. The title given on the cover of the 1992 issue
is 'The J. B. catalogue of stamps and postal history'. It is illustrated with facsimiles of
stamps.

885   **Malta. The stamps and postal history, 1576-1960.**
Edited by R. E. Martin.   London: Robson Lowe Ltd., for the Malta
Study Circle (Watford, England), 1980. 411p. bibliog.
This is the definitive handbook on its subject produced in painstaking detail by the
philatelists of the Malta Study Circle and elegantly presented in hardback. Every
aspect of the stamps, postal system, and postal history from the mail services of the
Knights up to the 1970s is dealt with comprehensively and illustrated. There is a bibli-
ography, p. 405-06. A twenty-eight-page *Supplement no. 1* appeared in 1985.

886   **Maritime mail.**
Edited by R. E. Martin.   Watford, England: Malta Study Circle, 1987.
15p. (Paper 22).
This paper, based on an original by J. G. C. Lander, deals with postmarks and the history of maritime postal services.

887   **Said S.M.O.M. stamp and coin catalogue 1994.**
Edited by Godwin Said.   Valletta: Said International, 1993/94. 274p.
This is the most comprehensive listing of stamps and coins issued by the Sovereign
Military Order of Malta (otherwise known as the Knights of St. John Rome). Messrs.
Emmanuel Said in Valletta have produced a number of catalogues and price lists pre-
viously.

888   **Franco-Maltese postal relations from their origins to 1870.**
Henri Tristant.   Valletta: Emmanuel Said, 1983. 56p. maps.
This is an amended translation of the French original (1982) which was based on
research in private collections and archives in France and Malta. The first French postmarks appeared in the early 18th century. A French postal administration functioned
briefly during Napoleon's occupation of the islands (1798-1800). During the 19th century, when much business was carried by steam packet-boats, Marseilles was the main
French centre for postal links with Malta.

Food and Drink

889   **Health at the Maltese table. A fresh approach to traditional cooking.**
Mary Bellizi, Peter Bellizi.   Valletta: Midsea Books, Klabb Kotba Maltin, 1992. 133p.

The writers argue that Malta has inherited a diet more British than Mediterranean – and one decidedly less healthy. Their illustrated book aims to restore the admirable Mediterranean dimension to cooking in Malta with dishes which are nourishing, delicious *and* authentic.

890   **Fenkata: an emblem of Maltese peasant resistance.**
Carmel Cassar.   Valletta: Ministry for Youth and Arts, 1994. 33p. bibliog.

An essay in cultural history focused on the political significance of rabbit stew as a popular Maltese dish. The illustrations are usually too small to convey much.

891   **Telecell restaurant guide: Malta and Gozo. 1995/6.**
Edited by Mario Dix.   St. Julian's, Malta: Mediterranean Multihull Ltd., 1994. 252p.

An independent guide to over 100 restaurants with substantial comment on establishments visited, plus basic information for visitors.

892   **A preliminary study of the nutritional status of the Maltese Islands.**
Frederick F. Fenech, Alfred Grech, Anthony P. Jaccarini, Luis Vassallo, Paul Vassallo-Agius.   In: *Human ecology in the Commonwealth.*   Edited by Howard Bowen-Jones.   London: Charles Knight & Co. Ltd., 1972, p. 75-94.

This pilot study is based on a stratified 2-stage random sample of 100 households. The first stage comprised localities and the second was made up of households sampled from electoral registers. The results group Malta with more developed countries but show a high incidence of obesity. The authors of the report demand action at the community level using public money.

893   **Food and nutrition policy in Malta.**
Leonard Mizzi.   Reading, England: University of Reading (European Association of Agricultural Economists), 1994. 21p.

Examines the context within which there remains a need to safeguard the interests of consumers and others. It argues for the implementation of a consumer protection act.

894   **Entrée to Malta and Gozo.**
Kay Orton, Emma Macleod-Johnstone (line-drawings), Paul Emra (area map).   London: Quiller, 1992. 126p.

This attractively written and illustrated volume is one of the 'Gatwick Guide Entrée Series', for which the general editor is Patricia Fenn. It surveys restaurant eating and gives a range of introductory information about food and catering in the islands.

895   **A taste of history: the food of the Knights of Malta.**
Pamela Parkinson-Large.   Lija, Malta: Melitensia Art Gallery (MAG) Publications, 1995. 190p. bibliog.

A discursive account drawn from many local and some other relevant accounts of aspects of dining with the Order. It is beautifully illustrated with chapter headings in black-and-white, and paintings in colour by George Large. However, the recipe section lacks precise instructions and quantities and is drawn from a variety of sources not necessarily related to the Order or to Malta.

896   **The best of Maltese cooking.**
Caroline Wirth.   Terni, Italy: Plurigraf (distributed by Miller, Valletta), 1991. 94p.

This is an attractively illustrated collection of recipes.

Mass Media

General

897 **Supplement to a checklist of Maltese periodicals and newspapers, covering the years 1974-1989.**
Ninette Camilleri, Romaine Petrocochino. Msida, Malta: University of Malta Press, 1990. 163p.
This lists 638 items to be added to those identified by Anthony F. Sapienza in 1977 (see item no. 901). It includes an explanatory introduction (p. i-xii).

898 **Australia's Maltese language press.**
Henry Frendo. In: *The ethnic press in Australia.* Edited by Abe (I.) Wade Ata and Colin Ryan. Melbourne: Academia Press, 1989, p. 125-36.
The 'invisibility' of the Maltese press in Australia was assisted by the use of English titles in some cases. Furthermore there is evidence that Maltese material – books as well as periodicals – was disregarded by those who made lists. However, although the Maltese-Australian press may lack professionalism, financial backing and effective distribution systems, its persistence and evolution augur well for survival.

899 **Maltese journalism 1838-1992: an historical overview.**
Henry Frendo. Valletta: Press Club (Malta), 1994. 129p. bibliog.
This collects together five articles originally published in *The Sunday Times* (of Malta) between 29 November and 27 December 1992. Frendo looks critically at newspapers as they originated and developed in Malta. The appendices include the Ordinance of 1839 abolishing censorship as well as subsequent ordinances and laws, the registration dates of Maltese newspapers, and the Press Club's *Code of Ethics* of 1889.

900 **Printing and censorship in Malta 1642-1839: a general survey.**
Joseph F. Grima. Valletta: Valletta Publishing Co. Ltd., 1991. 110p.
bibliog.
The vicissitudes of printing in Malta under its different regimes are outlined, as well
as the first newspapers during the French occupation and early years of British rule.
This succinct overview includes a useful bibliography (p. 97-103) and an index
(p. 105-10).

901 **A checklist of Maltese periodicals and newspapers in the National
Library of Malta (formerly Royal Malta Library) and University
of Malta Library.**
Anthony F. Sapienza. Msida, Malta: University of Malta Press, 1977.
37p.
Though not exhaustive, this list of 1,222 titles remains a very useful reference work.

902 **Maltese imprints: an inventory of Maltese publishers and places of
publication.**
Lillian Sciberras. Msida, Malta: University of Malta Library, 1992.
25p.
An alphabetical list of local publishers and their whereabouts (not full addresses) and
some Maltese imprints in Australia and Canada.

Newspapers and magazines

903 **The Malta Business Weekly.**
Sliema, Malta: Standard Publications Ltd., 1994- . weekly.
The leading Maltese business newspaper, this respected pink-coloured publication
(36p., in March 1997) surveys foreign, as well as local, economic developments. It
provides up-to-date coverage of stocks and finance generally in Malta and reports on
local companies and on political and social trends which have a bearing on economic
activity in the islands.

904 **Malta Economic Update.**
Valletta: October 1990- . monthly (with occasional gaps).
From March 1995 this was inserted in *The Malta Business Weekly* (q.v.) each month.
The issues in 1996 contained thirty to thirty-eight pages. They were edited by John
Formosa, printed at the Gutenberg Press and contained brief articles on topical sub-
jects.

905 **The Malta Independent.**
Sliema, Malta: Standard Publications Ltd., June 1992- . weekly.
This is a broad-ranging Sunday newspaper. In March 1997, two-fifths of its fifty-two pages presented general news about Malta, though nearly another third of the paper consisted of foreign news. The remaining space was divided about equally between business topics, sport, letters and advertising.

906 **The Sunday Times.**
Valletta: Allied Newspapers Ltd., 1929- . weekly.
Originally known as *The Sunday Times of Malta*, this durable and respected weekly reports and comments on all aspects of Maltese life in eighty-eight pages (March 1997). It publishes supplements on a range of topics. (Preceding *The Sunday Times*, from April 1840 to September 1927, there were weekly issues of *The Malta Times*, a determinedly pro-British paper.)

907 **The Times.**
Valletta: Allied Newspapers Ltd., 1935- . daily except Sundays.
The companion to *The Sunday Times* (q.v.), this daily was originally known as *The Times of Malta*. Its forty-eight pages (1997) give a broad-ranging coverage of Maltese news and opinion plus a varied selection of reporting of foreign developments (much of this from Reuter). After more than six decades, *The Times* remains the pre-eminent daily in the islands.

Periodicals

908 **The Accountant.**
Paceville, Malta: Crest Publicity Ltd. for the Malta Institute of Accountants, 1989-93?
The journal of the Malta Institute of Accountants, this contained articles on accountancy in Malta, plus advertising. The April 1992 issue (56p.) was edited by P. Mifsud-Cremona.

909 **The Architect.**
Paceville, Malta: Chamber of Architects and Civil Engineers, 1979-83; Valletta: Crest Publicity Ltd., for the Chamber of Architects and Civil Engineers, 1985-90.
This publication was intended to maintain a good rapport between the Council and members and as a place for articles of interest to the profession. Some of the articles were devoted to architectural history or current projects in Malta. The last issue, no. 14 (January 1990), was edited by Victor Torpiano and contained seventy-four pages plus advertising. (Much of Leonard Mahoney's historical research was first published in this journal and subsequently in item nos. 800, 801 and 828).

910   **Archivum. The Journal of Maltese Historical Research.**
       Valletta: Midsea Books, 1981.
No. 1 (1981), edited by Victor Mallia-Milanes and Austin Sammut, contained 156
pages of articles and book reviews (in English) by Maltese scholars. No subsequent
issues have been seen.

911   **Archivum Melitense: Journal of the Malta Historical and Scientific
       Society.**
       Valletta: Empire Press for the Malta Historical and Scientific Society,
       1910-49.
The final issue, vol. 10, no. 6 (February 1949) offered a characteristic range of articles
on the Islands and their history (in English, Italian and French).

912   **The Armed Forces of Malta Journal.**
       Malta, 1969-79. quarterly.
The final issue (no. 32, October 1979) was edited by Brigadier A. Samut-Tagliaferro.
During its decade of publication, the thirty-two issues of this bilingual journal
included articles on Maltese history, some of them with a military focus.

913   **Atrium: Mediterranean and Middle East Construction Review.**
       Malta: Graphic Services Ltd. with Associated News (M) Ltd., 1981- .
       twice yearly.
Some of the numbers have short illustrated articles on the architecture and urban characteristics of Malta.

914   **Ażad Perspektiv.**
       Sliema, Malta: Ażad, 1971-81. quarterly.
The last issue of this quarterly review (no. 14, January-March 1981) consisted of fifty-
six pages offering eight short articles (all but one in English) on socio-political
education: it was edited by Richard Muscat. Seventeen issues appeared during its publication.

915   **BASE: Journal of the Foundation for Human Resources
       Development.**
       Valletta: Foundation for Human Resources Development, 1992- .
       quarterly.
No. 15 (April-June 1996) contained twenty-eight pages of news and was edited by
Jacqueline Fenech, the Foundation's Chief Executive Officer. Most of the material is
in English and relates directly to Malta.

916   **Bird's Eye View.**
       Valletta: Ornithological Society, 1977- . annual (with gaps).
Offers news updates, technical articles and reports about the Ornithological Society.
No. 15 (Spring 1993) contained twenty pages, with advertising, and was edited by
Desirée Falzon.

917 **The Business Review.**
Ta'Xbiex, Malta: The Trade Club. monthly.
This 'Monthly Publication of the Trade Club' with short articles on Maltese business
and business people, carries advertising. The September 1996 issue (vol. 11, no. 9.
34p.) was edited by Stephen P. D'Alessandro.

918 **Civilization: an encyclopaedia on Maltese civilisation, history and contemporary arts.**
Hamrun, Malta: PEG Ltd., 1983-88.
This well-illustrated part-work included many sections that were serialized in episodes,
such as heraldry, early Maltese and Gozitan place-names, and others devoted to particular buildings, works of art, natural history, sports and Maltese personalities. It ceased
publication before all of these had been completed and the separate publication of
some is contemplated. Thirty-nine issues appeared in all.

919 **Cobweb: Economic Journal. The Journal of Aiesec (Malta).**
Valletta, 1971- . annual.
Recent issues of this glossy title (which appears not to be numbered by volume/issue)
have concentrated on particular themes: construction (1996), tourism (1995) and the
European Union (1994). The 1996 issue of this periodical was edited by Malcolm
Gingell and contains forty-two pages of economic and topical coverage, plus advertis-
ing.

920 **Commercial Courier.**
Valletta: The Malta Chamber of Commerce (in association with Crest
Publicity Ltd., 1947- . monthly.
Offers locally relevant news and comment (in English). Vol. 50, no. 10 (October
1996. 52p.) was edited by Stefano Mallia.

921 **Cyprus. Malta. Country Profile.**
London: Economist Intelligence Unit Ltd. annual.
Each issue offers a general review of economic and political trends in Malta.

922 **Cyprus. Malta. Country Report.**
London: Economist Intelligence Unit Ltd. quarterly.
Typically comprises a succinct overview of the political and economic scene in Malta
and trade tables. The issue for the third quarter of 1996 consisted of thirty-three pages
and advertising.

923 **Economic and Social Studies (New Series).**
Msida, Malta: University of Malta Press, 1983- .
This 'Journal of the Faculty of Economics, Management and Accountancy' at the university appeared – generally every two years – from 1983. It replaced a previous
series, consisting of four volumes, between 1971 and 1976. Recent issues of the new
series have been edited by E. P. Delia and E. L. Żammit and contain about seventy
pages each. The journal publishes articles on economic, sociological, industrial and

managerial issues in Malta and theoretical articles in these disciplines that are applicable to the local situation. (Several articles from this journal are noted individually in this volume.)

924 **Education: The Journal of the Faculty of Education, The University of Malta.**
Msida, Malta: Faculty of Education, The University of Malta, 1982- .
Aims to provide a forum for local and foreign educators to write about topics of relevance to the Maltese context and to be of direct use to those teaching in schools and considering new techniques and educational experiments. In recent years this publication has appeared once or twice annually. A third issue in 1995 (vol. 5, no. 3) focused on architecture and schooling: it was edited by R. G. Sultana.

925 **European Journal of Political Research: Special Issue: Political Data Yearbook.**
Dordrecht, the Netherlands: Kluwer Academic Publishers, 1973- .
annual.
Since 1992, this journal, produced by the European Consortium for Political Research, has included a review of political issues in Malta for the previous year.

926 **Heritage: An Encyclopaedia of Maltese Culture and Civilization.**
Edited by Paul Mizzi. Valletta: Midsea Publications, 1977- .
monthly, then intermittently.
A mine of information and illustrated material, much of which can also be found in larger or older books. The two regular entries are 'A concise history of Malta' by the late Professor Andrew Vella and 'Portrait gallery' by various authors on different past personalities. Each number is directed at the general reader interested in Maltese history and culture. But much original material is also published in concise and documented articles. An index was published at the end of each volume.

927 **Hyphen: A Journal of Melitensia and the Humanities.**
Msida, Malta: The New Lyceum, 1977- . 2-3 issues per year up to 1991, then very intermittent.
Initiated by staff of the upper secondary schools, this publication is intended to encourage students to study beyond the limits required by their formal examinations. The topics of the articles cover a wide range of academic subjects and often include reports of research bearing on local conditions, history and art.

928 **Id-Dritt (Formerly Law Journal).**
Msida, Malta: The University of Malta, Faculty of Law, 1971-90?
annual.
The official organ of the (students') Law Society at the university, this publication (formerly known as the *Law Journal*) reached no. 15 (97p.) in 1990, when it was edited by John Victor Mizzi and covered (in English) law and legal developments and cases affecting Malta.

929   **Il-Merill: Bulletin of the Malta Ornithological Society.**
      Valletta: 1968-91. annual.

The Malta Ornithological Society was founded in 1962 to publish 'the annual systematic list of birds recorded in the Maltese Islands and the annual ringing report'. The
last issue (no. 27, 1991) was edited by Charles Gauci: it contained fifty-eight pages of
(English) text, illustrations, reports on sightings, conservation, etc.

930   **Industry Today. Journal of the Malta Federation of Industry (New
      Series).**
      Msida, Malta: Crest Publicity Ltd. for the Federation of Industry,
      Floriana, Malta, 1983- . irregular.

No. 39 (80p. plus advertising) appeared in April 1996, edited by E. Calleja. With three
such issues annually, this glossy publication covers international trends relevant to
Malta, trade and investment opportunities, together with general industrial news about
Malta.

931   **Journal of the Malta Photographic Society.**
      Valletta: Malta Photographic Society, 1992- .

Recent quarterly issues, edited by Lionel M. Cassola for the Malta Photographic
Society, offer articles, local and society news, and advertising (all in English).
Between 1985 and 1991, this periodical was known as the *Photographic Society
(Malta) Journal*.

932   **Journal of Maltese Studies.**
      Msida, Malta: University of Malta, 1961- . irregular.

Published by the Department of Maltese in the Faculty of Arts at the university, this
irregular journal deals with language and culture in the islands. Vol. 23-24 (1993)
contained essays on M. K. Vassalli: it had 236 pages and an appendix. Oliver Friggieri
was general editor (see item no. 341).

933   **Journal of Mediterranean Studies (New Series).**
      Msida, Malta: Mediterranean Institute, University of Malta, 1991- .

Subtitled 'History, Culture, and Society in the Mediterranean World', this multidisci-
plinary publication is primarily aimed at an academic audience beyond Malta. Each
issue is devoted to a theme, with at least some contributions in each one likely to refer
to Malta. Also scheduled for two issues annually was the previous 'Old Series', entitled *Mediterranean Studies* which appeared from 1978-80 (see item no. 942). Earlier
still was the *Journal of the Faculty of Arts* (1957-77) first produced at the (then Royal)
University of Malta at its original location in Valletta. As with the later journals, this
one included some material relevant to Malta.

934   **Library of Mediterranean History.**
      Msida, Malta: Mireva Publications for the University of Malta, 1994- .

A scholarly journal (in English) designed to offer a specialist outlet for research into
the history of the ancient, mediaeval and modern Mediterranean world. It was edited
by Victor Mallia-Milanes at the Department of History, University of Malta, with
additional sections of research notes, communications and book reviews. One of the
five papers and both sets of research notes in vol. 1 (1994. 284p.) relate to Malta.

935   **Malta Archaeological Review. The Journal of the Archaeological Society.**
Valletta: The (Malta) Archaeological Society, 1996- .

The first number (8p.) is devoted to a report on the excavations in Gozo from 1987-94 by Caroline Malone and Simon Stoddart. This is illustrated with plans, photographs and measured drawings of the artifacts by Stephen Ashley. There is a short review of the study of archaeology in Malta by Anthony Bonanno, and a report of the society's activities in 1994. This publication represents part of the reinvigoration of archaeology in Malta and of the country's Museum's Department.

936   **Malta Football Association – Quarterly Review.**
Valletta: The Malta Football Association, 1987- . quarterly.

Vol. 9, no. 1 appeared in March 1995 with twenty-eight illustrated pages plus advertising on local football news and match reports.

937   **The Malta Government Gazette.**
Valletta: Department of Information, 1816-

The first issue of the *Gazetta del Governo di Malta* appeared on 27 October 1813. From 7 August 1816 it adopted its present title and was printed in Italian and English and then, more recently, in Maltese and English. The *Gazette* contains official notices, acts, bills, etc. By 30 October 1996 the series had reached no. 16,362.

938   **Malta Penny Magazine.**
Malta: James Richardson, 1839-41. weekly.

A magazine edited by M. Weiss of the Church Missionary Society. First published soon after the granting of freedom to the press in Malta, each issue consisted of only four pages with two or three illustrations, which fill some gaps before the introduction of photography. During the time it was published, 120 issues appeared.

939   **Malta Review of Foreign Affairs.**
Valletta: Ministry of Foreign Affairs, 1992- .

Recently there have been 2-3 issues annually, with some 120 pages in each one, offering documentation, diplomatic news, texts of official speeches, and articles on topics of concern to Malta. There is some illustration.

940   **Maltese Folklore Review.**
Balzan, Malta, 1962-73. irregular.

A periodical, containing articles in English (and Italian) on the social history, customs and traditions of Malta, edited by Joseph Cassar Pullicino.

941   **The Manoel.**
Valletta: Manoel Theatre Management Committee, 1996/97- .

Edited by Paul Xuereb, the first issue (vol. 1, no. 1) of this elegantly produced journal contains sixty-four pages of articles, information and illustrations reflecting the present and the past of the Manoel Theatre which was inaugurated in 1732 and today offers drama, music and dance. The Management Committee hope to publish issues annually.

942   **Mediterranean Studies.**
Valletta: Midsea Books Ltd., 1978-80. annual.

Three numbers of this journal were published before the demise of the old university, some articles in which are directly related to Malta and are noted separately in this volume. This publication replaced the *Journal of the Faculty of Arts* published annually at the University of Malta from 1957-77.

943   **Melita Historica: Journal of the Malta Historical Society.**
Malta: The Malta Historical Society, 1952- . annual.

This is the primary outlet for substantial articles on Maltese history as well as shorter research notes and book reviews. Some numbers include a bibliography of publications on Maltese history for that year. Most of the contents are in English, though Italian and French are also used – especially in earlier issues. The founding editor was the eminent Maltese scholar, Joseph Cassar Pullicino. More recently Mario Buhaġiar and Stanley Fiorini have edited this respected journal at the University of Malta. Many articles are listed separately in this volume.

944   **Melita Theologica: The Review of the Faculty of Theology and the Theology Students' Association, University of Malta.**
Msida, Malta: University of Malta, 1947-

All articles are in English (though Italian and Latin were used in earlier issues) and most contributors are Maltese. However, only a minority of contributions relate specifically to Malta. The 1995 issue (vol. 46) contained 203 pages (93p. in no. 1 with the rest in no. 2) and was produced by an editorial board consisting of A. Abela, E. M. Eminyan SJ, M. Bellizi, and C. Coleiro. Contributions relate to theology, scripture, canon law, and ecclesiastical history.

945   **The Pharmacist: The Journal of the Chamber of Pharmacists.**
Paceville, Malta: Chamber of Pharmacists, 1954-55, 1981-91.
irregular.

The first issue in 1954 (vol. 1, no. 1) contained eighteen pages (in English) relating to pharmacy in Malta, plus advertising.

946   **The Philatelic Society of Malta Magazine.**
Ta'Xbiex, Malta: The Philatelic Society, 1967- . irregular.

Contains articles and news, mostly about Malta, on stamps and postal history (in English). The April 1995 issue (vol. 24, no. 1. 46p.) was edited by A. Bonnici.

947   **Proceedings of History Week.**
Malta: The Historical Society,1981- . irregular.

The texts of papers presented at the annual conference of the Historical Society are irregularly published as funds permit. The format is that of an academic journal, whole numbers of which are sometimes listed separately here as well as specific articles.

948 **The Retailer.**
Valletta: Crest Publishing Co. for the Association of General Retailers
and Traders Union, 1962- . monthly.

Includes general material on markets, employment, competition, and union matters –
mostly in English.

949 **Society.**
Marsa, Malta: Marsa Press, 1989-91. quarterly.

This quarterly discussion of social, economic and political aspects of contemporary
life in Malta, with a view to debating the renewal of ideas and policies in the Malta
Labour Party, was edited by Alfred Sant (who became prime minister in 1996). Ten
issues were produced.

950 **The Teacher.**
Valletta: Malta Union of Teachers, 1981- . quarterly.

This publication, currently containing thirty-three pages, includes articles on educational practice and theory, together with some coverage of union matters.

951 **Tomorrow.**
Edited by Alfred Sant.   Sliema, Malta: Pragma Publishing Co. Ltd.,
December 1982-June 1985. monthly.

Each number comprised about ten articles or items devoted to Maltese current affairs
and lifestyles.

952 **Treasures of Malta.**
Edited by John Manduca.   Valletta: Fondazzjoni Patrimonju Malti,
1994- . thrice yearly.

The Foundation was set up in association with the National Tourism Organization to
give priority to Malta's cultural heritage and ensure 'a future for our past'. This well-
illustrated magazine primarily consists of a set of articles on aspects of Malta's
historic arts and architecture, as well as notes on recent outstanding items in the sale-
rooms, a local villa, forthcoming cultural events – especially the splendid exhibitions
organized annually by the Foundation – and relevant book reviews.

953 **Vigilo – Rivista ta' Din l'Art Helwa.** (Vigilo – Review of Din L'Art
Helwa.)
Valletta: Din l'Art Helwa, 1971-88, 1994- . irregular, up to 3 per year.
new format from February 1995.

This voluntary association plays the role of a civic society, although it is often mistakenly termed Malta's National Trust. It speaks out on local environmental issues,
especially those relating to historic buildings and the urban and rural landscape. It also
raises money and working parties for the restoration of historic buildings, several of
which are held by the association and opened to the public. This newsletter records its
activities and publicizes its concerns. It is mainly in English.

954 **Welcome: What's On in Malta and Gozo.**
Valletta: Associated Publicity Services Ltd., 1976- .
Nearly 400 issues of this inexpensive holiday guide for visitors have appeared and it
currently comes out at monthly intervals (1997). The pocket-size format presents basic
information about the islands and how to get about within them, together with updated
details of events and attractions. Advertising accounts for many of the several dozen
pages in each issue.

Directories and
Reference Works

955 Index of notaries (1465-1894).
Anthony Attard. Sliema, Malta: The Author, 1979. 22p.
A basic source for historical records, this short work lists the names of notaries exercising their profession in different Maltese localities as well as the index numbers of the original acts in the Notarial Archives and their transcribed registers which are held by various current keepers.

956 Directory of publishers, printers, book designers, book dealers.
Joseph M. Boffa. Floriana, Malta: *Għaqda Bibljotekarji* (Library Association), 1990. 55p.
This annotated list is preceded by an introduction.

957 The Malta year book – 1996.
Edited by Stanley J. A. Clews. Sliema, Malta: De La Salle Brothers Publications, St. Benild School, 1996. 536p.
This is the essential reference work of its type. Now in its forty-fourth year of publication since it first appeared in 1953, it has become the standard, accessible, comprehensive reference on Malta's history, government, administration, economy, finances, trade, private enterprise, religion, sport, etc. It includes a chronology of important events during the year covered, together with a number of illustrations. In addition there are special articles on selected topics. Everything is here from names of officials in government departments to times of church services.

958 Malta's timeline: a handbook of Maltese chronology.
Joseph Galea, edited by Raymond M. Cassar. Malta: Laga Co. Ltd., c.1989. 195p. bibliog.
A compendium of information, mainly relating to the period since the eviction of the Order of St. John by the French, listing officials, prime ministers, bishops, parish

priests since the foundation of their parish, a summary of census data, feudal lords and nobles of Malta, officers of the Maltese nationalist *Consiglio Popolare* and the *Università*, judicial appointments, and European heads of state and viceroys of Sicily.

959 *Il-Fiera tal-Ktieb*: **12th Malta Book Fair.**
Floriana, Malta: Ministry of Education and National Culture, 1996. 74p.
This is the latest in a series which has appeared in most years since 1979 when the first book fair was held in Valletta. Titles of this journal-like catalogue have varied, but all – including this one – contain articles on participating publishers, plus one or more articles on bibliographical, literary, or artistic topics related to Malta, some of which have been cited separately in this volume.

960 **Library guide.**
Msida, Malta: University of Malta Library, 1996. 7p.
This brief descriptive guide is in leaflet form. Six previous editions were issued as pamphlets.

961 **Malta Who's Who: 1987.**
Edited by John Manduca. Malta: Progress Press, 1987. 179p.
Six numbers were published during the years following Independence in 1964, but none was issued during the sixteen years of the Labour Government. This seventh volume is a useful source of information on those who have come to prominence during the intervening period in a range of fields – political, religious, professional, economic and educational. There has been no sequel to date.

962 **A directory of libraries and information units in Malta.**
Compiled by Anita Ragonesi and Laurence Zerafa. Msida, Malta: *Għaqda Bibljotekarji*, c/o University of Malta, 1996. xiii, 288p.
Based on a c.500 questionnaire survey (about fifty per cent response), this updates previous compilations. It gives details for 208 libraries and information units, describing locations, holdings, accessibility, etc., and includes indexes by name, subject, category and locality.

963 **Libraries and research in Malta.**
Edited by Paul Xuereb. Msida, Malta: Malta University Press, 1988. 53p.
A collection of short statements on an outline history (P. Xuereb), scientific research (R. Ellul Micallef), research in the humanities (A. Bonanno), the National Library (J. B. Sultana), the University of Malta Library (A. Mangion), special libraries (J. R. Grima), and inter-library co-operation (M. T. Baluci).

Bibliographies

964 Selected bibliography on the sociocultural environment of the Maltese Islands.
James Calleja. Valletta: International Environment Institute, Foundation for International Studies, University of Malta, 1986. 48p.
Derived from published and unpublished material available at six public, educational, and associational, libraries in Malta, this gives details of over 380 titles arranged by seven topics: culture and culture change, the economy, education, parties and politics, religion and social change, society and social change, and the family. Most of the titles are in English.

965 Malta in British periodicals 1915-1951 a select list.
Guzé Cassar Pullicino. *Melita Historica,* vol. 1, no. 2 (1953), p. 75-86.
This is a useful source of articles, etc. on Malta from a variety of periodicals. Being a select list, however, it does not claim to be comprehensive. The author was a librarian at the National Library.

966 *Index Historicus*: a classified index of articles in a select list of periodicals and collections of studies relating to Maltese history, including an author and an analytical index.
Carmel Cuschieri. Malta: The University Press, 1979. 151p.
For students of Maltese history this is an invaluable source of precise bibliographical information to be found in seventeen periodicals, most of them already discontinued by the date of this compilation. The 1985 edition of the *Malta* volume in the World Bibliographical Series did not include many such articles which all predate the years covered by this revised edition. We have included a greater selection from current periodicals. The *Index Historicus* contains 1,337 entries which, although not annotated, are presented in subject sections as follows: general history; archaeology; Malta and Gozo in Antiquity; the mediaeval period, 1090-1530; the Order of St. John;

French occupation, 1798-1800; contemporary history from 1800; ecclesiastical history; agriculture and horticulture; architecture; archives and documentation; biographies; economic and social history; education and culture; ethnology; fine arts; flora and fauna; folklore; geography and geology; language and literature; legal history; medical history; numismatics; the press; and visitors' accounts. Most of the entries were published in English or Italian by Maltese scholars, one of whom, Professor Godfrey Wettinger, has written a foreword.

967   *Melitensia* 1900-1975: a classified list of books and articles on Maltese history printed between 1900 and 1975.
Giovanni Mangion.   Malta: The Malta Historical Society, 1975.
This extensive compilation is divided into periodic and topical sections preceded by a list of journals containing articles of historical interest. Articles in locally published learned journals have normally been excluded, but publications in languages other than English are included.

968   *Melitensia*: books in print.
Valletta: Sapienza & Sons, 1996. 24p.
This bookshop in Republic Street, Valletta, publishes an annual list of books available in print on Malta and those published abroad. It includes titles in English and Maltese. Computerization will probably enable the list to be updated constantly.

969   Handlist of writings on art in Malta.
Edward Sammut.   Valletta: The Library Association, 1978. 39p.
This revised and enlarged edition of the author's 1964 work is divided into topographical and historical sections as well as those on particular artists. There are artist and author indexes.

970   Malta in British periodicals 1952-1973.
Marie Schinas.   *Melita Historica,* vol. 6, no. 4 (1975), p. 411-30.
This bibliography of 335 items is divided into 22 sections, the longest of which are antiquities, architecture, economics and politics. It is an invaluable source for which the previous edition of this bibliography provides no substitute. Entries were taken from *The British Humanities Index* (London: The Library Association, 1962- . quarterly & annual), previously the *Subject Index to Periodicals* (1915-61). It is designed to update that compiled by G. Cassar Pullicino (1915-51) (see item no. 965).

971   A marketing tool for the information industry: Malta and its national bibliography.
Lillian Sciberras.   *Library Management,* vol. 7, no. 3 (1986). 40p.
This very useful issue starts with a chronology of major library and bibliographical trends in Malta and reviews the recent development of the library system. A map shows thirty-one libraries, of which nineteen are in Valletta and ten are elsewhere in Malta. Gozo accounts for two libraries. The writer discusses the book trade (p. 14-18), and 'the bibliographic habit' (p. 19-26) where she includes references to bibliographies and book-lists. She concludes with an account of the *Malta National Bibliography* (q.v.) and indicates some important sources on p. 39 and p. 40.

972   **Academic dissertations, theses, long assignments and projects in Maltese library and information studies.**
Compiled by Lillian Sciberras.   Msida, Malta: University of Malta, 1995. 19p.
This list was produced for limited distribution but is a useful means of access to a difficult source area.

973   **A checklist of British official publications relating to Malta 1801-1950.**
Donald H. Simpson.   *Melita Historica*, vol. 1, no. 3 (1954), p. 150-55.
This unannotated list is based on UK Parliamentary Papers, the bibliography of the *Cambridge history of the British Empire*, vol. II, edited by Holland Rose (Cambridge, England: Cambridge University Press, reprinted 1961), the *Catalogue of Parliamentary papers 1801-1900*, published by P. S. King (London, 1904, 1912), and material in the library of the Royal Empire Society.

974   **Malta National Bibliography.**
Edited by John B. Sultana et al.   Valletta: National Library of Malta, 1983- .
The first issue of this major source covered items (with at least eight pages) published in Malta in 1983 and received in the National Library by way of legal deposit: it appeared in 1984. Also included are some works about the Maltese Islands and others written by Maltese but published abroad. The first issue indicated 264 titles, overwhelmingly in either English or Maltese, together with a select list of periodical articles. There are indexes of authors, titles, series and subjects. Full reference details are given, though there are no annotations. Annual issues continued to appear in the same format up to that for 1992 (published in 1995) though the size increased from 41 pages in 1983 to 80 for 1992 – which issue shows 405 titles in the classified section and a longer list of periodical articles than hitherto. The 1993 issue had not appeared by 1997 when it was said that there were continuing production difficulties. A resumption of the annual issues is earnestly awaited in view of the very great value of the National Bibliography to students of Malta.

975   **Malta.**
Compiled by John R. Thackrah.   Oxford: Clio Press, 1985. 164p.
(World Bibliographical Series, vol. 64).
This represents the first edition of which the current volume is the second. It includes 588 entries divided into subject areas similar to this volume. However, although some items are included in both volumes, the first covered the whole era of printing up to about 1983/84 and most of its items are not duplicated here. It therefore remains an important and useful annotated source of information prior to the period of publication covered by this second volume.

976   *Melitensia*: a catalogue of printed books and articles in the
      University of Malta Library referring to Malta.
      Paul Xuereb.   Msida, Malta: University of Malta Press, 1974. 76p.
This bibliography covers a wide range of topics and similar lists of *Melitensia* in the
University of Malta Library appeared in later years. More recently, information on
material in the library became available in computer print-out form, and for some time
in 1995-96 this information also appeared as monthly *Acquisition Lists*.

977   Theses and dissertations submitted for the degrees of the Royal
      University of Malta.
      Paul Xuereb.   *Journal of Educational Affairs*, vol. 2 (1976), p. 72-86.
Lists titles, classified by the degree for which they were awarded and alphabetically by
author, to be found in the library of the University of Malta.

978   A bibliography of Maltese bibliographies.
      Paul Xuereb.   Msida, Malta: University of Malta Library, 1978. 18p.
This work details 121 bibliographies on Malta, plus a listing of some unpublished dissertations.

979   The bibliographical control and acquisition of Maltese books, with
      special reference to literary works in the English language.
      Paul Xuereb.   In: *Conference on the acquisition and bibliography of
      Commonwealth and Third World literatures in English, 21-22 October,
      1982: proceedings.*   London: Commonwealth Institute (Working
      Party on Library Holdings of Commonwealth Literature), 1983,
      p. 273-82.
A well-researched study covering Maltese literature.

980   Promoters of information: the first twenty years of the *Għaqda
      Bibljotekarji*, 1969-1989.
      Paul Xuereb.   Valletta: *Għaqda Bibljotekarji*, 1989. 87p.
This offers a history of the *Għaqda Bibljotekarji* (Library Association) during the first
two decades of its existence (p. 3-48), together with the text of the Association's constitution, and an annotated bibliography, compiled by Lillian Sciberras, on libraries
and librarianship in Malta.

Indexes

There follow three separate indexes: authors (personal and corporate); titles; and subjects. Title entries are italicized and refer either to the main titles, or to many of the other works cited in the annotations. The numbers refer to bibliographical entry rather than page numbers. Individual index entries are arranged in alphabetical sequence.

Index of Authors

A

Abel, C. 816-17
Abela, A. 944
Abela, A. E. 1, 218, 267-68, 820
Abela, A. M. 370-72, 433
Abela, C. 818
Abela, G. F. 2
Abela, J. S. 139
Adam, P. 158
Adams, O. B. 861
Agius, A. J. 219
Agius, D. 335
Agius, D. A. 312
Agius, E. 346
Agius Ferrante, A. 713
Agius Muscat, H. 434
Agius-Vadala, M. 198
Aiesec 919
Aikema, B. 68
Air Malta 617
Alden, S. 578
Alexander, D. 23
Alexander, J. (Lady Carnwath) 449
Allen, D. F. 199-200, 220
Allied Newspapers Ltd. 906-07
Alliott, E. A. 747
Amico, V. 48
Andersen, H. C. 58

Anderson, E. W. 17, 491, 654
Apap Bologna, A. 840
Aquilina, E. 49
Aquilina, G. 149, 175
Aquilina, J. 308-09, 313-16, 395-96, 718
Aquilina Ross, G. 34, 49, 52
Aquilina, S. 576
Arberry, A. J. 729
Archer, B. 638
Ashley, S. 935
Ashton, S. E. 45, 568-69
Associated News (M) Ltd. 913
Associated Publicity Services Ltd. 954
Association of General Retailers and Traders Union 948
Atkins, P. J. 17
Attard, Anthony 955
Attard, C. 631
Attard, F. A. 35
Attard, Joe 872
Attard, Joseph 163, 221, 239
Attard, Joseph 632
Attard, L. E. 288-89
Attard, P. A. 676
Audit Office (Malta) 555
Austin, D. 450

Ażad 914
Azzopardi, Aldo E. 50-51
Azzopardi, Anton 18, 22
Azzopardi, C. 841
Azzopardi, Emmanuel 874
Azzopardi, Ernest 295, 515
Azzopardi, F. 861
Azzopardi, J. 347-48, 740, 753-54, 764, 770-72, 804, 820, 842, 862
Azzopardi, M. 730, 733

B

Badger, G. P. 222
Baggett, I. R. 17
Baldacchino, A. E. 75
Baldacchino, C. 577
Baldacchino, Godfrey 373-74, 390, 482, 558, 633-38, 653, 696
Baldacchino, J. G. 123
Balm, R. 655
Baluci, M. T. 963
Bank of Valletta 534, 544-45, 630
Bannerman, D. A. 76
Barber, M. 199
Barnes, S. 415
Bartholemew Clyde 21
Bartholy, H. 387

233

240

Index of Titles

243

255

257

264

Index of Subjects

A

Abela, Gian Francesco
(1582-1655) 144
Acta Originalia 350
Adams, Andrew Leith
(1872-82) 33
Adult education 688, 696
Age, elderly 435
Agius, Anton (b. 1933)
788
Agriculture 159, 602,
604-08, 611-15
Air Malta 617
Air transport 263, 617, 628,
631
Al-Himyari (14th century)
151
Alphabet 323
Alternativa Demokratika
476
Andersen, Hans Christian
(1805-75) 58, 62
Animal husbandry 159,
224, 415
Apap, Marchese
Felicissimo 464
Apap, Vincent (b. 1909)
778
Apap, Willie (1918-70)
783, 787
Arab period 157, 162, 876
Arabic language *see*
Language
Archaeology,
archaeological sites 2,
6-7, 93-104, 106-11,
115, 119, 123, 130,
136, 680, 935
Architecture 33, 54, 138,
141-42, 175, 237,
664-65, 680, 744, 746,
793, 797, 800-03,
805-13, 815-18,
820-21, 823-28, 830,
865, 909, 913

Archives 153-56, 160, 164,
174, 177, 217, 347,
350, 425, 463, 746,
868, 873, 955
Armed Forces of Malta
266, 491, 912
Armoury, Valletta 810
Art 105, 237, 742, 744-45,
756-90, 829, 840, 842,
844, 849, 918, 969
Auberge de Bavière 808
Auberge de Provence 853
Austin, John (1790-1859)
233
Austin, Sarah (1793-1867)
233
Australia 288-89, 303,
305-07, 898, 902
Autobiography 67, 415,
465, 470, 479
Aviation *see* Air transport
Azzopardi, Francesco
(1749-1809) 861
Azzopardi, Mario (b. 1944)
730, 733, 735

B

Ball, Sir Alexander John
(1756-1809) 231
Band clubs 352
Bank of Valletta 544-45
Banks and banking 488,
515, 544-47, 550,
552-53, 908
Baroque 744, 746, 749,
801, 807, 809,
814-15
Barraca Lift 620
Barry, E.M. (1830-80) *see*
Opera House
Barth, Joseph (1746-1818)
422
Barthet, Esprit (b. 1919)
778

Battle of Lepanto (1571)
767
Beach sediments 32
Belli, Andrea (1703-72)
800
Benedict XIV, Pope
(1730-40) 200
Bible 332
Bibliographies 12, 209,
243, 328-29, 463, 612,
745, 964-80
Bighi (hospital) 824
Bilingualism 336-37, 339,
345
Biogeography 89
Biographies 67, 423, 449,
456, 483, 713, 770,
777, 779, 789
Birds 76, 88, 916, 929
Bird shooting/trapping 88,
580-81, 589
Birgu (Vittoriosa) *see*
Vittoriosa
Blue Clay 28
Book Fair (*Il-Fiera tal-
Ktieb*) 959
Borġ Olivier, G. (1911-80)
14
Bormla (Cospicua) *see*
Cospicua
Brazil 288
British period 7, 142-43,
217-18, 220-24, 230,
232, 234, 237-38, 259,
261, 263-64, 267, 299,
340, 358, 362-63, 450,
454, 460-64, 469, 487,
527, 535, 762, 771,
819, 821-22, 830, 837,
839, 958, 973
see also Fortifications;
Navy; World War
Broadcasting Authority 622
Brocktorff Circle Mortuary
Complex 106
Bronze Age 101

265

Brougham (Lord
    Chancellor)
    (1778-1868) 233
Brucellosis (undulant fever)
    414-16, 432, 615
Buġibba 21
Built environment 6, 141,
    210, 664, 794, 798,
    801-02, 818-19, 825,
    913
Buonamici, Francesco
    (1596-1677) 807
Buses 619
Business 598, 903-04, 917,
    919
Busuttil, Salvatore
    (1798-1854) 750
Byron, Lord (1788-1824)
    72
Byzantines 118-19

C

Cabreo (de Vilhena) 210
Caesarean Section 411
Calì, Giuseppe (1846-1930)
    782
Calleja, Giuseppe
    (1828-1915) 775
Calleja, Maria 11
Camilleri, Antoine 778
Camilleri, Charles
    (b. 1931) 14, 863,
    865-66, 871-72
Camilleri, Nicola
    (c.1773-1860) 781
Canada 288-89, 344, 902
Cancer 407
Carnival 201
Car tours 45
Caravaggio, Michelangelo
    Merisi da (1569-1609)
    452, 749, 764, 766,
    768
Caricature 784
Carthaginians, Punic
    influence 96, 115
'Cart tracks' 101, 109
Caruana Dingli, Edward
    (1876-1950) 750
Casa Rocca Piccola 795
Casanova, Vincenzo

(c.1645-1706) 814
Casino Maltese 782
Cassar, Giuseppe
    (b. 1917) 774
Cassar, Girolomo
    (c.1520-86) 812
Cassar, Vittorio (d. 1609)
    812
Catacombs, hypogea
    116-18, 680, 793
Cathedral of Malta see
    Mdina, Cathedral
Cathedral Museum, Mdina
    626, 740-41, 753,
    756, 758, 770, 774-75,
    779, 842, 854, 861,
    868
Cauchi, Joe (1913-92)
    753
Cave dwellings 126
Caxaro, Peter (d. 1485)
    333
Cemeteries 822
Censorship 900
Census 279, 280-81,
    283-86, 294, 384, 435,
    445, 591, 605
Central Bank of Malta
    546-47
Chamber of Commerce
    207
Charts see Maps
Chigi, Fabio (subsequently
    Pope Alexander VII:
    1655-67) 201
Child workers 646
Cholera 417
Church (Catholic) 2, 141,
    237, 283, 346, 349-50,
    353-55, 359, 362-64,
    366-69, 371, 452, 454,
    503
Churches 102, 126, 137,
    359, 623, 755, 792,
    799, 814-15, 817, 823,
    826-28, 843
Clausiliidae 89
Climate 17, 660, 662
Climbing 578, 582
Clocks 853
Coasts 654
Coinage 188, 874-77, 880
Cole, Leslie (1910-76) 750

Coleridge, Samuel Taylor
    (1772-1834) 65, 231
Collegium Melitense see
    University of Malta
Comino 19, 835
Comitato Patriotico
    Maltese 456
Commanderies 171, 185,
    204
Commerce 13, 485, 489,
    500, 512, 593, 598,
    919-23
Commission for the
    Advancement of
    Women 648
Community care 433
Commun Tesoro 204
Congenital anomalies 404
Conservation
    antiquities 128-36, 138,
    835, 953
    environment 571, 589,
    654, 673, 953
Constantinople 786
Constitution 451, 461,
    463, 467, 484, 487,
    490
Constitutional Party 453
Container Port, Kalafrana
    599, 670
Contraception 406
Cooke, John Henry
    (1862-1933) 33
Cooking 889-90, 896
Co-operative Movement
    636
Copper Age 104
Coralline see Limestone
Corn monopoly 223
Cospicua (Bormla) 20,
    684-85
Cotton 207
Cottonera 625, 685
Council of Trent 353
Cremona, Emvin (1919-87)
    778
Cultural heritage 10,
    131-33, 136, 573, 926,
    933, 952
Curia (Archdiocesan
    offices) 854
Currency 878-79
Curriculum 692-95

266

Ferry (Malta-Gozo) 618
Fertility cult 94
Festa (fiesta) 237, 351-52, 387
Filfla 19
Finance 204, 223, 514, 518, 520, 522, 524-25, 530, 532, 535, 544-57, 908
First World War (1914-18) *see* World War
Fish, Fisheries 84, 93, 603-05, 609, 616
Flora 7, 74-75, 77, 82-83, 85
Floriana 1, 20, 214, 382
Flour production 7
Folklore 6, 395, 399-402, 940
Folk music 870
Folk tales 397, 399
Fondazzjoni Patrimonju Malti 773, 840, 854, 952
Food and drink 17, 434, 604, 892-93, 895
Football (soccer) 577, 583, 585, 588, 936
Foreign relations 142, 148, 168, 175, 213, 216, 232, 491-97, 499-510, 512-14, 939
Forsskål, Petrus (1732-63) 74
Fort Chambrai, Gozo 835
Fortifications 797, 804-09, 811-13, 819, 821-22, 830-39
Fort St. Elmo, Valletta 831
Fossils 16, 28, 402
Foundation of Human Resource Development 637
Foundation for International Studies 683
Franciscans, Franciscanism 149, 175
Freeport (Kalafrana) 599, 670
Freemasonry 219, 227
French Revolution 232
French Rule 209, 217, 231, 234, 460

Frere, John Hookham (1769-1846) 71, 228, 424, 739
Frere, William (1775-1836) 71
Friggieri, Joe (b. 1946) 730
Friggieri, Oliver (b. 1947) 720-21, 730
Fruit trees 602, 610
Furniture 850-51

G

Gafà, Lorenzo (1639-1703) 873
Galea, Joseph (1904-85) 750
Gallipoli 264
Ganado, Albert (b. 1924) 745
Gardens 159, 228, 656, 825
Gender 385-86, 388, 712
General Workers' Union 504, 634, 644-45, 653
Geography 4, 17-18, 22, 169, 222, 529, 654, 657
Geology 7, 24-26, 30, 32-33, 77, 89, 657
Geomorphology 17, 23, 27
George Cross 242, 268
Gerada, Alfred (1895-1968) 750
German Knights of Malta 178
Germany 387
Ġgantija 99
Għaqda Bibljotekarji see Library Association
Għajnsielem huts 99
Għar Dalam (cave) 112
Għawdex see Gozo
Gianni, Girolamo (1837-c.1895) 750, 773
Gimach, Carlo (1651-1730) 744, 808
Girna (stone hut) 796, 827
Globigerina see Limestone
Gobelin Tapestries 846
Goddess, Great Goddess 93, 108

Gold 844
Gonzi, Michael, Archbishop (1885-1984) 363
Government, Administration 451, 481-82, 937
Gozo 5-7, 11, 13, 18, 21, 55, 95, 99, 104, 122, 222, 298, 312, 315, 349-50, 369, 397, 534, 560, 564, 567, 571, 618, 630, 667-68, 731, 812, 833, 835, 841, 918, 935
Gozo Cathedral 833
Gozo Citadel 95, 833
Gozo Museum 95
Grain 610
Grammar (Maltese) 314, 317, 320, 325, 334
Grand Harbour 8, 13, 68, 255-57, 262, 819, 829
Grand Masters' Palace 846
Great Siege (1565) *see* Siege (1565)
Grech, Giuseppe (1755-87) 175
Greek Catholics 195, 755
Greece (classical) 113-14
Guides, guidebooks 34, 36, 37-46, 50, 222, 954, 957

H

Ħal Far 250
'Ħal Farruġ' *see* Kirkop
Ħal Milieri 125, 137
Ħal Saflieni Hypogeum 110, 130, 135
Ħamrun 828
Harbours 599, 756-57, 771, 773, 819
see also Grand Harbour; Marsamxett Harbour
Hastings, Marquis of, Governor (1824-27) 236
Health 403, 416, 427, 434, 440-42, 889
Heart disease 414

Henin, Gabriele
(1696-1754) 423
Heraldry 270, 272-75, 278
History 4, 6, 13, 139-40,
142-43, 181, 202-05,
212, 217, 222, 226,
230, 238, 259-61, 267,
291, 293, 304, 346-47,
349, 360, 383, 427,
457-58, 516, 658, 745,
767, 791-92, 797,
800-01, 804-06, 811,
813, 823, 910-18, 926,
943, 947, 952, 958,
966-67, 973
see also Order of St.
John; British period
Honour and shame 394
Hospitals 408, 419, 428
Hotels 63, 558
see also Guides
Households 382
Housing 104, 281, 444,
795, 798, 801-02,
818
Human capital 443, 520,
678, 915
Human rights 486

I

Il-Bidni (Marsascala) 131
Immigration 297
Income 524, 633
Industry 540, 591, 593,
595, 597, 601, 632
642, 930
Infant feeding 409
Inglott, Anton (1915-45)
772
Inquisition 141, 150, 166,
189-91, 355, 854
Institute of Health Care 448
International relations *see*
Foreign relations
Isouard, Nicolò (1773 or
1775-1818) 862
Istanbul *see* Constantinople
Istanbul State Archives 193
Italian language *see*
Language
Italy 340, 358

J

Jesuit 354
Jews 161
Journalism 325, 899
Journals *see* Periodicals

K

Kalafrana (container port)
599, 670
Kalleya, Josef (b. 1898)
778
Karm, Dun *see* Psaila
(Psajla), Dun Karm
Karstic terrain 24
King's Own Malta
Regiment 266
King's Own Malta Rifles
258
Kinship 376
Kirkop 352, 376
Knights' Holy Infirmary
see Sacra Infermeria
Knights of St. John *see*
Order of St. John
Krasnoff, Nicholas (20th
century) 750

L

Labour, employment 390,
518-19, 632-33, 635,
637-38, 640, 642, 644,
649-53
Labour Party *see* Malta
Labour Party
Lace 841
Lampedusa (island) 232
Landscape 45, 52, 674, 776
Land use 606-07, 665
Language 235, 331, 334-35,
345, 400
Arabic 336-37, 339,
342-43
English 325, 334, 342-43
Italian 142, 308-34,
336-38, 341-42
Maltese 344-45, 387, 390,
680, 694, 898, 932
Sicilian 327, 331, 400

Language planning 337
Language question 340,
343, 858
Laparelli, Francesco
(1521-71) 804-05, 812
Lascaris Bastion, Valletta
64
Lascaris Castellar, Grand
Master (1636-57) 808
La Valette, Grand Master
see De la Valette,
Grand Master
Laverack, John
(19th-century
Methodist minister)
229
Law and legal system
485-86, 488-89,
531, 535, 572-73, 928
Lazzaretto *see* Quarantine
Lear, Edward (1812-88)
750
Leisure *see* Tourism
Leo XIII, Pope
(1878-1903) 358
Lepanto *see* Battle of
Lepidoptera 90-91
Letters 727
Libraries 424, 960, 962-63,
971-72, 980
Library Association (Malta)
956, 980
Libya 494, 511
Limestone 23-24, 31, 134,
138
Linguistics (Maltese) 151,
316
L'Isla *see* Senglea
Literature 142, 719-20,
722, 724, 979
see also Novels; Poetry;
Short stories
Lombard Bank (Malta)
Limited 550
London, Maltese in 296
Luftwaffe 241, 864
Luqa 250

M

McFall, Albert (1862-1923)
750

Magazines *see* Periodicals

Magri, Fr. Manwel (1851-1907) 136

Maitland, Sir Thomas, Governor (1813-24) 232, 824

Malta Amateur Dramatic Company (M.A.D.C.) 859

Malta Archaeological Project 103

Malta Development Corporation 593

Malta Drydocks *see* Drydocks

Malta Export Trade Corporation 594

Malta Federation of Industry 595, 601, 930

Malta Historical Society 175

Malta Labour Party 352, 362, 453, 462-63, 472-73, 476, 501, 509-10, 645, 711

Malta Literary Award 7

Malta National Bibliography 974

Malta Siege Bell 829

Malta Society of Arts, Manufacturers and Commerce 779

Malta Study Circle (Philatelic) 885-86

Malta Union of Teachers *see* Movement of United Teachers

Maltese language *see* Language

Maltese Corps of the British Army 259

Maltese Dog (*Kelb tal-Fenek*) 79

Maltese Protestant College 236

Mandati documents 154, 849

Manduca, Girolamo (1574-1643) 144

Manikata Church 817, 827

Manoel Theatre, Valletta 782, 858, 860, 862, 941

Manufacturing 528, 592-97

Maps, plans, charts, atlases 20-21, 26, 35, 146, 152, 165, 188, 197-98, 210, 280, 445, 579, 654, 657, 659, 745, 794, 800, 811, 830, 836, 838

Marchese, Count Saverio (1757-1833) 770

Marine pollution 670

Maritime boundaries *see* Sea boundaries

Maritime Museum, Vittoriosa (Birgu) 98, 626, 743, 781

Marriage 202-03, 376, 379, 388

Marsamxett Harbour 8, 256, 262, 426, 819

Marsascala 131, 133

Marsaxlokk 131, 133, 616

Massa, Antonio (1590-1624) 854

Massa, Daniel (b. 1936) 730

Mdina 21, 47, 115, 154, 214, 333, 561, 713, 740-41, 753-54, 756, 758, 774, 779-80, 791-92, 794, 804, 828, 842, 861

Mdina Cathedral 154-55, 177, 347, 745, 754, 780, 791, 849 *see also* Cathedral Museum, Mdina; Mdina

Media *see* Press

Mediaeval period 142, 144, 159-61, 345, 347, 800-01, 869

Medical Association of Malta 641

Medical conditions 192, 420, 425, 680

Medical unionism 641

Medicine 423-24

Mediterranean (region) 17, 142, 158, 168, 194, 230, 232, 248, 322, 492-93, 496, 502, 636, 771, 784, 819, 821, 913, 933-34, 942

Mellieha 559

Mental health 441

Methodism 229

Mġarr, Gozo 812

Micallef, Luciano (b. 1954) 790

Mid-Med Bank 553

Migration 295, 299-300, 302, 304, 344

Millipedes 80

Minerals 32

Mintoff, Dom (b. 1916) 14, 363-64, 471-72, 499, 505, 641

Miocene 26, 28, 31

Misrah Strejnu 133

Missionary work 332, 335

Mizzi, Achille (b. 1939) 730

Molluscs 78, 81, 87

Mondrogon Co-operatives 515

Mortality 416

Mosaics 120

Mosta 147

Movement for the Promotion of Literature 735

Movement of United Teachers 7-8

Msida 772, 788, 822

M.U.S.E.U.M. 688

Museum of Fine Arts, Valletta *see* National Museum of Fine Arts, Valletta

Museums Department 134, 935

Music 7, 383, 861-63, 865-70, 872-73

N

Naples 217

Nasoni, Nicolo (1691-1773) 744

National Accounts 554-55

National Library of Malta 210, 424, 901

National Museum, Valletta 101, 125

National Museum of Fine Arts, Valletta 452, 743, 751-52, 759, 785

Map of Malta and Gozo

This map shows the more important features.

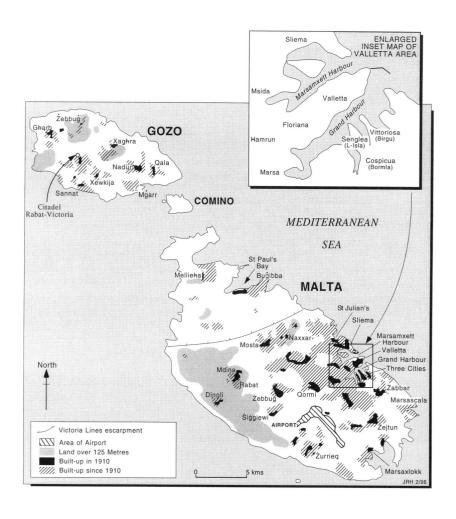

ALSO FROM CLIO PRESS

INTERNATIONAL ORGANIZATIONS SERIES

Each volume in the International Organizations Series is either devoted to one specific organization, or to a number of different organizations operating in a particular region, or engaged in a specific field of activity. The scope of the series is wide-ranging and includes intergovernmental organizations, international non-governmental organizations, and national bodies dealing with international issues. The series is aimed mainly at the English-speaker and each volume provides a selective, annotated, critical bibliography of the organization, or organizations, concerned. The bibliographies cover books, articles, pamphlets, directories, databases and theses and, wherever possible, attention is focused on material about the organizations rather than on the organizations' own publications. Notwithstanding this, the most important official publications, and guides to those publications, will be included. The views expressed in individual volumes, however, are not necessarily those of the publishers.

VOLUMES IN THE SERIES

Catching Breath

P
s